ROCKS

ROCKS

EDITED BY JOHN P. RAFFERTY, ASSOCIATE EDITOR,
EARTH AND LIFE SCIENCES

Britannica
Educational Publishing

IN ASSOCIATION WITH

ROSEN
EDUCATIONAL SERVICES

Published in 2012 by Britannica Educational Publishing
(a trademark of Encyclopædia Britannica, Inc.)
in association with Rosen Educational Services, LLC
29 East 21st Street, New York, NY 10010.

For a listing of additional Britannica Educational Publishing titles, call toll free (800) 237-9932.

First Edition

Britannica Educational Publishing
Michael I. Levy: Executive Editor
J.E. Luebering: Senior Manager
Marilyn L. Barton: Senior Coordinator, Production Control
Steven Bosco: Director, Editorial Technologies
Lisa S. Braucher: Senior Producer and Data Editor
Yvette Charboneau: Senior Copy Editor
Kathy Nakamura: Manager, Media Acquisition
John P. Rafferty: Associate Editor, Earth and Life Sciences

Rosen Educational Services
Hope Lourie Killcoyne: Senior Editor and Project Manager
Nelson Sá: Art Director
Cindy Reiman: Photography Manager
Matthew Cauli: Designer, Cover Design
Introduction by John P. Rafferty

Library of Congress Cataloging-in-Publication Data

Rocks / edited by John P. Rafferty. — 1st ed.
   p. cm. — (Geology : landforms, minerals, and rocks)
"In association with Britannica Educational Publishing, Rosen Educational Services."
Includes bibliographical references and index.
ISBN 978-1-61530-492-9 (lib. bdg.)
1. Rocks. 2. Petology. I. Rafferty, John P.
QE431.2.R63 2012
552—dc22

                                                                  2010045807

Manufactured in the United States of America

On the cover (front and back): Marble quarry at Carrara, Italy. *Gjon Mili/Time & Life
Pictures/Getty Images*

On the cover (front top), p. iii: Rocks fall into three major classes, determined by how
they were formed: sedimentary (far left), metamorphic (centre images), and igneous (far
right). *Shutterstock.com*

On pages 1, 50, 111, 191, 259, 260, 264, 267: With some rocks dating back nearly four billion
years, the Grand Canyon in northern Arizona provides a wealth of historic information
about the geologic events of that area. Rock types in this immense canyon include Archean
granite and schist, Proterozoic limestones, sandstones, and shales, and Paleozoic freshwater
shales, cemented sandstones, and limestones. *iStockphoto/Thinkstock*

CONTENTS

2

29

65

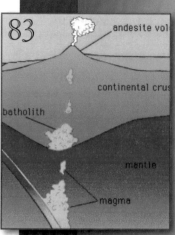

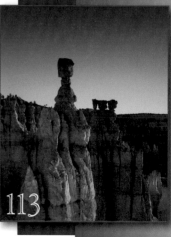

145

199

217

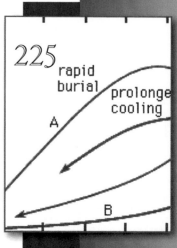

INTRODUCTION

Rocks are the foundations upon which humans and other forms of life on Earth stand. Rock makes up the solid outer skin of planet Earth, as well as the molten and solid layers of Earth's interior. Across the wide span of geologic time, no rock remains the same. Rocks begin as volumes of magma (hot, fluidlike mixtures of minerals, gases, and steam) that slowly rise and cool into igneous rocks at or near Earth's surface. Exposed to the elements on the surface over long time intervals, igneous rocks may crack, flake, and break apart to provide the basic materials for deposits of sedimentary rock. After being subjected to high temperatures, high pressures, or bathed in chemical solutions, igneous and sedimentary rock may become metamorphic rock or revert into magma if conditions are particularly intense. The first part of this book provides the reader with a general treatment of rocks and their important properties, while the remainder of the book considers the three major types of rocks: igneous, sedimentary, and metamorphic.

For any given rock, the path of its formation determines how it is classified. Igneous rocks form from magma that cools either within Earth's interior or on Earth's surface. Sedimentary rocks are derived from bits of preexisting rock and compounds that precipitate from chemical reactions at or near Earth's surface. Lastly, metamorphic rock is produced when a rock is later transformed by temperature, pressure, reactions with chemical solutions, or a combination of these phenomena into rocks with properties that differ from the original material.

All rocks are classified according to their texture, which is an aggregation of the size, shape, and pattern of their characteristic grains and crystals. A rock's texture can

Wave Rock in Australia, one of that country's most famous landforms, is a massive formation of granite, an igneous rock. Steve Allen/Brand X Pictures/ Getty Images

provide clues to its identity and how it was formed. The crystals of igneous and metamorphic rocks are divided according to size. Pegmatic rocks have relatively large crystals, whereas phaneritic and aphanitic rocks contain medium-sized and small crystals, respectively. Similarly, sedimentary rocks are classified in part by the size of their grains. Porosity, or the volume of the rock not taken up by grains, crystals, or cementing material—that is, the spaces in between those elements—is another important feature of rocks.

The physical properties of rocks are important to geologists, materials scientists, seismologists, and the mining industry. The knowledge of a rock's characteristics allows these practitioners to better predict the behaviour of the rock under different conditions. For example, a rock's density, or the mass of the rock per unit of its volume, is important because it can provide clues to the identity of a given rock as well as the structure of the geology occurring below Earth's surface. Rocks can be altered by mechanical forces—which include stress and strain, confining pressure, internal pore pressure, and temperature—that occur within Earth's interior, and each type of rock responds differently to these forces. There are those rocks that conduct heat and electricity better than others, and those that contain magnetic minerals. Certain rocks are under enormous pressure from incremental movements of Earth's tectonic plates, whereas others experience less stress and strain. The ability to predict the behaviour of a given rock exposed to various combinations of mechanical forces allows geologists to better understand the organizational structure of the rock layers under the surface, discover and extract rocks containing valuable minerals or other resources, and more accurately foretell the location and intensity of earthquakes.

Igneous rocks are closely tied to the behaviour of magma, the material from which they arise. They are formed by the cooling and crystallization of magma at or near Earth's surface. These processes occur most often near the boundaries of Earth's tectonic plates. Magma extruded onto the surface is called lava, and thus the rocks formed by lava are called extrusive, or volcanic, rocks. Igneous rocks that form within other layers of other rocks are called intrusive, or plutonic, rocks.

The relationship between heat, pressure, and water within deep layers of rock determines how igneous rocks are formed. In general, new magma is generated by the melting of solid rocks as they are driven deep into Earth and thus closer to the planet's internal heat source. At the atomic level, heating causes the molecules in the rock to vibrate. If enough heat is added, the bonds between molecules will break and the rock will change from a solid to a liquid. Since rocks are made up of different minerals with different melting points, some minerals melt earlier than others, and rocks are said to partially melt. Although Earth's temperatures rise with depth, melting can be confounded by increases in pressure. In dry rocks, the tremendous weight of the surrounding rock holds the molecules in the rock together, and more energy is needed to melt the rock. Thus, with added pressure, the melting point of the various minerals in the rock increases. On the other hand, the melting point of minerals in wet rocks—that is, rocks with a high water content—is lowered. (Water dissolves relatively easily into magmas, and any undissolved water in the rock helps to break the bonds that stabilize the crystal structures in the rock's minerals.) Also, under high pressure conditions, wet rocks melt faster than dry rocks.

After the magma is created, it has a tendency to rise, because the rocks above are less dense (and thus easier to move through) than the ones below. As it travels upward, it cools and crystallizes. Since this magma is made up of different minerals with different freezing temperatures, some minerals will crystallize earlier than others. Minerals, which are essentially solid forms of chemical compounds, are constructed by the elements available in the magma. Those that form early in the crystallization process remove different elements from the magma, changing the chemistry of the magma that remains. Consequently, different types of rocks will form from the same volume of magma.

All igneous rocks are classified by their dominant chemical composition. Those with high levels of silica are called felsic rocks. Granite and rhyolite are examples of common felsic rocks in plutonic and volcanic settings, respectively. On the other end of the spectrum, rocks made up of less than 40 percent silica are called ultramafic rocks. These rocks contain relatively high proportions of magnesium and iron. Peridotite and komatiite are common ultramafic rocks that occur in plutonic and volcanic settings, respectively.

The creation of sedimentary rocks, however, is only indirectly related to the behaviour of magma. Such rocks are derived from weathering—that is, the decomposition of rock. Weathering can occur mechanically from the actions of wind, water, gravity, and ice that remove bits and pieces of rock from their parent material. These pieces, which may be as large as boulders or as fine as bits of sand and silt, are transported to new areas and deposited. After layer upon layer of sediment accumulates in an area such as a basin, some of the loose material may be converted to solid rock, a process called lithification. The weight of the accumulated layers of material above compacts the lower levels of sediment. Water that filters through the compacted sediment may dissolve some of the material, creating a type of cement that binds different particles together. Chemical weathering can also produce sedimentary rock. In this process, minerals precipitate from solutions to form rock.

Sedimentary rocks can be divided into three broad categories. The first contains terrigenous clastic sedimentary rocks, that is, sedimentary rocks that contain broken fragments of decomposed rocks called clasts. Terrigenous clastic rocks are classified by their grain size and texture. Those with small grains are called mudrocks. Sedimentary rocks with progressively larger particle sizes are classified in turn as sandstones, breccias, and conglomerates. The second category, the carbonates, are inorganic sedimentary rocks that form from chemical weathering. Common examples of carbonate rocks include limestones and dolomites. The noncarbonated chemical sedimentary rocks make up the third category. This group includes the cherts and phosporites, as well as iron-rich rocks and organic-rich rocks (such as coal).

Metamorphic rocks are derived from igneous, sedimentary, or other metamorphic rocks. Metamorphic rocks are rocks that undergo extreme changes to their crystal structure. They are similar to igneous rocks in that they are affected by heat and pressure, but, they are unlike igneous rocks in that they do not melt. Metamorphic rocks are not transformed by overhauling their internal chemistry or material state. (Recrystallization takes place while the rock is in solid form.) However, they are affected by the materials that surround them, as well as the composition of the parent rock. The process of metamorphism occurs within a range of temperature, pressure, and chemical conditions, and the intensity of the transformation, reflected in the metamorphic grade of the rock, depends on the environmental conditions that surround the rock.

There are four types of metamorphism. Contact metamorphism occurs when a rock is subject to heating, such as when hot igneous material touches or surrounds cooler rock. The parts of the rock that make contact with the magma will undergo the greatest transformation and thus will likely become high-grade metamorphic rocks, whereas the parts of the rock farther away from the heat source will exhibit a low-grade transformation. Quartzite, which results from sandstone or chert coming into direct contact with hot magma, and marble, which results from the placement of limestone or dolostone under these same conditions, are examples of high-grade metamorphic rocks. In contrast, slate, which results from shale placed in milder temperature and pressure conditions, is an example of a low-grade metamorphic rock.

Other types of metamorphism do not require direct contact between the magma and the rock. In hydrothermal metamorphism, magma-heated seawater and groundwater become the agents of metamorphism. The remaining two, dynamic and regional metamorphism, emphasize the role pressure plays in transforming a rock. Dynamic metamorphism results from the actions of directed pressure or stress, such as the changes that occur in rocks that are buried under several layers of rock or smashed along a fault plane. Regional metamorphism is similar, but it considers rock transformations over wide areas, such as beneath landscape-sized deposits of sedimentary rock or between two colliding tectonic plates.

The study of rocks goes well beyond their classification and identification. The placement and orientation of rocks within mountains, along the sides of cliffs, and on the floors of lake and ocean basins can explain a great deal about the environments they emerged from, as well as the environments that shaped them into their current forms. Rocks also contain clues to the evolution of life on Earth. Layers of sedimentary rock often contain fossils, or remnants or imprints of long-dead organisms. Fossils and the rocks that hold them are snapshots of moments in time. Both can be dated and placed with other fossils and rocks to construct evolutionary timelines that span many millions of years. From these timelines, paleontologists can better understand how Earth, as well as the groups of life-forms that inhabit it, changed from the periods following the planet's initial formation to the present day.

CHAPTER 1

A WORLD OF ROCK

Rocks are naturally occurring and coherent aggregates of one or more minerals. Such aggregates constitute the basic unit of which the solid Earth is comprised and typically form recognizable and mappable volumes. Rocks are commonly divided into three major classes according to the processes that resulted in their formation. These classes are (1) igneous rocks, which have solidified from molten material called magma;

Porphyry, an igneous rock. DEA/A. Rizzi/De Agostini Picture Library/ Getty Images

(2) sedimentary rocks, those consisting of fragments derived from preexisting rocks or of materials precipitated from solutions; and (3) metamorphic rocks, which have been derived from either igneous or sedimentary rocks under conditions that caused changes in mineralogical composition, texture, and internal structure. These three classes, in turn, are subdivided into numerous groups and types on the basis of various factors, the most important of which are chemical, mineralogical, and textural attributes.

GENERAL CONSIDERATIONS

Igneous rocks are those that solidify from magma, a molten mixture of rock-forming minerals and usually

Seashell fossil embedded in limestone. A sedimentary rock, limestone sometimes hosts fossil animal shells—from microscopic fragments to full specimens. Shutterstock.com

volatiles such as gases and steam. Since their constituent minerals are crystallized from molten material, igneous rocks are formed at high temperatures. They originate from processes deep within Earth—typically at depths of about 50 to 200 km (30 to 120 miles)—in the mid- to lower-crust or in the upper mantle. Igneous rocks are subdivided into two categories: intrusive (emplaced in the crust), and extrusive (extruded onto the surface of the land or ocean bottom), in which case the cooling molten material is called lava.

Sedimentary rocks are those that are deposited and lithified (compacted and cemented together) at the Earth's surface, with the assistance of running water, wind, ice, or living organisms. Most are deposited from the land surface to the bottoms of lakes, rivers, and

Marble, a metamorphic rock. Shutterstock.com

oceans. Sedimentary rocks are generally stratified—i.e., they have layering. Layers may be distinguished by differences in colour, particle size, type of cement, or internal arrangement.

Metamorphic rocks are those formed by changes in preexisting rocks under the influence of high temperature, pressure, and chemically active solutions. The changes can be chemical (compositional) and physical (textural) in character. Metamorphic rocks are often formed by processes deep within Earth that produce new minerals, textures, and crystal structures. The recrystallization that takes place does so essentially in the solid state, rather than by complete remelting, and can be aided by ductile deformation and the presence of interstitial fluids such as water. Metamorphism often produces apparent layering, or banding, because of the segregation of minerals into separate bands. Metamorphic processes can also occur at Earth's surface due to meteorite impact events and pyrometamorphism taking place near burning coal seams ignited by lightning strikes.

LAVA

Lava is molten rock originating as magma in Earth's mantle that pours out onto Earth's surface through volcanic vents at temperatures of about 700–1,200 °C (1,300–2,200 °F). Mafic lavas, such as basalt, form flows known by the Hawaiian names *pahoehoe* and *aa*. *Pahoehoe* is smooth and gently undulating; the lava moves through natural pipes known as lava tubes. *Aa* is very rough, covered with a layer of loose, irregular fragments called clinker, and flows in open channels. Lava that starts out as *pahoehoe* may turn into *aa* as it cools. Lavas of intermediate composition form a block lava flow, which also has a top consisting largely of loose rubble, but the fragments are fairly regular in shape, mostly polygons with relatively smooth sides.

Geologic materials—mineral crystals and their host rock types—are cycled through various forms. The process depends on temperature, pressure, time, and changes in environmental conditions in Earth's crust and at its surface. The rock cycle reflects the basic relationships among igneous, metamorphic, and sedimentary rocks. Erosion includes weathering (the physical and chemical breakdown of minerals) and transportation to a site of deposition. Diagenesis is, as previously explained, the process of forming sedimentary rock by compaction and natural cementation of grains, or crystallization from water or solutions, or recrystallization. The conversion of sediment to rock is termed lithification.

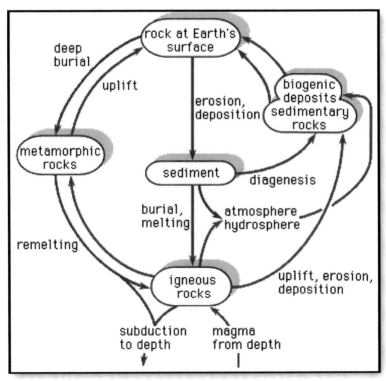

The rock cycle. Copyright Encyclopædia Britannica, Inc.; rendering for this edition by Rosen Educational Services

TEXTURE

The texture of a rock is the size, shape, and arrangement of the grains (for sedimentary rocks) or crystals (for igneous and metamorphic rocks). Also of importance are the rock's extent of homogeneity (i.e., uniformity of composition throughout) and the degree of isotropy. The latter is the extent to which the bulk structure and composition are the same in all directions in the rock.

Analysis of texture can yield information about the rock's source material, conditions and environment of deposition (for sedimentary rock) or crystallization and recrystallization (for igneous and metamorphic rock, respectively), and subsequent geologic history and change.

CLASSIFICATION BY GRAIN OR CRYSTAL SIZE

The common textural terms used for rock types with respect to the size of the grains or crystals, are given in

Common Textural Terms for Rocks*

size (in millimetres)	igneous and metamorphic	sedimentary		pyroclastic	
		sediment	rock	sediment	rock
256 128 64	very coarse (pegmatitic)	boulder		block bomb	breccia
		cobble			
32 16 8 4 2	coarse	conglomerate			
		pebble		lapilli cinder	lapilli
	medium	granule			
1 1/2 1/4 1/8 1/16	fine	sand	coarse sandstone	coarse ash	coarse tuff
			fine sandstone		
1/32 1/64 1/128 1/256	dense	silt	siltstone	fine ash	fine tuff
		clay	shale		

(phaneritic / aphanitic indicated at left)

*Diagonal lines in the table reflect the variability in size limits of certain grades resulting from the use of different values by different authors.

Copyright Encyclopædia Britannica, Inc.; rendering for this edition by Rosen Educational Services

the table. The particle-size categories are derived from the Udden-Wentworth scale developed for sediment. For igneous and metamorphic rocks, the terms are generally used as modifiers—e.g., medium-grained granite. Aphanitic is a descriptive term for small crystals (from the Greek *aphanēs*, meaning "invisible"), and phaneritic for larger ones. (Applied to those crystals viewable without the aid of a microscope, phaneritic comes from the Greek *phaneros*, meaning "visible"). Very coarse crystals (those larger than 3 cm, or 1.2 inches) are termed pegmatitic.

For sedimentary rocks, the broad categories of sediment size are coarse (greater than 2 mm, or 0.08 inch), medium (between 2 and $\frac{1}{16}$ mm, or 0.08 and 0.0025 inch), and fine (under $\frac{1}{16}$ mm, or 0.0025 inch). The latter includes silt and clay, which both have a size indistinguishable by the human eye and are also termed dust. Most shales (the lithified version of clay) contain some silt. Pyroclastic rocks are those formed from clastic (from the Greek word for broken) material ejected from volcanoes. Blocks are fragments broken from solid rock, while bombs are molten when ejected.

CRYSTALLINE ROCK

A crystalline rock is any rock composed entirely of crystallized minerals without glassy matter. Intrusive igneous rocks—those that congeal at depth—are virtually always crystalline, whereas extrusive igneous rocks, or volcanic rocks, may be partly to entirely glassy. Many factors influence the ability of a magma to crystallize, but the length of time during which cooling occurs is the controlling factor. Metamorphic rocks are almost always crystalline; the term crystalline schists has been applied to indicate all rocks of metamorphic origin, and thus the term crystalline rocks may be taken to mean an igneous origin. Sedimentary rocks can also be crystalline, such as the crystalline limestones precipitated directly from solution; the term is not generally applied to the clastic sediments, even though they are formed largely from the accumulation of crystalline materials.

POROSITY

The term rock refers to the bulk volume of the material, including the grains or crystals as well as the contained void space. The volumetric portion of bulk rock that is not occupied by grains, crystals, or natural cementing material is termed porosity. That is to say, porosity is the ratio of void volume to the bulk volume (grains plus void space). This void space consists of pore space between grains or crystals, in addition to crack space. In sedimentary rocks, the amount of pore space depends on the degree of compaction of the sediment (with compaction generally increasing with depth of burial), on the packing arrangement and shape of grains, on the amount of cementation, and on the degree of sorting. Typical cements are siliceous, calcareous or carbonate, or iron-bearing minerals.

Sorting is the tendency of sedimentary rocks to have grains that are similarly sized—i.e., to have a narrow range of sizes. Poorly sorted sediment displays a wide range of grain sizes and hence has decreased porosity. Well-sorted sediment indicates a grain size distribution that is fairly

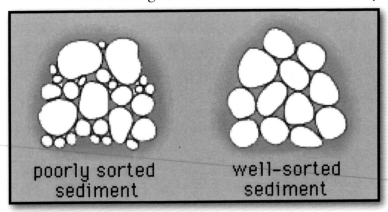

Sorting. Copyright Encyclopædia Britannica, Inc.; rendering for this edition by Rosen Educational Services

uniform. Depending on the type of close-packing of the grains, porosity can be substantial. It should be noted that in engineering usage—e.g., geotechnical or civil engineering—the terminology is phrased oppositely and is referred to as grading. A well-graded sediment is a (geologically) poorly sorted one, and a poorly graded sediment is a well-sorted one.

Total porosity encompasses all the void space, including those pores that are interconnected to the surface of the sample as well as those that are sealed off by natural cement or other obstructions. Thus the total porosity (ϕT) is

$$\varphi_T = 100 \left(1 - \frac{\text{Vol}_G}{\text{Vol}_B} \right) \% ,$$

where Vol$G$ is the volume of grains (and cement, if any) and Vol$B$ is the total bulk volume. Alternatively, one can calculate ϕT from the measured densities of the bulk rock and of the (mono)mineralic constituent. Thus,

$$\varphi_T = 100 \left(1 - \frac{\rho_B}{\rho_G} \right) \% ,$$

where ρB is the density of the bulk rock and ρG is the density of the grains (i.e., the mineral, if the composition is monomineralogic and homogeneous). For example, if a sandstone has a ρB of 2.38 grams per cubic cm (1.37 ounces per cubic inch) and is composed of quartz (SiO_2) grains having ρG of 2.65 grams per cubic cm (1.37 ounces per cubic inch), the total porosity is

$$\varphi_T = 100 \left(1 - \frac{2.38}{2.65} \right) = 10.2\% .$$

Apparent (effective, or net) porosity is the proportion of void space that excludes the sealed-off pores. It thus measures the pore volume that is effectively interconnected and accessible to the surface of the sample, which is important when considering the storage and movement of subsurface fluids such as petroleum, groundwater, or contaminated fluids.

PHYSICAL PROPERTIES

Physical properties of rocks are of interest and utility in many fields of work, including geology, petrophysics, geophysics, materials science, geochemistry, and geotechnical engineering. The scale of investigation ranges from the molecular and crystalline up to terrestrial studies of Earth and other planetary bodies. Geologists are interested in the radioactive age dating of rocks to reconstruct the origin of mineral deposits; seismologists formulate prospective earthquake predictions using premonitory physical or chemical changes; crystallographers study the synthesis of minerals with special optical or physical properties; exploration geophysicists investigate the variation of physical properties of subsurface rocks to make possible detection of natural resources such as oil and gas, geothermal energy, and ores of metals; geotechnical engineers examine the nature and behaviour of the materials on, in, or of which such structures as buildings, dams, tunnels, bridges, and underground storage vaults are to be constructed; solid-state physicists study the magnetic, electrical, and mechanical properties of materials for electronic devices, computer components, or high-performance ceramics; and petroleum reservoir engineers analyze the response measured on well logs or in the processes of deep drilling at elevated temperature and pressure.

Since rocks are aggregates of mineral grains or crystals, their properties are determined in large part by the properties of their various constituent minerals. In a rock these general properties are determined by averaging the relative properties and sometimes orientations of the various grains or crystals. As a result, some properties that are anisotropic (i.e., differ with direction) on a submicroscopic or crystalline scale are fairly isotropic for a large bulk volume of the rock. Many properties are also dependent on grain or crystal size, shape, and packing arrangement, the amount and distribution of void space, the presence of natural cements in sedimentary rocks, the temperature and pressure, and the type and amount of contained fluids (e.g., water, petroleum, gases). Because many rocks exhibit a considerable range in these factors, the assignment of representative values for a particular property is often done using a statistical variation.

Some properties can vary considerably, depending on whether measured in situ (in place in the subsurface) or in the laboratory under simulated conditions. Electrical resistivity, for example, is highly dependent on the fluid content of the rock in situ and the temperature condition at the particular depth.

Density

Density varies significantly among different rock types because of differences in mineralogy and porosity. Knowledge of the distribution of underground rock densities can assist in interpreting subsurface geologic structure and rock type.

DRY BULK DENSITIES FOR VARIOUS ROCK TYPES

ROCK TYPE	NUMBER OF SAMPLES	MEAN (GRAMS PER CUBIC CM)	STANDARD DEVIATION	MODE (GRAMS PER CUBIC CM)	MEDIAN (GRAMS PER CUBIC CM)
all rocks	1,647	2.73	0.26	2.65	2.86
andesite	197	2.65	0.13	2.58	2.66
basalt	323	2.74	0.47	2.88	2.87
diorite	68	2.86	0.12	2.89	2.87
dolerite (diabase)	224	2.89	0.13	2.96	2.90
gabbro	98	2.95	0.14	2.99	2.97
granite	334	2.66	0.06	2.66	2.66
quartz porphyry	76	2.62	0.06	2.60	2.62
rhyolite	94	2.51	0.13	2.60	2.49
syenite	93	2.70	0.10	2.67	2.68
trachyte	71	2.57	0.10	2.62	2.57
sandstone	107	2.22	0.23	2.22	2.22

Source: After data from H.S. Washington (1917) and R.J. Piersol, L.E. Workman, and M.C. Watson (1940) as compiled by Gary R. Olhoeft and Gordon R. Johnson in Robert S. Carmichael, ed., *Hand-book of Physical Properties of Rocks*, vol. III, CRC Press, Inc. (1984).

In strict usage, density is defined as the mass of a substance per unit volume; however, in common usage, it is taken to be the weight in air of a unit volume of a sample at a specific temperature. Weight is the force that gravitation exerts on a body (and thus varies with location), whereas mass (a measure of the matter in a body) is a fundamental property and is constant regardless of location. In routine density measurements of rocks, the sample weights are considered to be equivalent to their masses, because the discrepancy between weight and mass would result in less error on the computed density than the experimental errors introduced in the measurement of volume. Thus, density is often determined using weight rather than mass. Density should properly be reported in kilograms per cubic metre (kg/m³), but is still often given in grams per cubic cm (g/cm³).

Another property closely related to density is specific gravity. It is defined, as noted above, as the ratio of the weight or mass in air of a unit volume of material at a stated temperature to the weight or mass in air of a unit volume of distilled water at the same temperature. Specific gravity is dimensionless (i.e., has no units).

The bulk density of a rock is $\rho B = W_G/V_B$, where W_G is the weight of grains (sedimentary rocks) or crystals (igneous and metamorphic rocks) and natural cements, if any, and V_B is the total volume of the grains or crystals plus the void (pore) space. The density can be dry if the pore space is empty, or it can be saturated if the pores are filled with fluid (e.g., water), which is more typical of the subsurface (in situ) situation. If there is pore fluid present,

$$\text{(saturated)} \quad \rho_B = \frac{W_G + W_{fl}}{V_B},$$

where W_{fl} is the weight of pore fluid. In terms of total porosity, saturated density is

$$\text{(saturated)} \quad \rho_B = \rho_G(1 - \varphi_T) + \rho_{fl}\varphi_T,$$

and thus

$$\varphi_T = \frac{\rho_G - \rho_B}{\rho_G - \rho_{fl}},$$

where ρ_{fl} is the density of the pore fluid. Density measurements for a given specimen involve the determination of any two of the following quantities: pore volume, bulk volume, or grain volume, along with the weight.

A useful way to assess the density of rocks is to make a histogram plot of the statistical range of a set of data. The representative value and its variation can be expressed as follows: (1) mean, the average value, (2) mode, the most common value (i.e., the peak of the distribution curve), (3) median, the value of the middle sample of the data set (i.e., the value at

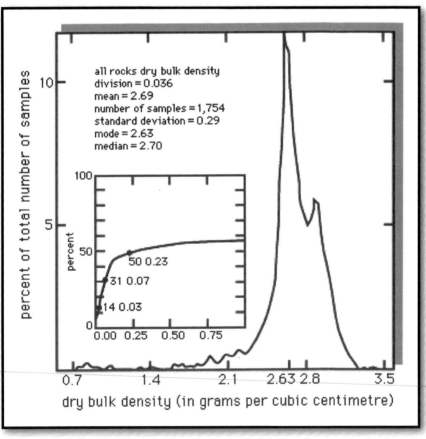

Dry bulk densities (distribution with density) for all rocks given in the dry bulk densities table. Copyright Encyclopædia Britannica, Inc.; rendering for this edition by Rosen Educational Services

which half of the samples are below and half are above), and (4) standard deviation, a statistical measure of the spread of the data (plus and minus one standard deviation from the mean value includes about two-thirds of the data).

TYPICAL DENSITY RANGES FOR SOME OTHER ROCK TYPES	
ROCK TYPE	DENSITY (GRAMS PER CUBIC CM)
amphibolite	2.79–3.14
andesite glass	2.40–2.57
anhydrite	2.82–2.93
anorthosite	2.64–2.92
basalt glass	2.70–2.85
chalk	2.23
dolomite	2.72–2.84
dunite	2.98–3.76
eclogite	3.32–3.45
gneiss	2.59–2.84
granodiorite	2.67–2.78
limestone	1.55–2.75
marble	2.67–2.75
norite	2.72–3.02
peridotite	3.15–3.28
quartzite	2.65
rock salt	2.10–2.20
schist	2.73–3.19
shale	2.06–2.67
slate	2.72–2.84

Source: After data from R.A. Daly, G.E. Manger, and S.P. Clark, Jr. (1966); A.F. Birch (1966); F. Press (1966); and R.N. Schock, B.P. Bonner, and H. Louis (1974) in Robert S. Carmichael, ed., *Handbook of Physical Properties of Rocks*, vol. III, CRC Press, Inc. (1984).

The density distributions for granite, basalt, and sandstone are often compared. Granite is an intrusive igneous rock with low porosity and a well-defined chemical (mineral) composition; its range of densities is narrow. Basalt is, in most cases, an extrusive igneous rock that can exhibit a large variation in porosity (because entrained gases leave voids called vesicles), and thus some highly porous samples can have low densities. Sandstone is a clastic sedimentary rock that can have a wide range of porosities depending on the degree of sorting, compaction, packing arrangement of grains, and cementation. The bulk density varies accordingly.

The density of clastic sedimentary rocks increases as the rocks are progressively buried. This is because of the increase of overburden pressure, which causes compaction, and the progressive cementation with age. Both compaction and cementation decrease the porosity.

The densities for rock-forming minerals and rocks are represented by the variables r_G and r_B, respectively. The bulk densities for sedimentary rocks, which typically have variable porosity, are often presented as ranges of both dry r_B and (water-) saturated r_B. The pore-filling fluid is usually briny water, often indicative of the presence of seawater when the rock was being deposited or lithified. It should be noted that the bulk density is less than the grain density of the constituent mineral (or mineral assemblage), depending on the porosity. For example, sandstone (characteristically quartzose) has a typical dry bulk density of 2.0–2.6 g/cm^3, with a porosity that can vary from low to more than 30 percent. The density of quartz itself is 2.65 g/cm^3. If porosity were zero, the bulk density would equal the grain density.

Saturated bulk density is higher than dry bulk density, owing to the added presence of pore-filling fluid.

MECHANICAL PROPERTIES

Rocks can be altered mechanically through a variety of processes. The stress of a force upon a rock can deform, or strain, the rock. Such forces include confining pressure, internal pore pressure, temperature, the rate of loading, and time.

STRESS AND STRAIN

When a stress σ (force per unit area) is applied to a material such as rock, the material experiences a change in dimension, volume, or shape. This change, or deformation, is called strain (ε). Stresses can be axial—e.g., directional tension or simple compression—or shear (tangential), or all-sided (e.g., hydrostatic compression). The terms stress and pressure are sometimes used interchangeably, but often stress refers to directional stress or shear stress and pressure (*P*) refers to hydrostatic compression. For small stresses, the strain is elastic (recoverable when the stress is removed and linearly proportional to the applied stress). For larger stresses and other conditions, the strain can be inelastic, or permanent.

ELASTIC CONSTANTS

In elastic deformation, there are various constants that relate the magnitude of the strain response to the applied stress. These elastic constants include the following:

(1) Young's modulus (*E*) is the ratio of the applied stress to the fractional extension (or shortening) of the sample length parallel to the tension (or compression). The strain is the linear change in dimension divided by the original length.

(2) Shear modulus (μ) is the ratio of the applied stress to the distortion (rotation) of a plane originally perpendicular to the applied shear stress; it is also termed the modulus of rigidity.

(3) Bulk modulus (k) is the ratio of the confining pressure to the fractional reduction of volume in response to the applied hydrostatic pressure. The volume strain is the change in volume of the sample divided by the original volume. Bulk modulus is also termed the modulus of incompressibility.

(4) Poisson's ratio (σp) is the ratio of lateral strain (perpendicular to an applied stress) to the longitudinal strain (parallel to applied stress).

For elastic and isotropic materials, the elastic constants are interrelated. For example,

$$\sigma_p = \frac{E}{2\mu} - 1;$$

$$E = 3k(1 - 2\sigma_p);$$

and

$$\mu = \frac{3}{2} k \left(\frac{1 - 2\sigma_p}{1 + \sigma_p} \right).$$

The following are the common units of stress:

1 bar $= 10^6$ dynes per square centimetre
$= 10^5$ newtons per square metre, or pascals (Pa)
$= 0.1$ megapascal (*i.e.*, 0.1×10^6 Pa).

Thus 10 kilobars = 1 gigapascal (i.e., 10^9 Pa).

ROCK MECHANICS

The study of deformation resulting from the strain of rocks in response to stresses is called rock mechanics. When the scale of the deformation is extended to large geologic structures in Earth's crust, the field of study is known as geotectonics.

The mechanisms and character of the deformation of rocks and Earth materials can be investigated through laboratory experiments, development of theoretical models based on the properties of materials, and study of deformed rocks and structures in the field. In the laboratory, one can simulate—either directly or by appropriate scaling of experimental parameters—several conditions. Two types of pressure may be simulated: confining (hydrostatic), due to burial under rock overburden, and internal (pore), due to pressure exerted by pore fluids contained in void space in the rock. Directed applied stress, such as compression, tension, and shear, is studied, as are the effects of increased temperature introduced with depth in Earth's crust. The effects of the duration of time and the rate of applying stress (i.e., loading) as a function of time are examined. Also, the role of fluids, particularly if they are chemically active, is investigated.

Some simple apparatuses for deforming rocks are designed for biaxial stress application: a directed (uniaxial) compression is applied while a confining pressure is exerted (by pressurized fluid) around the cylindrical specimen. This simulates deformation at depth within Earth. An independent internal pore-fluid pressure also can be exerted. The rock specimen can be jacketed with a thin, impermeable sleeve (e.g., rubber or copper) to separate the external pressure medium from the internal pore fluids (if any). The specimen is typically a few centimetres in dimension.

Another apparatus for exerting high pressure on a sample was designed in 1968 by Akira Sawaoka, Naoto Kawai, and Robert Carmichael to give hydrostatic confining pressures up to 12 kilobars (1.2 gigapascal), additional directed stress, and temperatures up to a few hundred degrees Celsius. The specimen is positioned on the base-plate; the pressure is applied by driving in pistons with a hydraulic press. The end caps can be locked down to hold the pressure for time experiments and to make the device portable.

Apparatuses have been developed, typically using multianvil designs, which extend the range of static experimental conditions—at least for small specimens and limited times—to pressures as high as about 1,700 kilobars (170 gigapascal) and temperatures of about 2,000 °C (about 3,600 °F). Such work has been pioneered by researchers such as Peter M. Bell and Ho-Kwang Mao, who conducted studies at the Geophysical Laboratory of the Carnegie Institution in Washington, D.C. Using dynamic techniques (i.e., shock from explosive impact generated by gun-type designs), even higher pressures up to 7,000 kilobars (700 gigapascal)—which is nearly twice the pressure at Earth's centre and seven million times greater than the atmospheric pressure at Earth's surface—can be produced for very short times. A leading figure in such ultrapressure work is A. Sawaoka at the Tokyo Institute of Technology.

In the upper crust of the planet, hydrostatic pressure increases at the rate of about 320 bars (0.032 gigapascal) per km (0.6 mile), and temperature increases at a typical rate of 20–40 °C (68–104 °F) per km, depending on recent crustal geologic history. Additional directed stress, as can be generated by large-scale crustal deformation (tecto-nism), can range up to 1 to 2 kilobars (0.1 to 0.2 gigapascal). This is approximately equal to the ultimate strength (before fracture) of solid crystalline rock at surface temperature and pressure. The stress released in a single major earthquake—a shift on a fault plane—is about 50–150 bars.

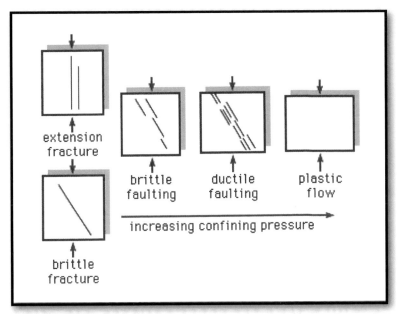

Deformation as affected by increased confining pressure. Copyright Encyclopædia Britannica, Inc.; rendering for this edition by Rosen Educational Services

In studying the deformation of rocks one can start with the assumption of ideal behaviour: elastic strain and homogeneous and isotropic stress and strain. In reality, on a microscopic scale there are grains and pores in sediments and a fabric of crystals in igneous and metamorphic rocks. On a large scale, rock bodies exhibit physical and chemical variations and structural features. Furthermore, conditions such as extended length of time, confining pressure, and subsurface fluids affect the rates of change of deformation.

STRESS-STRAIN RELATIONSHIPS

The deformation of materials is characterized by stress-strain relations. For elastic-behaviour materials, the strain is proportional to the load (i.e., the applied stress). The strain is immediate with stress and is reversible (recoverable) up to the yield point stress, beyond which permanent strain results. For viscous material, there is laminar (slow, smooth, parallel) flow; one must exert a force to maintain motion because of internal frictional resistance to

SOME TYPICAL VALUES OF ELASTIC CONSTANTS AND PROPERTIES		
	elastic constants (at room temperature and pressure)	
MATERIAL	YOUNG'S MODULUS (IN 106 BARS)	SHEAR MODULUS (IN 106 BARS)
ice	0.1	0.03
shale	0.2–0.3	0.15
limestone	0.4–0.7	0.22–0.26
granite	0.3–0.6	0.2
basalt	0.7–0.9	0.3
steel	2.1	0.83
	TEMPERATURE (DEGREES CELSIUS)	COEFFICIENT OF VISCOSITY (POISES)
lava (Mount Vesuvius)	1,100 1,400	28,300 250
lava (Oshima, Japan)	1,038 1,125	230,000 5,600
andesite lava	1,400	150–1,500
	COMPRESSIVE STRENGTH (AT ROOM TEMPERATURE AND PRESSURE, IN KILOBARS)	
shale	0.8–1.8	
sandstone	0.5–2	
limestone	1–2	
granite	1.7–2.5	
basalt	1–3.4	

flow, called the viscosity. Viscosity varies with the applied stress, strain rate, and temperature. In plastic behaviour, the material strains continuously (but still has strength) after the yield point stress is reached; however, beyond this point there is some permanent deformation. In elasticoviscous deformation, there is combined elastic and viscous behaviour. The material yields continuously (viscously) for a constant applied load. An example of such behaviour is creep, a slow, permanent, and continuous deformation occurring under constant load over a long time in such materials as crystals, ice, soil and sediment, and rocks at depth. In firmoviscous behaviour, the material is essentially solid but the strain is not immediate with application of stress; rather, it is taken up and released exponentially. A plasticoviscous material exhibits elastic behaviour for initial stress (as in plastic behaviour), but after the yield point stress is reached, it flows like a viscous fluid.

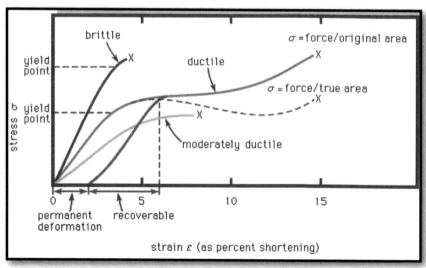

Typical stress-strain curves for rock materials. Each X represents the point of fracture for the corresponding material. Copyright Encyclopædia Britannica, Inc.; rendering for this edition by Rosen Educational Services

Rheology is the study of the flow deformation of materials. The concept of rheidity refers to the capacity of a material to flow, arbitrarily defined as the time required with a shear stress applied for the viscous strain to be 1,000 times greater than the elastic strain. It is thus a measure of the threshold of fluidlike behaviour. Although such behaviour depends on temperature, relative comparisons can be made.

The ability to undergo large permanent deformation before fracture is called ductility. Stress is force per unit area, whereas strain can be defined as fractional shortening of the specimen parallel to the applied compression. Brittle material behaves elastically nearly until the point of fracture, whereas the ductile (plastically deformable) material is elastic up to the yield point but then has a range of plastic deformation before fracturing. For plastic deformation, the flow mechanisms are intracrystalline (slip and twinning within crystal grains), intercrystalline motion by crushing and fracture (cataclasis), and recrystallization by solutioning or solid diffusion.

If the applied stress is removed while a ductile material is in the plastic range, part of the strain is recoverable (elastically), but there is permanent deformation. The

RHEIDITY THRESHOLD OF FLUIDLIKE DEFORMATION	
MATERIAL	APPROXIMATE TIME
ice (e.g., glacier)	2 weeks
gypsum	1 year
rock salt (e.g., saltdome)	10–20 years
serpentine (a mafic silicate mineral)	10,000 years

ultimate strength is the highest point (stress) on a stress-strain curve, often occurring at fracture (which is the complete loss of cohesion). The strength of a material is its resistance to failure (destruction of structure) by flow or fracture; it is a measure of the stress required to deform a body.

EFFECT OF ENVIRONMENTAL CONDITIONS

The behaviour and mechanical properties of rocks depend on a number of environmental conditions. (1) Confining pressure increases the elasticity, strength (e.g., yield point and ultimate fracture stress), and ductility. (2) Internal pore-fluid pressure reduces the effective stress acting on the sample, thus reducing the strength and ductility. The effective, or net, confining pressure is the external hydrostatic pressure minus the internal pore-fluid pressure. (3) Temperature lowers the strength, enhances ductility, and may enhance recrystallization. (4) Fluid solutions can enhance deformation, creep, and recrystallization. (5) Time is an influential factor as well. (6) The rate of loading (i.e., the rate at which stress is applied) influences mechanical properties. (7) Compaction, as would occur with burial to depth, reduces the volume of pore space for sedimentary rocks and the crack porosity for crystalline rocks.

Rocks, which are typically brittle at Earth's surface, can undergo ductile deformation when buried and subjected to increased confining pressure and temperature for long periods of time. If stress exceeds their strength or if they are not sufficiently ductile, they will fail by fracture—as a crystal, within a bed or rock, on an earthquake fault zone, and so on—whereas with ductility they can flow and fold.

ROCK STRENGTHS, WITH VARYING TEMPERATURE AND PRESSURE

ROCK TYPE	TEMPER-ATURE (°C)	CONFINING PRESSURE (KILOBARS)	PLASTIC YIELD STRENGTH (KILOBARS)	ULTIMATE STRENGTH (KILOBARS)
granite	500	5	10	11.5
	800	5	5	6
gabbro	500	5	4	8
peridotite	500	5	8	9
	800	5	5.5	8
basalt	500	5	8	10
	800	5	2	2.5
marble	24	2	2.5	5.5
	500	3	1	2
limestone	24	2	4.5	5.5
	500	3	2.5	3
dolomite	24	2	6	7
	500	5	4	6.5
shale	24	2	1.5	2.5
rock salt	24	1	0.5	1

An increase in confining pressure causes brittle fracture to become shear slippage and eventually causes flow (ductile) behaviour. This transition is also aided by higher temperature, decreased internal pore-fluid pressure, and slower strain rate.

VARIATION OF SOME ELASTIC CONSTANTS (IN 106 BARS) WITH ROCK TYPE AND CONFINING PRESSURE

ROCK TYPE	BULK MODULUS	YOUNG'S MODULUS	SHEAR MODULUS	POISSON'S RATIO
at pressure = 1 bar				
granite	0.1	0.3	0.2	0.05
gabbro	0.3	0.9	0.6	0.1
dunite	1.1	1.5	0.5	0.3
obsidian	0.4	0.7	0.3	0.08
basalt	0.5	0.8	0.3	0.23
gneiss	0.1	0.2	0.1	0.05
marble	0.1	0.4	0.2	0.1
quartzite				
sandstone	0.07	0.2	0.08	0.1
shale	0.04	0.1	0.05	0.04
limestone	0.8	0.6	0.2	0.3
at pressure = 3,000 bars				
rock type	bulk modulus	Young's modulus	shear modulus	Poisson's ratio
granite	0.5	0.6	0.4	0.25
gabbro	0.9	0.8	0.5	0.2
dunite	1.2	1.7	0.7	0.27
obsidian				
basalt	0.8	1.2	0.4	0.25
gneiss	0.5	0.7	0.3	
marble	0.8	0.7	0.3	0.3
quartzite	0.5	1.0	0.4	0.07
sandstone				
shale				
limestone				

Thermal Properties

Heat flow (or flux), q, in Earth's crust or in rock as a building material, is the product of the temperature gradient (change in temperature per unit distance) and the material's thermal conductivity (k, the heat flow across a surface per unit area per unit time when a temperature difference exists in unit length perpendicular to the surface). Thus,

$$q = \frac{dT}{dz} \times k.$$

The units of the terms in this equation are given below, expressed first in the centimetre-gram-second (cgs) system and then in the International System of Units (SI) system, with the conversion factor from the first to the second given between them.

q, heat flow:

calories per square centimetre per second (cal/cm² · sec) $\times \dfrac{1}{23.9} \times 10^{-6} =$ watts per square metre (W/m²)

$\dfrac{dT}{dz}$, temperature gradient:

degrees Celsius per kilometre (°C/km, practical unit for Earth) $\times 10^{-3} =$ degrees Celsius per metre (°C/m)

k, thermal conductivity:

calories per square centimetre per second per degree Celsius (cal/cm² · sec · °C) $\times \dfrac{1}{23.9} \times 10^{-3} =$ watts per metre per degree Celsius (W/m · °C)

INTRUSIVE AND EXTRUSIVE ROCKS

Reddish volcanic rock on the coast of Tanna Island, Vanuatu. Allan Power—Bruce Coleman Inc.

Intrusive rocks, which are also called plutonic rocks, are igneous rocks formed from magma forced into older rocks at depths within Earth's crust. The intruded magma then slowly solidifies below Earth's surface, though it may later be exposed by erosion. Igneous intrusions form a variety of rock types.

In contrast, extrusive rocks are rocks derived from magma (molten silicate material) that have been poured out or ejected at Earth's surface. Extrusive rocks are usually distinguished from intrusive rocks on the basis of their texture and mineral composition.

Both lava flows and pyroclastic debris (fragmented volcanic material) are extrusive; they are commonly glassy (obsidian) or finely crystalline (basalts and felsites). Many extrusive rocks also contain intrusive components; this mixture of fine- and coarse-grained textures is described as porphyritic.

THERMAL CONDUCTIVITY

Thermal conductivity can be determined in the laboratory or in situ, as in a borehole or deep well, by turning on a heating element and measuring the rise in temperature with time. It depends on several factors: (1) chemical composition of the rock (i.e., mineral content), (2) fluid content (type and degree of saturation of the pore space);

TYPICAL VALUES OF THERMAL CONDUCTIVITY
(in 0.001 calories per centimetre per second per degree Celsius)

MATERIAL	AT 20 °C	AT 200 °C
typical rocks	4–10	
granite	7.8	6.6
gneiss		
(perpendicular to banding)	5.9	5.5 (100 °C)
(parallel to banding)	8.2	7.4 (100 °C)
gabbro	5.1	5.0
basalt	4.0	4.0
dunite	12.0	8.1
marble	7.3	5.2
quartzite	15.0	9.0
limestone	6.0	
one sandstone		
(dry)	4.4	
(saturated)	5.4	
shale	3–4	
rock salt	12.8	
sand		
(dry)	0.65	
(30% water)	3.94	
water	1.34 (0 °C)	1.6 (80 °C)
ice	5.3 (0 °C)	9.6 (-130 °C)
magnetite	12.6	
quartz	20.0	
feldspars	5.0	

the presence of water increases the thermal conductivity (i.e., enhances the flow of heat), (3) pressure (a high pressure increases the thermal conductivity by closing cracks which inhibit heat flow), (4) temperature, and (5) isotropy and homogeneity of the rock. For crystalline silicate rocks—the dominant rocks of the "basement" crustal rocks—the lower values are typical of ones rich in magnesium and iron (e.g., basalt and gabbro) and the higher values are typical of those rich in silica (quartz) and alumina (e.g., granite). These values result because the thermal conductivity of quartz is relatively high, while that for feldspars is low.

THERMAL EXPANSION

The change in dimension—linear or volumetric—of a rock specimen with temperature is expressed in terms of a coefficient of thermal expansion. This is given as the ratio of dimension change (e.g., change in volume) to the original dimension (volume, V) per unit of temperature (T) change:

$$\frac{1}{V}\frac{\Delta V}{\Delta T}.$$

THERMAL EXPANSION OF ROCKS	
ROCK TYPE	LINEAR-EXPANSION COEFFICIENT (IN 10^{-6} PER DEGREE CELSIUS)
granite and rhyolite	8 ± 3
andesite and diorite	7 ± 2
basalt, gabbro, and diabase	5.4 ± 1
sandstone	10 ± 2
limestone	8 ± 4
marble	7 ± 2
slate	9 ± 1

Most rocks have a volume-expansion coefficient in the range of 15–33 × 10^{-6} per degree Celsius under ordinary conditions. Quartz-rich rocks have relatively high values because of the higher volume expansion coefficient of quartz. Thermal-expansion coefficients increase with temperature. Linear expansion coefficients may be calculated using the equation,

$$\frac{1}{L}\frac{\Delta L}{\Delta T},$$

where L represents length.

Radioactive Heat Generation

The spontaneous decay (partial disintegration) of the nuclei of radioactive elements provides decay particles and energy. The energy, composed of emission kinetic energy and radiation, is converted to heat; it has been an important factor in affecting the temperature gradient and thermal evolution of Earth. Deep-seated elevated temperatures provide the heat that causes rock to deform plastically and to move, thus generating to a large extent the processes of plate tectonics—plate motions, seafloor spreading, continental drift, and subduction—and most earthquakes and volcanism.

Some elements, or their isotopes (nuclear species with the same atomic number but different mass numbers), decay with time. These include elements with an atomic number greater than 83—of which the most important are uranium-235, uranium-238, and thorium-232—and a few with a lower atomic number, such as potassium-40.

The heat generated within rocks depends on the types and abundances of the radioactive elements and their host minerals. Such heat production, A, is given in calories per cubic cm per second, or 1 calorie per gram

SOME RADIOACTIVE DECAY SERIES

ELEMENT	RADIO-ACTIVE ISOTOPE	FINAL PRODUCT	ISOTOPIC ABUNDANCE (%)	HALF-LIFE (IN 10⁹ YEARS)
uranium	U-235	Pb-207	0.72	0.7
	U-238	Pb-206	99.28	4.5
thorium	Th-232	Pb-208	100.0	14.0
potassium	K-40	(89%) Ca-40	0.01	1.4*
		(11%) Argon-40		11.9*
rubidium	Rb-87	Sr-87	27.8	48.8

*half-life for K-40 as a whole is $1.25(10^9)$ years.

per year = 4.186×10^7 ergs per gram per year = 1.327 ergs per gram per second. The rate of radioactive decay, statistically an exponential process, is given by the half-life, $t_{1/2}$. The half-life is the time required for half the original radioactive atoms to decay for a particular isotope.

HEAT PRODUCTIVITIES

ISOTOPE	HEAT PRODUCTIVITY, A (CALORIES PER GRAM PER YEAR)
U-235	4.29
U-238	0.71
natural uranium	0.73
Th-232	0.20
K-40	0.22
natural potassium	$27(10^{-6})$
Rb-87	$130(10^{-6})$
natural rubidium	$36(10^{-6})$

HEAT PRODUCTIVITIES

MAJOR ROCK PROVINCE	ABUNDANCES			
	U PPM	TH PPM	K %	HEAT PRODUCTIVITY, A (IN 10^{-13} CALORIES PER CUBIC CENTIMETRE PER SECOND)
oceanic crust	0.42	1.68	0.69	0.71
continental shield crust (old)	1.00	4.00	1.63	1.67
continental upper crust (young)	1.32	5.28	2.15	2.20

HEAT PRODUCTIVITIES OF VARIOUS ROCKS

ROCK TYPE	ABUNDANCES			
	U PPM	TH PPM	RB PPM	K %
granite	3.4	50	220	4.45
andesite	1.9	6.4	67	2.35
oceanic basalt	0.5	0.9	9	0.43
peridotite	0.005	0.01	0.063	0.001
average upper-continental crust	2.5	10.5	110	2.7
average continental crust	1.0	2.5	50	1.25

ROCK TYPE	HEAT PRODUCTION			
	FROM U	FROM TH	FROM K	TOTAL A (in 10^{-6} calories per gram per year)
granite	2.52	9.95	1.16	13.63
andesite	1.41	1.27	0.61	3.29
oceanic basalt	0.37	0.18	0.11	0.66

ROCK TYPE	HEAT PRODUCTION			
	FROM U	FROM TH	FROM K	TOTAL A (in 10-6 calories per gram per year)
average upper-continental crust	1.85	2.09	0.7	4.64
average continental crust	0.74	0.5	0.33	1.56

Source: Modified from compilation by William Van Schmus in Robert S. Carmichael, ed., *Handbook of Physical Properties of Rocks*, vol. III, CRC Press, Inc. (1984).

The radioactive elements are more concentrated in the continental upper-crust rocks that are rich in quartz (i.e., felsic, or less mafic). This results because these rocks are differentiated by partial melting of the upper-mantle and oceanic-crust rock. The radioactive elements tend to be preferentially driven off from these rocks for geochemical reasons.

CONTINENTAL DRIFT

The large-scale horizontal movement of continents relative to one another and to the ocean basins during one or more episodes of geologic time is called continental drift. This concept was an important precursor to the development of the theory of plate tectonics, which incorporates it.

The idea of a large-scale displacement of continents has a long history. Noting the apparent fit of the bulge of eastern South America into the bight of Africa, the German naturalist Alexander von Humboldt theorized about 1800 that the lands bordering the Atlantic Ocean had once been joined. Some 50 years later, Antonio Snider-Pellegrini, a French scientist, argued that the presence of identical fossil plants in both North American and European coal deposits could be explained if the two continents had formerly been connected, a relationship otherwise difficult to account for. In 1908 Frank B. Taylor of the United States invoked the notion of continental collision to explain the formation of some of the world's mountain ranges.

The first truly detailed and comprehensive theory of continental drift was proposed in 1912 by Alfred Wegener, a German meteorologist. Bringing together a large mass of geologic and paleontological data, Wegener postulated that throughout most of geologic time there was only one continent, which he called Pangea. Late in the Triassic Period (an interval which lasted from approximately 251 million to 199.6 million years ago), Pangea fragmented, and the parts began to move away from one another. Westward drift of the Americas opened the Atlantic Ocean, and the Indian block drifted across the Equator to merge with Asia. In 1937 Alexander L. Du Toit, a South African geologist, modified Wegener's hypothesis by suggesting two primordial continents: Laurasia in the north and Gondwana in the south.

Aside from the congruency of continental shelf margins across the Atlantic, modern proponents of continental drift have amassed impressive geologic evidence to support their views. Indications of widespread glaciation from 380 to 250 million years ago are evident in Antarctica, southern South America, southern Africa, India, and Australia. If these continents were once united around the south polar region, this glaciation would become explicable as a unified sequence of events in time and space. Also, fitting the Americas with the continents across the Atlantic brings together similar kinds of rocks, fossils, and geologic structures. A belt of ancient rocks along the Brazilian coast, for example, matches one in West Africa. Moreover, the earliest marine deposits along the Atlantic coastlines of either South America or Africa are Jurassic in age (approximately 199.6 million to 145.5 million years old), which suggests that the ocean did not exist before that time.

ELECTRICAL PROPERTIES

The electrical nature of a material is characterized by its conductivity (or, inversely, its resistivity) and its dielectric constant, and coefficients that indicate the rates of change of these with temperature, frequency at which measurement is made, and so on. For rocks with a range of chemical composition as well as variable physical properties of porosity and fluid content, the values of electrical properties can vary widely.

Resistance (R) is defined as being one ohm when a potential difference (voltage; V) across a specimen of one volt magnitude produces a current (i) of one ampere; that is, $V = Ri$. The electrical resistivity (ρ) is an intrinsic property of the material. In other words, it is inherent and not dependent on sample size or current path. It is related to resistance by $R = \rho L/A$ where L is the length of specimen, A is the cross-sectional area of specimen, and units of ρ are ohm-centimetre; 1 ohm-centimetre equals 0.01 ohm-metre. The conductivity (σ) is equal to $1/\rho$ ohm $^{-1} \cdot$ cm^{-1} (or termed mhos/cm). In SI units, it is given in mhos/metre, or siemens/metre.

Materials that are generally considered as "good" conductors have a resistivity of 10^{-5}–10 ohm-centimetre (10^{-7}–10^{-1} ohm-metre) and a conductivity of 10–10^{7} mhos/metre. Those that are classified as intermediate conductors have a resistivity of 100–10^{9} ohm-centimetre (1–10^{7} ohm-metre) and a conductivity of 10^{-7}–1 mhos/metre. "Poor" conductors, also known as insulators, have a resistivity of 10^{10}–10^{17} ohm-centimetre (10^{8}–10^{15} ohm-metre) and a conductivity of 10^{-15}–10^{-8}. Seawater is a much better conductor (i.e., it has lower resistivity) than fresh water owing to its higher content of dissolved salts; dry rock is very resistive. In the subsurface, pores are typically filled to some degree by fluids. The resistivity of materials has a wide range—copper is, for example, different from quartz by 22 orders of magnitude.

For high-frequency alternating currents, the electrical response of a rock is governed in part by the dielectric constant, ε. This is the capacity of the rock to store electric charge; it is a measure of polarizability in an electric

TYPICAL RESISTIVITIES	
MATERIAL	**RESISTIVITY (OHM-CENTIMETRE)**
seawater (18 °C)	21
uncontaminated surface water	$2(10^4)$
distilled water	$0.2-1(10^6)$
water (4 °C)	$9(10^6)$
ice	$3(10^8)$
Rocks (in situ)	
sedimentary	
clay, soft shale	$100-5(10^3)$
hard shale	$7-50(10^3)$
sand	$5-40(10^3)$
sandstone	$(10^4)-(10^5)$
glacial moraine	$1-500(10^3)$
porous limestone	$1-30(10^4)$
dense limestone	$>(10^6)$
rock salt	$(10^8)-(10^9)$
igneous	$5(10^4)-(10^8)$
metamorphic	$5(10^4)-5(10^9)$
Rocks (laboratory)	
dry granite	10^{12}
Minerals	
copper (18 °C)	$1.7(10^{-6})$
graphite	$5-500(10^{-4})$
pyrrhotite	$0.1-0.6$
magnetite crystals	$0.6-0.8$
pyrite ore	$1-(10^5)$
magnetite ore	$(10^2)-5(10^5)$
chromite ore	$>10^6$
quartz (18 °C)	$(10^{14})-(10^{16})$

field. In cgs units, the dielectric constant is 1.0 in a vacuum. In SI units, it is given in farads per metre or in terms of the ratio of specific capacity of the material to specific capacity of vacuum (which is 8.85×10^{-12} farads per metre). The dielectric constant is a function of temperature, and of frequency, for those frequencies well above 100 hertz (cycles per second).

Electrical conduction occurs in rocks by (1) fluid conduction—i.e., electrolytic conduction by ionic transfer in briny pore water—and (2) metallic and semiconductor (e.g., some sulfide ores) electron conduction. If the rock has any porosity and contained fluid, the fluid typically dominates the conductivity response. The rock conductivity depends on the conductivity of the fluid (and its chemical composition), degree of fluid saturation, porosity and permeability, and temperature. If rocks lose water, as with compaction of clastic sedimentary rocks at depth, their resistivity typically increases.

MAGNETIC PROPERTIES

The magnetic properties of rocks arise from the magnetic properties of the constituent mineral grains and crystals. Typically, only a small fraction of the rock consists of magnetic minerals. It is this small portion of grains that determines the magnetic properties and magnetization of the rock as a whole, with two results: (1) the magnetic properties of a given rock may vary widely within a given rock body or structure, depending on chemical inhomogeneities, depositional or crystallization conditions, and what happens to the rock after formation; and (2) rocks that share the same lithology (type and name) need not necessarily share the same magnetic characteristics. Lithologic classifications are usually based on the abundance of dominant silicate minerals, but the magnetization is determined by the minor fraction of such magnetic mineral grains as iron oxides. The major rock-forming magnetic minerals are iron oxides and sulfides.

Although the magnetic properties of rocks sharing the same classification may vary from rock to rock, general magnetic properties do nonetheless usually depend on rock type and overall composition. The magnetic properties of a particular rock can be quite well understood provided one has specific information about the magnetic properties of crystalline materials and minerals, as well as about how those properties are affected by such factors as temperature, pressure, chemical composition, and the size of the grains. Understanding is further enhanced by information about how the properties of typical rocks are dependent on the geologic environment and how they vary with different conditions.

APPLICATIONS OF THE STUDY OF ROCK MAGNETIZATION

An understanding of rock magnetization is important in at least three different areas: prospecting, geology, and materials science. In magnetic prospecting, one is interested in mapping the depth, size, type, and inferred composition of buried rocks. The prospecting, which may be done from ground surface, ship, or aircraft, provides an important first step in exploring buried geologic structures and may, for example, help identify favourable locations for oil, natural gas, and economic mineral deposits.

Rock magnetization has traditionally played an important role in geology. Paleomagnetic work seeks to determine the remanent magnetization and thereby ascertain the character of Earth's field when certain rocks were formed. The results of such research have important ramifications in stratigraphic correlation, age

MAGNETIC SURVEY

A magnetic survey is one of the tools used by the exploration geophysicist in his or her search for mineral-bearing ore bodies or even oil-bearing sedimentary structures. The essential feature is the measurement of the magnetic-field intensity and sometimes the magnetic inclination, or dip, and declination (departure from geographic north) at several stations. If the object of the survey is to make a rapid reconnaissance of an area, a magnetic-intensity profile is made only over the target area. If the object of the survey is to delineate already discovered structures, the geophysicist sets up a grid over the area and makes measurements at each station on the grid. The corrected data he records is then entered on a scale drawing of the grid, and contour lines are drawn between points of equal intensity to give a magnetic map of the target area that may clearly indicate the size and extent of the anomalous body to the trained eye of the interpreting geophysicist.

dating, and reconstructing past movements of Earth's crust. Indeed, magnetic surveys of the oceanic crust provided for the first time the quantitative evidence needed to cogently demonstrate that segments of the crust had undergone large-scale lateral displacements over geologic time, thereby corroborating the concepts of continental drift and seafloor spreading, both of which are fundamental to the theory of plate tectonics.

The understanding of magnetization is increasingly important in materials science as well. The design and manufacture of efficient memory cores, magnetic tapes, and permanent magnets increasingly rely on the ability to create materials having desired magnetic properties.

BASIC TYPES OF MAGNETIZATION

There are six basic types of magnetization: (1) diamagnetism, (2) paramagnetism, (3) ferromagnetism, (4) antiferromagnetism, (5) ferrimagnetism, and (6) superparamagnetism.

Diamagnetism arises from the orbiting electrons surrounding each atomic nucleus. When an external magnetic field is applied, the orbits are shifted in such a way that the atoms set up their own magnetic field in opposition to the applied field. In other words, the induced diamagnetic field opposes the external field. Diamagnetism is present in all materials, is weak, and exists only in the presence of an applied field. The propensity of a substance for being magnetized in an external field is called its susceptibility (k) and it is defined as J/H, where J is the magnetization (intensity) per unit volume and H is the strength of the applied field. Since the induced field always opposes the applied field, the sign of diamagnetic susceptibility is negative. The susceptibility of a diamagnetic substance is on the order of -10^{-6} electromagnetic units per cubic cm (emu/cm³). It is sometimes denoted κ for susceptibility per unit mass of material.

Paramagnetism results from the electron spin of unpaired electrons. An electron has a magnetic dipole moment—which is to say that it behaves like a tiny bar magnet—and so when a group of electrons is placed in a magnetic field, the dipole moments tend to line up with the field. The effect augments the net magnetization in the direction of the applied field. Like diamagnetism, paramagnetism is weak and exists only in the presence of an applied field, but since the effect enhances the applied field, the sign of the paramagnetic susceptibility is always positive. The susceptibility of a paramagnetic substance is on the order of 10^{-4} to 10^{-6} emu/cm³.

Ferromagnetism also exists because of the magnetic properties of the electron. Unlike paramagnetism, however, ferromagnetism can occur even if no external field is applied. The magnetic dipole moments of the atoms spontaneously line up with one another because it is energetically favourable for them to do so. A remanent magnetization can be retained. Complete alignment of the dipole moments would take place only at a temperature of absolute zero (o kelvin [K], or -273.15 °C, or -459.67 °F). Above absolute zero, thermal motions begin to disorder the magnetic moments. At a temperature called the Curie temperature, which varies from material to material, the thermally induced disorder overcomes the alignment, and the ferromagnetic properties of the substance disappear. The susceptibility of ferromagnetic materials is large and positive. It is on the order of 10 to 10^4 emu/cm³. Only a few materials—iron, cobalt, and nickel—are ferromagnetic in the strict sense of the word and have a strong residual magnetization. In general usage, particularly in engineering, the term ferromagnetic is frequently applied to any material that is appreciably magnetic.

Antiferromagnetism occurs when the dipole moments of the atoms in a material assume an antiparallel arrangement in the absence of an applied field. The result is that the sample has no net magnetization. The strength of the susceptibility is comparable to that of paramagnetic materials. Above a temperature called the Néel temperature, thermal motions destroy the antiparallel arrangement, and the material then becomes paramagnetic. Spin-canted (anti)ferromagnetism is a special condition which occurs when antiparallel magnetic moments are deflected from the antiferromagnetic plane, resulting in a weak net magnetism. Hematite (α-Fe_2O_3) is such a material.

Ferrimagnetism is an antiparallel alignment of atomic dipole moments which does yield an appreciable net magnetization resulting from unequal moments of the magnetic sublattices. Remanent magnetization is detectable. Above the Curie temperature the substance becomes paramagnetic. Magnetite (Fe_3O_4), which is the most magnetic common mineral, is a ferrimagnetic substance.

Superparamagnetism occurs in materials having grains so small (about 100 angstroms) that any cooperative alignment of dipole moments is overcome by thermal energy.

TYPES OF REMANENT MAGNETIZATION

Rocks and minerals may retain magnetization after the removal of an externally applied field, thereby becoming permanent weak magnets. This property is known as remanent magnetization and is manifested in different forms, depending on the magnetic properties of the rocks and minerals and their geologic origin and history. Delineated below are the kinds of remanent magnetization frequently observed.

CRM (chemical, or crystallization, remanent magnetization) can be induced after a crystal is formed and undergoes one of a number of physicochemical changes, such as oxidation or reduction, a phase change, dehydration, recrystallization, or precipitation of natural cements. The induction, which is particularly important in some (red) sediments and metamorphic rocks, typically takes place at constant temperature in Earth's magnetic field.

DRM (depositional, or detrital, remanent magnetization) is formed in clastic sediments when fine particles are deposited on the floor of a body of water. Marine sediments, lake sediments, and some clays can acquire DRM. Earth's magnetic field aligns the grains, yielding a preferred direction of magnetization.

IRM (isothermal remanent magnetization) results from the application of a magnetic field at a constant (isothermal) temperature, often room temperature.

NRM (natural remanent magnetization) is the magnetization detected in a geologic in situ condition. The NRM of a substance may, of course, be a combination of any of the other remanent magnetizations described here.

PRM (pressure remanent, or piezoremanent, magnetization) arises when a material undergoes mechanical deformation while in a magnetic field. The process of deformation may result from hydrostatic pressure, shock impact (as produced by a meteorite striking Earth's surface), or directed tectonic stress. There are magnetization changes with stress in the elastic range, but the most pronounced effects occur with plastic deformation when the structure of the magnetic minerals is irreversibly changed.

TRM (thermoremanent magnetization) occurs when a substance is cooled, in the presence of a magnetic field, from above its Curie temperature to below that temperature. This form of magnetization is generally the most important, because it is stable and widespread, occurring in igneous and sedimentary rocks. TRM also can occur when dealing exclusively with temperatures below the Curie temperature. In PTRM (partial thermoremanent magnetization) a sample is cooled from a temperature below the Curie point to yet a lower temperature.

VRM (viscous remanent magnetization) results from thermal agitation. It is acquired slowly over time at low temperatures and in Earth's magnetic field. The effect is weak and unstable but is present in most rocks.

Hysteresis and Magnetic Susceptibility

The concept of hysteresis is fundamental when describing and comparing the magnetic properties of rocks. Hysteresis is the variation of magnetization with applied field and illustrates the ability of a material to retain its magnetization, even after an applied field is removed.

Magnetic susceptibility is a parameter of considerable diagnostic and interpretational use in the study of rocks. This is true whether an investigation is being conducted in the laboratory or magnetic fields over a terrain are being studied to deduce the structure and lithologic character of buried rock bodies. Susceptibility for a rock type can vary widely, depending on magnetic mineralogy, grain size and shape, and the relative magnitude of remanent magnetization present, in addition to the induced magnetization from Earth's weak field. The latter is given as $J_{induced} = kH_{ex}$, where k is the (true) magnetic susceptibility and H_{ex} is the external (i.e., Earth's) magnetic field. If there is an additional remanent magnetization with its ratio (Q_n) to induced magnetization being given by

$$Q_n = \frac{J_{remanent}}{kH_{ex}},$$

then the total magnetization is

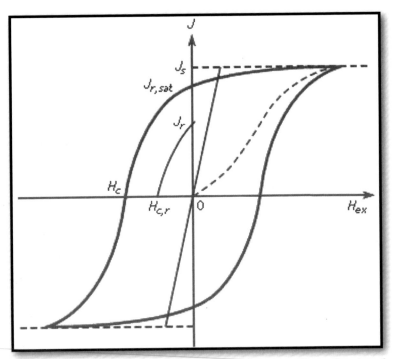

General magnetic hysteresis curve, showing magnetization (J) as a function of the external field (H_{ex}). J_s is the saturation (or "spontaneous") magnetization; $J_{r,sat}$ is the remanent magnetization that remains after a saturating applied field is removed; J_r is the residual magnetization left by some magnetization process other than IRM saturation; H_c is the coercive field; and H_{cr} is the field necessary to reduce J_r to zero. Copyright Encyclopædia Britannica, Inc.; rendering for this edition by Rosen Educational Services

$$J = J_{induced} + J_{remanent}$$

$$= kH_{ex} + Q_n kH_{ex}$$

$$= k(1 + Q_n)H_{ex}$$

$$= k_{app} H_{ex},$$

where k_{app}, the "apparent" magnetic susceptibility, is $k(1 + Q_n)$.

MAGNETIC MINERALS AND MAGNETIC PROPERTIES OF ROCKS

The major rock-forming magnetic minerals are the following iron oxides: the titanomagnetite series, $x\mathrm{Fe_2TiO_4} \cdot (1 - x)\mathrm{Fe_3O_4}$, where $\mathrm{Fe_3O_4}$ is magnetite, the most magnetic mineral; the ilmenohematite series, $y\mathrm{FeTiO_3} \cdot (1 - y)\mathrm{Fe_2O_3}$, where $\alpha\text{-}\mathrm{Fe_2O_3}$ (in its rhombohedral structure) is hematite; maghemite, $\gamma\text{-}\mathrm{Fe_2O_3}$ (in which some iron atoms are missing in the hematite structure); and limonite (hydrous iron oxides). They also include sulfides—namely, the pyrrhotite series, $y\mathrm{FeS} \cdot (1 - y)\mathrm{Fe_{1-x}S}$.

APPROXIMATE "APPARENT SUSCEPTIBILITIES" FOR ROCK TYPES	
ROCK	APPARENT MAGNETIC SUSCEPTIBILITY (electromagnetic units per cubic centimetre)
iron ores	over 0.1
basalt	10^{-2}
andesite	10^{-3}
dacite	10^{-4}
metamorphic rocks	10^{-4}
sedimentary rocks	10^{-5}

Source: From T. Nagata, ed., *Rock Magnetism*, Maruzen Co., Tokyo (1961).

MEASURED SUSCEPTIBILITIES FOR ROCK TYPES

ROCK TYPE	% OF SAMPLES WITH MAGNETIC SUSCEPTIBILITY (in 10^{-6} electromagnetic units per cubic centimetre)			
	LESS THAN 100	100–1,000	1,000–4,000	GREATER THAN 4,000
Basic extrusive (e.g., basalt)	5	29	47	19
Basic intrusive (e.g., gabbro)	24	27	28	21
Granite	60	23	16	1
Metamorphic (gneiss, schist, slate)	71	22	7	0
Sedimentary	73	19	4	4

Source: After D.H. Lindsley, G.E. Andreasen, and J.R. Balsley, "Magnetic Properties of Rocks and Minerals" in *Handbook of Physical Constants*, S.P. Clark, ed., Memoir 97, Geological Society of America, 1966, and L.B. Slichter, "Magnetic Properties of Rocks" in *Handbook of Physical Constants*, F. Birch, ed. (1942).

TYPICAL MAGNETIC PROPERTIES OF ROCKS

ROCK	J_n NATURAL REMANENT MAGNETIZATION (10^{-5} electromagnetic units per cubic centimetre)	K MAGNETIC SUSCEPTIBILITY (10^{-5} electromagnetic units per cubic centimetre)	RATIO* $Q_n = J_n/k \cdot H_{ex}$
Igneous			
granite	10–80	50–400	0.3–1
diabase	190–400	100–230	2–3.5

ROCK	J_n NATURAL REMANENT MAGNETIZATION (10^{-5} electromagnetic units per cubic centimetre)	K MAGNETIC SUSCEPTIBILITY (10^{-5} electromagnetic units per cubic centimetre)	RATIO* $Q_n = J_n/k \cdot H_{ex}$
Igneous			
seafloor basalt (1–6 metres)	500–800	30–60	25–45
typical (average)	10–4,000	5–500	1–40
Sedimentary			
red sediments	0.2–2	0.04–6	2–4
sandstone		1–40	
shale		1–50	
limestone		0.5–20	
typical (average)	0.1–10	0.3–30	0.02–10
Ores			
magnetite ore	300,000–1,000,000	30,000–100,000	~10–50
hematite ore		10–70	

*For external magnetic field (H_{ex}) = 0.5 oersted, the cgs electromagnetic unit of magnetic field intensity.
Source: After Robert S. Carmichael, ed., *Handbook of Physical Properties of Rocks*, vol. II, CRC Press, Inc. (1982).

Rocks may be tested for their apparent magnetic susceptibility. The calculated values usually include some remanent as well as induced magnetization. Values are higher for mafic igneous rocks, especially as the content of magnetite increases.

CHAPTER 2
IGNEOUS ROCK

I gneous rocks are crystalline or glassy rocks formed by the cooling and solidification of molten earth material. They comprise one of the three principal classes of rocks, the others being metamorphic and sedimentary. Igneous rocks are formed from the solidification of magma, which is a hot (600 to 1,300 °C, or 1,100 to 2,400 °F) molten or partially molten rock material. Earth is composed predominantly of a large mass of igneous rock with a very thin veneer of weathered material—namely, sedimentary rock. Whereas sedimentary rocks are produced by processes operating mainly at Earth's surface by the disintegration of mostly older igneous rocks, igneous—and metamorphic—rocks are formed by internal processes that cannot be directly observed and that necessitate the use of physical-chemical arguments to deduce their origins. Because of the high temperatures within Earth, the principles of chemical equilibrium are applicable to the study of igneous and metamorphic rocks, with the latter being restricted to those rocks formed without the direct involvement of magma.

Magma is thought to be generated within the plastic asthenosphere (the layer of partially molten rock underlying Earth's crust) at a depth below about 60 km (40 miles). Because magma is less dense than the surrounding solid rocks, it rises toward the surface. It may settle within the crust or erupt at the surface from a volcano as a lava flow. Rocks formed from the cooling and solidification of magma deep within the crust are distinct from those erupted at the surface mainly owing to the differences in physical and chemical conditions prevalent in

Towering columns of basalt, an igneous rock, make up the unusual formation known as the Devils Postpile, part of a national monument in east-central California. It formed within the last 100,000 years, when a lava flow filled a valley floor and then very slowly cooled and cracked into many-sided columns. Glaciers later eroded most of the hardened lava, revealing the sides of the remaining columns. Shutterstock.com

the two environments. Within Earth's deep crust the temperatures and pressures are much higher than at its surface; consequently, the hot magma cools slowly and crystallizes completely, leaving no trace of the liquid magma. The slow cooling promotes the growth of minerals large enough to be identified visually without the aid of a microscope. On the other hand, magma erupted at the surface is chilled so quickly that the individual minerals have little or no chance to grow. As a result, the rock is either composed of minerals that can be seen only with the aid of a microscope or contains no minerals at all (in the latter case, the rock is composed of glass, which is a highly viscous liquid). This results in two groups: (1) plutonic intrusive igneous rocks that solidified deep within the crust and (2) volcanic, or extrusive, igneous rocks formed at Earth's surface. Some intrusive rocks, known as subvolcanic, were not formed at great depth but were instead injected near the surface where lower temperatures result in a more rapid cooling process; these tend to be aphanitic and are referred to as hypabyssal intrusive rocks.

The deep-seated plutonic rocks can be exposed at the surface for study only after a long period of denudation or by some tectonic forces that push the crust upward or by a combination of the two conditions. (Denudation is the wearing away of the terrestrial surface by processes including weathering and erosion.) Generally, the intrusive rocks have cross-cutting contacts with the country rocks that they have invaded, and in many cases the country rocks show evidence of having been baked and thermally metamorphosed at these contacts. The exposed intrusive rocks are found in a variety of sizes, from small veinlike injections to massive dome-shaped batholiths, which extend for more than 100 square km (40 square miles) and make up the cores of the great mountain ranges.

Extrusive rocks occur in two forms: (1) as lava flows that flood the land surface much like a river and (2) as fragmented pieces of magma of various sizes (pyroclastic materials), which often are blown through the atmosphere and blanket Earth's surface upon settling. The coarser pyroclastic materials accumulate around the erupting volcano, but the finest pyroclasts can be found as thin layers located hundreds of kilometres from the opening. Most lava flows do not travel far from the volcano, but some low-viscosity flows that erupted from long fissures have accumulated in thick (hundreds of metres) sequences, forming the great plateaus of the world (e.g., the Columbia River plateau of Washington and Oregon and the Deccan plateau in India). Both intrusive and extrusive magmas have played a vital role in the spreading of the ocean basin, in the formation of the oceanic crust, and in the formation of the continental margins. Igneous processes have been active since the onset of Earth's formation some 4.6 billion years ago. Their emanations have provided the water for the oceans, the gases for the primordial oxygen-free atmosphere, and many valuable mineral deposits.

COMPOSITION

Igneous rocks are made up of various chemical and mineralogical components. These rocks can be divided into two groups: felsic (from *fel*dspar and *si*lica) and mafic (from *ma*gnesium and *f*errous iron). Silicate minerals make up the bulk of the chemical ingredients in igneous rocks.

CHEMICAL COMPONENTS

The great majority of the igneous rocks are composed of silicate minerals (meaning that the basic building blocks for the magmas that formed them are made of silicon [Si] and oxygen [O]), but minor occurrences of carbonate-rich igneous rocks are found as well. Indeed, in 1960 a sodium carbonate (Na_2CO_3) lava with only 0.05 weight percent silica (SiO_2) was erupted from Ol Doinyo Lengai, a volcano in northern Tanzania, Africa. Because of the limited occurrence of such carbonate-rich igneous rocks, however, the following discussion will consider the chemistry of silicate rocks only. The major oxides of the rocks generally correlate well with their silica content: those rocks with low silica content are enriched in magnesium oxide (MgO) and iron oxides (FeO, Fe_2O_3, and Fe_3O_4) and are depleted in soda (Na_2O) and potash (K_2O); those with a large amount of silica are depleted in magnesium oxide and iron oxides but are enriched in soda and potash. Both calcium oxide (CaO) and alumina (Al_2O_3) are depleted in the rocks that have a silica content of less than about 45 weight percent, but, above 45 percent, calcium oxide can be as high as 10 percent; this amount decreases gradually as the silica increases. Alumina in rocks that contain more than 45 percent silica is generally above approximately 14 weight percent, with the greatest abundance occurring at an intermediate silica content of about 56 weight percent. Because of the importance of silica content, it has become common practice to use this feature of igneous rocks as a basis for subdividing them into the following groups: silicic or felsic (or acid, an old and discredited but unfortunately entrenched term), rocks having more than 66 percent silica; intermediate, rocks with 55 to 66 percent silica; and subsilicic, rocks containing less than 55 percent silica. The latter may be further divided into two groups: mafic, rocks with 45 to 55 percent silica and ultramafic, those containing less than 45 percent. The subsilicic rocks, enriched as they are in iron (Fe) and magnesium (Mg), are termed femic (from *fe*rrous iron and *m*agnesium), whereas the silicic rocks are referred to as sialic (from *si*lica and *al*uminum, with which they are enriched) or salic (from *s*ilica and *al*uminum). The terms mafic (from *ma*gnesium and *f*errous iron) and felsic (*fel*dspar and *s*ilica) are used interchangeably with femic and sialic.

The silica content also reflects the mineral composition of the rocks. As the magma cools and begins to crystallize, silica is taken from the magma to be combined with the other cationic oxides to form the silicate minerals. For example, one mole of SiO_2 is combined with one mole of MgO to make the magnesium-rich pyroxene, $MgSiO_3$ (enstatite): $SiO_2 + MgO \rightarrow MgSiO_3$. Two moles of SiO_2 are needed to be combined with one mole each of CaO and Al_2O_3 to make the calcium-rich plagioclase, $CaAl_2Si_2O_8$ (anorthite). However, in a case where magma does not have enough silica relative to the magnesium oxide to produce the pyroxene, the magma will compensate by making a magnesium-olivine (forsterite; Mg_2SiO_4), along with the pyroxene, since the olivine requires only one-half as much silica for every mole of magnesium oxide. On the other hand, a silicic magma may have excess silica such that some will be left after all the silicate minerals were formed from the combination of the oxides; the remaining "free" silica crystallizes as quartz or its polymorphs. The former case usually occurs in subsilicic rocks that characteristically will have silicate minerals like magnesium-olivine, sodium-nepheline ($NaAlSiO_4$, which requires only one mole of silicon for every mole of sodium [Na]), and leucite ($KAlSi_2O_6$, which requires only two moles of silicon to one mole of potassium [K]). These three minerals substitute in part for enstatite, albite ($NaAlSi_3O_8$, requiring three moles of silicon for one mole of sodium), and orthoclase feldspar ($KAlSi_3O_8$, requiring three moles of silicon for one mole of potassium), respectively. Quartz clearly will not be present in these rocks. Minerals such as magnesium-olivine, nepheline, and leucite are termed undersaturated (with respect to

FELSIC AND MAFIC ROCKS

Felsic and mafic rocks are igneous rocks categorized on the basis of their silica content. Chemical analyses of the most abundant components in rocks usually are presented as oxides of the elements; igneous rocks typically consist of approximately 12 major oxides totaling over 99 percent of the rock. Of the oxides, silica (SiO_2) is usually the most abundant. Because of this abundance and because most igneous minerals are silicates, silica content was used as a basis of early classifications; it remains widely accepted today. Within this scheme, rocks are described as felsic, intermediate, mafic, and ultramafic (in order of decreasing silica content).

In a widely accepted silica-content classification scheme, rocks with more than 65 percent silica are called felsic; those with between 55 and 65 percent silica are intermediate; those with between 45 and 55 percent silica are mafic; and those with less than 45 percent are ultramafic. Compilations of many rock analyses show that rhyolite and granite are felsic, with an average silica content of about 72 percent; syenite, diorite, and monzonite are intermediate, with an average silica content of 59 percent; gabbro and basalt are mafic, with an average silica content of 48 percent; and peridotite is an ultramafic rock, with an average of 41 percent silica. Although there are complete gradations between the averages, rocks tend to cluster about the averages. In general, the gradation from felsic to mafic corresponds to an increase in colour index (dark-mineral percentage).

The fine-grained or glassy nature of many volcanic rocks makes a chemical classification such as the felsic-mafic taxonomy very useful in distinguishing the different types. Silica content is especially useful because the density and refractive index of natural glasses have been correlated with silica percentage; this makes identification possible in the absence of chemical data. For similar determinations, glasses can also be prepared in the laboratory from crystalline rocks.

The influence of silica content on the particular minerals that crystallize from a rock magma is a complex interaction of several parameters, and it cannot be assumed that rocks with the same silica content will have the same mineralogy. Silica saturation is a classification of minerals and rocks as oversaturated, saturated, or undersaturated with respect to silica. Felsic rocks are commonly oversaturated and contain free quartz (SiO_2), intermediate rocks contain little or no quartz or feldspathoids (undersaturated minerals), and mafic rocks may contain abundant feldspathoids. This broad grouping on the basis of mineralogy related to silica content is used in many modern classification schemes.

silica), and the subsilicic rocks that contain them are termed undersaturated as well. In the case of rocks that have excess silica, the silicic rocks will have quartz and magnesium-pyroxene, which are considered saturated minerals, and the rocks that contain them are termed supersaturated.

MINERALOGICAL COMPONENTS

The felsic minerals include quartz, tridymite, cristobalite, feldspars (plagioclase and alkali feldspar), feldspathoids (nepheline and leucite), muscovite, and corundum. Because felsic minerals lack iron and magnesium, they are generally light in colour and consequently are referred to as such or as leucocratic. The mafic minerals include olivine, pyroxenes, amphiboles, and biotites, all of which are dark in colour. Mafic minerals are said to be melanocratic. These terms can be applied to the rocks, depending on the relative proportion of each type of mineral present. In this regard, the term colour index, which refers to the total percentage of the rock occupied by mafic minerals, is useful. Felsic rocks have a colour index of less than 50, while mafic rocks have a colour index above 50. Those rocks that have a colour index above 90 are referred to as ultramafic. These terms are to be used only for the mineralogical content of igneous rocks because they do not necessarily correlate directly with chemical terms. For example, it is common to find a felsic rock composed almost entirely of the mineral plagioclase, but in chemical terms, such a rock is a subsilicic mafic rock. Another example is an igneous rock consisting solely of pyroxene. Mineralogically it would be termed ultramafic, but chemically it is a mafic igneous rock with a silica content of about 50 percent.

The influence of supersaturation and undersaturation on the mineralogy of a rock was noted above. During the crystallization of magmas, supersaturated minerals will not be formed along with undersaturated minerals. Supersaturated minerals include quartz and its polymorphs and a low-calcium orthorhombic pyroxene. These cannot coexist with any of the feldspathoids (e.g., leucite and nepheline) or magnesium-rich olivine. In volcanic rocks that have been quenched (cooled rapidly) such that only a small part of the magma has been crystallized, it is possible to find a forsterite (magnesium-rich olivine) crystal surrounded by a glass that is saturated or supersaturated. In this case, the outer rim of the olivine may be corroded or replaced by a magnesium-rich pyroxene (called a reaction rim). The olivine was the first to be crystallized, but it was in the process of reacting with the saturated magma to form the saturated mineral when an eruption halted the reaction. Had the magma been allowed to crystallize fully, all the forsterite would have been transformed into the magnesium-rich pyroxene and quartz may have been crystallized.

Accessory minerals present in igneous rocks in minor amounts include monazite, allanite, apatite, garnets, ilmenite, magnetite, titanite, spinel, and zircon. Glass may be a major phase in some volcanic rock but, when present, is usually found in minor amounts. Igneous rocks that were exposed to weathering and circulating groundwater have undergone some degree of alteration. Common alteration products are talc or serpentine formed at the expense of olivine, chlorites replacing pyroxene and amphiboles, iron oxides replacing any mafic mineral, clay minerals and epidote formed from the feldspars, and calcite that may be formed at the expense of any calcium-bearing mineral by interaction with a carbon dioxide (CO_2)-bearing solution. Glass is commonly altered to clay minerals and zeolite. In some cases, however, glass has undergone a devitrification process (in which it is transformed into a crystalline material) initiated by reaction of the glass with water or by subsequent reheating. Common products of devitrification include quartz and its polymorphs, alkali feldspar, plagioclase, pyroxene, zeolite, clays, and chlorite.

TEXTURAL FEATURES

The texture of an igneous rock normally is defined by the size and form of its constituent mineral grains and by the spatial relationships of individual grains with one another and with any glass that may be present. Texture can be described independently of the entire rock mass, and its geometric characteristics provide valuable insights into the conditions under which the rock was formed.

CRYSTALLINITY

Among the most fundamental properties of igneous rocks are crystallinity and granularity, two terms that closely

CRYSTALLINITY CATEGORIES OF IGNEOUS ROCKS	
CRYSTALLINITY	ROCK TERM
entirely crystalline	holocrystalline
crystalline material and subordinate glass	hemicrystalline or hypocrystalline
glass and subordinate crystalline material	hemihyaline or hypohyaline
entirely glassy	holohyaline or hyaline

CATEGORIES OF ROCK GRAIN SIZE

TERMS IN COMMON USE	GENERAL GRAIN SIZE IGNEOUS ROCKS IN GENERAL	PEGMATITES
fine-grained	<1 mm	<1 in.
medium-grained	1–5 mm	1 in.–4 in.
coarse-grained	5 mm–2 cm	4 in.–12 in.
very coarse-grained	>2 cm	>12 in.

reflect differences in magma composition and the differences between volcanic and various plutonic environments of formation. Entirely crystallized, or holocrystalline, rocks in which mineral grains can be recognized with the unaided eye are called phanerites, and their texture is called phaneritic. Those with mineral grains so small that their outlines cannot be resolved without the aid of a hand lens or microscope are termed aphanites, and their texture is termed aphanitic. Aphanitic rocks are further described as either microcrystalline or cryptocrystalline, according to whether or not their individual constituents can be resolved under the microscope. The subaphanitic, or hyaline, rocks are referred to as glassy, or vitric, in terms of granularity.

Aphanitic and glassy textures represent relatively rapid cooling of magma and, hence, are found mainly among the volcanic rocks. Slower cooling, either beneath Earth's surface or within very thick masses of lava, promotes the formation of crystals and, under favourable circumstances of magma composition and other factors, their growth to relatively large sizes. The resulting phaneritic rocks are so widespread and so varied that it is convenient to specify their grain size.

GRANULARITY

In general, granularity refers to the size of a rock's constituent grains or crystals. While size is important, other factors, such as the fabric (pattern) and the articulation of these grains, also contribute to the understanding of a rock's texture.

GRAIN SIZE

The general grain size ordinarily is taken as the average diameter of dominant grains in the rock; for the pegmatites, which are special rocks with extremely large crystals, it can refer to the maximum exposed dimensions of dominant grains. Most aphanitic rocks are characterized by mineral grains less than 0.3 mm (0.01 inch) in diameter, and those in which the average grain size is less than 0.1 mm (0.004 inch) are commonly described as dense.

FABRIC

A major part of rock texture is fabric or pattern, which is a function of the form and outline of its constituent grains, their relative sizes, and their mutual relationships in space. Many specific terms have been employed to shorten the description of rock fabrics, and even the sampling offered here may seem alarmingly extensive. It should be noted, however, that fabric provides some of the most useful clues to the nature and sequence of magmatic crystallization.

The degree to which mineral grains show external crystal faces can be described as euhedral or panidiomorphic (fully crystal-faced), subhedral or hypidiomorphic (partly faced), or anhedral or allotriomorphic (no external crystal faces). Quite apart from the presence or absence of crystal faces, the shape, or habit, of individual mineral grains is described by such terms as equant, tabular, platy, elongate, fibrous, rodlike, lathlike, needlelike, and irregular. A more general contrast can be drawn between grains of equal (equant) and inequal dimensions. Even-grained, or equigranular, rocks are characterized by essential minerals that all exhibit the same order of grain size, but this implied equality need not be taken too literally. For such rocks the combination terms panidiomorphic-granular, hypidiomorphic-granular, and allotriomorphic-granular are applied according to the occurrence of euhedral, subhedral, and anhedral mineral grains within them. Many fine-grained allotriomorphic-granular rocks are more simply termed sugary, saccharoidal, or aplitic.

Rocks that are unevenly grained, or inequigranular, are generally characterized either by a seriate fabric, in which the variation in grain size is gradual and essentially continuous, or by a porphyritic fabric, involving more than one distinct range of grain sizes. Both of these kinds of texture are common. The relatively large crystals in a porphyritic rock ordinarily occur as separate entities, known as phenocrysts, set in a groundmass or matrix of much finer-grained crystalline material or glass. Quite commonly in many volcanic rocks, phenocrysts are aggregated. When this is observed, the term glomeroporphyritic is used to describe the texture, and the aggregate is referred to as a glomerocryst. In some cases, such glomerocrysts are monomineralic, but more commonly they are composed of two or more minerals. Based on chemical composition, texture, and other criteria such as isotopic analysis, it has been demonstrated that some phenocrysts and glomerocrysts were not crystallized from the host magma but rather were accidentally torn from the country rock by the magma as it rose to the surface. When this has occurred, these phenocrysts are referred to as xenocrysts, while the aggregates can be termed xenoliths. The size of phenocrysts is essentially independent of their abundance relative to the groundmass, and they range in external form from euhedral to anhedral. Most of them are best described as subhedral. Because the groundmass constituents span almost the full ranges of crystallinity and granularity, porphyritic fabric is abundantly represented among the phaneritic, aphanitic, and glassy rocks.

The sharp break in grain size between phenocrysts and groundmass reflects a corresponding change in the conditions that affected the crystallizing magma. Thus, the phenocrysts of many rocks probably grew slowly at depth, following which the nourishing magma rose to Earth's surface as lava, cooled much more rapidly, and congealed to form a finer-grained or glassy groundmass. A porphyritic volcanic rock with a glassy groundmass is described as having a vitrophyric texture and the rock can be called a vitrophyre. Other porphyritic rocks may well reflect less drastic shifts in position and perhaps more subtle and complex changes in conditions of temperature, pressure, or crystallization rates. Many phenocrysts could have developed at the points where they now occur, and some may represent systems with two fluid phases, magma and coexisting gas. Appraisals of the composition of phenocrysts, their distribution, and their periods of growth relative to the accompanying groundmass constituents are important to an understanding of many igneous processes.

IMPORTANT TEXTURAL TYPES

The articulation of mineral grains is described in terms of planar, smoothly curved, sinuous, sutured, interlocked, or irregular surfaces of mutual boundary. The distribution and orientation of mineral grains and of mineral grains and glass are other elements of fabric that can be useful in estimating the conditions and sequence of mineral formation in igneous rocks. The following are only a few of the most important examples:

Directive textures are produced by the preferred orientation of platy, tabular, or elongate mineral grains to yield grossly planar or linear arrangements; they are generally a result of magmatic flowage.

Graphic texture refers to the regular intergrowth of two minerals, one of them generally serving as a host and the other appearing on surfaces of the host as striplike or cuneiform units with grossly consistent orientation; the graphic intergrowth of quartz in alkali feldspar is a good example.

Ophitic texture is the association of lath-shaped euhedral crystals of plagioclase, grouped radially or in an irregular mesh, with surrounding or interstitial large anhedral crystals of pyroxene; it is characteristic of the common rock type known as diabase.

Poikilitic texture describes the occurrence of one mineral that is irregularly scattered as diversely oriented crystals within much larger host crystals of another mineral.

Reaction textures occur at the corroded margins of crystals, from the corrosive rimming of crystals of one mineral by finer-grained aggregates of another, or as a result of other features that indicate partial removal of crystalline material by reaction with magma or other fluid.

Pyroclastic texture results from the explosive fragmentation of volcanic material, including magma (commonly the light, frothy pumice variety and glass fragments called shards), country rock, and phenocrysts. Fragments less than 2 mm (0.08 inch) in size are called ash, and the rock formed of these is called tuff; fragments between 2 and 64 mm are lapilli and the rock is lapillistone; fragments greater than 64 mm (2.5 inches) are called bombs if rounded or blocks if angular, and the corresponding rock is termed agglomerate or pyroclastic breccia, respectively. Commonly, many of these pyroclastic rocks have been formed by dense hot clouds that hug the ground and behave much like a lava flow and hence are given the name pyroclastic flow. Most of these flows are composed of ash-size material; therefore, they are called ash flows and the rocks deposited by them are called ash-flow tuffs. A more general term for rocks deposited by these flows that does not specify size of fragments is ignimbrite. Ash-flow tuffs and other ignimbrites often have zones in which the fragments have been welded. These zones are termed welded tuffs and display a directive planar texture (called eutaxitic) that results from compaction and flattening of pumice fragments. Such pyroclastic flows were responsible for many of the deposits of the eruption of Mount St. Helens in Washington State, U.S., on May 18, 1980. Most eruptions eject fragments that are borne by the wind and deposited subaerially (on the land surface). These deposits are said to be ash-fall tuffs and are recognized by their lamination (formation in thin layers that differ in grain size or composition). They commonly blanket the topography

A volcanic peak in the Cascade Range, Mount St. Helens is situated in southwestern Washington state. Dormant since 1857, it erupted on May 18, 1980, in one of the most violent volcanic eruptions ever recorded in North America. Peter Lipman/U.S. Geological Survey

in contrast to the ash-flow deposits, which flow around topographic highs and which are completely unsorted.

Replacement textures occur where a mineral or mineral aggregate has the external crystal form of a preexisting different mineral (pseudomorphism) or where the juxtaposition of two minerals indicates that one was formed at the expense of the other.

Finally, crystal zoning describes faintly to very well-defined geometric arrangements of portions within individual crystals that differ significantly in composition (or some other property) from adjacent portions; most common are successive shells grouped concentrically about the centres of crystals, presumably reflecting shifts in conditions during crystal growth.

STRUCTURAL FEATURES

The structure of an igneous rock is normally taken to comprise the mutual relationships of mineral or mineral-glass aggregates that have contrasting textures, along with layering, fractures, and other larger-scale features that transect or bound such aggregates. Structure often can be described only in relation to masses of rock larger than a hand specimen, and most of its individual expressions can be closely correlated with physical conditions that existed when the rock was formed.

SMALL-SCALE STRUCTURAL FEATURES

Among the most widespread structural features of volcanic rocks are the porelike openings left by the escape of gas from the congealing lava. Such openings are called vesicles, and the rocks in which they occur are said to be vesicular. Where the openings lie close together and form a large part of the containing rock, they impart to it a slaglike, or scoriaceous, structure. Their relative abundance is even greater in the type of sialic glassy rock known as pumice, which is essentially a congealed volcanic froth. Most vesicles can be likened to peas or nuts in their ranges of size and shape; those that were formed when the lava was still moving tend to be flattened and drawn out in the direction of flow. Others are cylindrical, pearlike, or more irregular in shape, depending in part on the manner of escape of the gas from the cooling lava; most of the elongate ones occur in subparallel arrangements.

Many vesicles have been partly or completely filled with quartz, chalcedony, opal, calcite, epidote, zeolites, or other minerals. These fillings are known as amygdules, and the rock in which they are present is amygdaloidal. Some are concentrically layered, others also include centrally disposed series of horizontal layers, and still others are featured by central cavities into which well-formed crystals project.

Spherulites are light-coloured subspherical masses that commonly consist of tiny fibres and plates of alkali feldspar radiating outward from a centre. Most range from pinpoint to nut size, but some are as much as several feet in diameter. The relatively large ones tend to be internally complex and to contain concentric shells of feldspar fibres with or without accompanying quartz, tridymite, or glass. Spherulites occur mainly in glassy volcanic rocks; they also are present in some partly or wholly crystalline rocks that include shallow-seated intrusive types. Many evidently are products of rapid crystallization, perhaps at points of gas concentration in the freezing magmas. Others, in contrast, were formed more slowly, by devitrification of volcanic glasses, presumably not long after they congealed and while they were still relatively hot.

Lithophysae, also known as stone bubbles, consist of concentric shells of finely crystalline alkali feldspar separated by empty spaces; thus, they resemble an onion or a newly blooming rose. Commonly associated with spherulites in glassy and partly crystalline volcanic rocks of salic composition, many lithophysae are about the size of walnuts. They have been ascribed to short episodes of rapid crystallization, alternating with periods of gas escape when the open spaces were developed by thrusting the feldspathic shells apart or by contraction associated with cooling. The curving cavities commonly are lined with tiny crystals of quartz, tridymite, feldspar, topaz, or other minerals deposited from the gases.

Some glassy rocks of silicic composition are marked by domains of strongly curved, concentrically disposed fractures that promote breakage into rounded masses of pinhead to walnut size. Because their surfaces often have a pearly or shiny lustre, the name perlite is applied to such rocks. Perlite is most common in glassy silicic rocks that have interacted with water to become hydrated. During the hydration process, water enters the glass, breaking the silicon-oxygen bonds and causing an expansion of the glass structure to form the curved cracks. The extent of hydration of glass, indicating the amount of perlite that has been formed from the glass, depends on the climate and on time. In a given area where the climate is expected to be consistent, the thickness of the hydration of the glass surface has been used by archaeologists to date artifacts such as arrowheads composed of the dark volcanic glass known as obsidian and made by early native Americans.

Numerous structural features of comparably small scale occur among the intrusive rocks; these include miarolitic, orbicular, plumose, and radial structures. Miarolitic rocks are felsic phanerites distinguished by scattered pods or layers, ordinarily several centimetres in maximum thickness, within which their essential minerals are coarser-grained, subhedral to euhedral, and otherwise pegmatitic in texture. Many of these small interior bodies, called miaroles, contain centrally disposed crystal-lined cavities that are known as druses or miarolitic cavities. An internal zonal disposition of minerals also is common, and the most characteristic sequence is alkali feldspar with graphically intergrown quartz, alkali feldspar, and a central filling of quartz. Miarolitic structure probably represents local concentration of gases during very late stages in consolidation of the host rocks.

The term orbicular is applied to rounded, onionlike masses with distinct concentric layering that are distributed in various ways through otherwise normal-appearing phaneritic rocks of silicic to mafic composition. The layers within individual masses are typically thin, irregular, and sharply defined, and each differs from its immediate neighbours in composition or texture. Some layers contain tabular or prismatic mineral grains that are oriented radially with respect to the containing orbicule and, hence, are analogous to spherulitic layers in volcanic rocks. The minerals of most orbicules are the same as those of the enclosing rock, but they are not necessarily present in the same proportions. The concentric structure appears to reflect rhythmic crystallization about specific centres, commonly at early stages in consolidation of the general rock mass.

The normal fabric of some relatively coarse-grained plutonic rocks is interrupted by clusters of crystals with radial grouping but without concentric layering. A characteristic plumelike, spraylike, or rosettelike structure is imparted by the markedly elongate form of the participating crystals or crystal aggregates, which seem to have developed outward from common centres by direct crystallization from magma or by replacement of preexisting solid material.

Large-Scale Structural Features

Many kinds of larger-scale features occur among both the intrusive and the extrusive rocks. Most of these are mentioned later in connection with rock occurrence or are discussed in other articles, but several are properly introduced here:

Clastic Structures

These are various features that express the accumulation of fragments or the rupturing and dislocation of solid material. In volcanic environments they generally result from explosive activity or the incorporation of solid fragments by moving lava; as such, they characterize the pyroclastic rocks. Among the plutonic rocks, they appear chiefly as local to very extensive zones of pervasive shearing, dislocation, and granulation, commonly best recognized under the microscope. Those developed prior to final consolidation of the rock are termed protoclastic; those developed after final consolidation, cataclastic.

Flow Structures

These are planar or linear features that result from flowage of magma with or without contained crystals. Various forms of faintly to sharply defined layering and lining typically reflect compositional or textural inhomogeneities, and they often are accentuated by concentrations or preferred orientation of crystals, inclusions, vesicles, spherulites, and other features.

Fractures

These are straight or curving surfaces of rupture directly associated with the formation of a rock or later superimposed upon it. Primary fractures generally can be related to emplacement or to subsequent cooling of the host rock mass. The columnar jointing found in many mafic volcanic rocks is a typical result of contraction upon cooling.

INCLUSIONS

These are rounded to angular masses of solid material enclosed within a rock of recognizably different composition or texture. Those consisting of older material not directly related to that of their host are known as xenoliths, and those representing broken-up and detached older parts of the same igneous body that encloses them are termed cognate xenoliths or autoliths.

PILLOW STRUCTURES

These are aggregates of ovoid masses, resembling pillows or grain-filled sacks in size and shape, that occur in many basic volcanic rocks. The masses are separated or interconnected, and each has a thick vesicular crust or a thinner and more dense glassy rind. The interiors ordinarily are coarser-grained and less vesicular. Pillow structure is formed by rapid chilling of highly fluid lava in contact with water or water-saturated sediments, accompanied by the development of budlike projections with tough, elastic crusts. As additional lava is fed into each bud, it grows into a pillow and continues to enlarge until rupture of the skin permits escape of fresh lava to form a new bud and a new pillow.

SEGREGATIONS

These are special types of inclusions that are intimately related to their host rocks and in general are relatively rich in one or more of the host-rock minerals. They range from small pods to extensive layers and from early-stage crystal accumulations formed by gravitational settling in magma to very late-stage concentrations of coarse-grained material developed in place.

These are arrangements of rock units with contrasting composition, or texture, in an igneous body, commonly in a broadly concentric pattern. Chilled margins, the fine-grained or glassy edges along the borders of many extrusive and shallow-seated intrusive bodies, represent quenching of magma along contacts with cooler country rock. Other kinds of zones generally reflect fractional crystallization of magma and are useful in tracing courses of magmatic differentiation, as will be noted later.

An interesting type of zonal structure is an orbicular configuration that has alternating light and dark repeating bands in an oval arrangement found in some diorites and granodiorites. Pegmatites also often have zonal structures due to fluctuations in fluid composition. This results in "pockets" that may contain gems or other unusual minerals.

CLASSIFICATION OF IGNEOUS ROCKS

Igneous rocks are classified on the basis of mineralogy, chemistry, and texture. As discussed earlier, texture is used to subdivide igneous rocks into two major groups: (1) the plutonic rocks, with mineral grain sizes that are visible to the naked eye, and (2) the volcanic and hypabyssal types, which are usually too fine-grained or glassy for their mineral composition to be observed without the use of a petrographic microscope. Being rather coarsely grained, phaneritic rocks readily lend themselves to a classification based on mineralogy since their individual mineral components can be discerned, but the volcanic rocks are more difficult to classify because either their mineral composition is not visible or the rock has not fully crystallized owing to fast cooling. As a consequence, various methods employ chemical composition as the criterion for volcanic igneous rock classification. A commonly used technique was introduced at the beginning of the 20th century by the American geologists C. Whitman Cross, Joseph P. Iddings, Louis V. Pirsson, and Henry S. Washington. In this method, the mineral composition of the rock is recalculated into a standard set of typically occurring minerals that theoretically could have developed from the complete equilibrium crystallization at low temperatures of a magma of the indicated bulk composition. The calculated hypothetical mineral composition is called the norm, and the minerals constituting the standard set are termed normative minerals, since they are ordinarily found in igneous rocks. The rock under analysis may then be classified according to the calculated proportions of the normative minerals.

Because other methods for calculating the norm have been devised, this original norm is referred to as the CIPW norm after the initials of the four petrologists who devised the system. The norm calculation allows the petrologist studying an aphanitic rock to "see" the mineral assemblage that corresponds well with the actual mineral assemblage of a plutonic rock of the same composition that had crystallized under equilibrium conditions. Moreover, the norm has been shown to have a thermodynamic basis. The concept of silica saturation discussed above is incorporated into the norm, which will show whether a magma of a certain composition is supersaturated, saturated, or undersaturated by the presence or absence of normative minerals such as quartz, orthopyroxene, olivine, and the feldspathoids.

CLASSIFICATION OF PLUTONIC ROCKS

A plutonic rock may be classified mineralogically based on the actual proportion of the various minerals of which it is composed (called the mode). In any classification scheme, boundaries between classes are set arbitrarily; however, if the boundaries can be placed closest to natural divisions or gaps between classes, they will seem less random and subjective, and the standards will facilitate universal understanding. In order to set boundaries nearest to the population lows (of constituent minerals) and to achieve an international consensus, a poll among the world's petrologists was conducted and a modal classification for plutonic igneous rocks was devised. Based mainly on this poll, the International Union of Geological Sciences (IUGS) Subcommission on the Systematics of Igneous Rocks in 1973 suggested the use of the modal composition for all plutonic igneous rocks with a colour index less than 90 and for those plutonic ultramafic rocks with a colour index greater than 90.

The rock modes of various mineral components can be plotted on a graph. Each component is represented by the corners of the equilateral triangle, the length of whose sides are divided into 100 equal parts. Any composition plotting at a corner, therefore, has a mode of 100 percent of the corresponding component. Any point on the sides of the triangle represents a mode composed of the two adjacent corner components.

For example, in a comparison of quartz, alkali feldspar, and plagioclase, if the colour index is less than 90 and quartz (Q) is present, then the three components, Q + A (alkali feldspar) + P (plagioclase), are recalculated from the mode to sum to 100 percent and plotted to a region on the graph. A rock with 60 percent Q and 40 percent A will plot on the QA side at a location 60 percent of the distance from A to Q. A rock containing all three components will plot within the triangle. Since the sides of the triangle are divided into 100 parts, a rock having a mode of 20 percent Q and 80 percent A + P (in unknown proportions for the moment) will plot on the

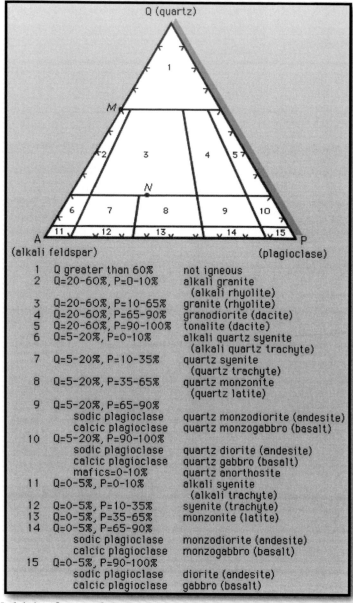

1	Q greater than 60%	not igneous
2	Q=20-60%, P=0-10%	alkali granite
		(alkali rhyolite)
3	Q=20-60%, P=10-65%	granite (rhyolite)
4	Q=20-60%, P=65-90%	granodiorite (dacite)
5	Q=20-60%, P=90-100%	tonalite (dacite)
6	Q=5-20%, P=0-10%	alkali quartz syenite
		(alkali quartz trachyte)
7	Q=5-20%, P=10-35%	quartz syenite
		(quartz trachyte)
8	Q=5-20%, P=35-65%	quartz monzonite
		(quartz latite)
9	Q=5-20%, P=65-90%	
	sodic plagioclase	quartz monzodiorite (andesite)
	calcic plagioclase	quartz monzogabbro (basalt)
10	Q=5-20%, P=90-100%	
	sodic plagioclase	quartz diorite (andesite)
	calcic plagioclase	quartz gabbro (basalt)
	mafics=0-10%	quartz anorthosite
11	Q=0-5%, P=0-10%	alkali syenite
		(alkali trachyte)
12	Q=0-5%, P=10-35%	syenite (trachyte)
13	Q=0-5%, P=35-65%	monzonite (latite)
14	Q=0-5%, P=65-90%	
	sodic plagioclase	monzodiorite (andesite)
	calcic plagioclase	monzogabbro (basalt)
15	Q=0-5%, P=90-100%	
	sodic plagioclase	diorite (andesite)
	calcic plagioclase	gabbro (basalt)

Modal classification of plutonic igneous rocks with less than 90 percent mafic minerals. The names in parentheses are the equivalent volcanic rocks. After IUGS Subcommission on the Systematics of Igneous Rocks, "Plutonic Rocks, Classification and Nomenclature," Geotimes, 18, no. 10 (1973). Reprinted with permission from Geotimes. Copyright Encyclopædia Britannica, Inc.; rendering for this edition by Rosen Educational Services

line that parallels the AP side and lies 20 percent of the distance toward Q from the side AP. If this same rock has 30 percent P and 50 percent A, the rock mode will plot at the intersection of the 20 percent Q line described above, with a line paralleling the QA side at a distance 30 percent toward P from the QA side. The third intersecting line for the point is necessarily the line paralleling the QP side at 50 percent of the distance from the side QP toward A.

A rock with 25 percent Q, 35 percent P, and 40 percent A plots in the granite field, whereas one with 25 percent Q, 60 percent P, and 15 percent A plots in the granodiorite field. The latter is close to the average composition of Earth's continental crust. Igneous rocks normally do not exceed about 50 percent quartz, and the feldspathoidal rocks are relatively rare. The most common plutonic rocks are those in fields numbered 3, 4, 5, 8, 9, 10, and 15. These are found in what have been called granite (used in a loose sense) batholiths, which are irregularly shaped large bodies covering an area greater than 100 square km (about 39 square miles). Batholiths constitute the cores of the great mountain ranges, such as the Rockies in western North America and the Sierra Nevada in California, U.S. Typically these batholiths are composites of smaller intrusions, each of which may display several different rock types. The average composition is close to that of a granodiorite, but in many batholiths the sequence of intrusions progresses from basic to acidic, with gabbro or quartz diorite being emplaced first. In the Sierra Nevada batholith, the dominant rocks are quartz monzonite and granodiorite, with intrusions including quartz diorite in the far western rim and granite in the east. Batholiths contain medium- to coarse-grained rocks with hypidiomorphic-granular texture. The rocks are generally leucocratic; diorites and quartz diorites typically contain less than 30 percent mafic minerals—e.g., hornblende and biotite. Pyroxenes are rare but are more commonly found in the gabbros. Mineralogically the ratio of hornblende to biotite, the colour index, the calcium content of the plagioclase feldspar, and the ratio of plagioclase to alkali feldspar decrease from diorite to quartz diorite to granodiorite and granite. Common accessory minerals include apatite, titanite, and an opaque mineral such as magnetite or ilmenite. Ideally it would be preferable to use the same modal scheme for volcanic rocks.

GRANITE

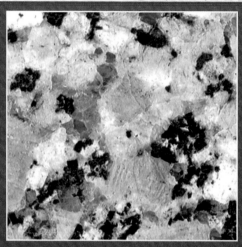

Cut and polished surface of granite (magnified 1.5×). Large, slightly pink grains are microcline feldspar; white grains are sodium-rich plagioclase feldspar; smaller smoky grains are quartz; black spots are biotite and hornblende. D.L. Weide

Granite is a coarse- or medium-grained intrusive igneous rock that is rich in quartz and feldspar; it is the most common plutonic rock of Earth's crust, forming by the cooling of magma (silicate melt) at depth.

Because of its use as paving block and as a building stone, the quarrying of granite was, at one time, a major industrial activity. Except for tombstones, however, for which there is a continuing demand, the present production of granite is geared to the fluctuating market for curbing in highway construction and veneer used in the facing of large industrial and commercial buildings.

Granite may occur in dikes or sills (tabular bodies injected in fissures and inserted between other rocks), but more characteristically it forms irregular masses of extremely variable size, ranging from less than 8 km (5 miles) in maximum dimension to larger masses (batholiths) that are often hundreds or thousands of square kilometres in area.

The principal constituent of granite is feldspar. Both plagioclase feldspar and alkali feldspar are usually abundant in it, and their relative abundance has provided the basis for granite classifications. In most granite, the ratio of the dominant to the subdominant feldspar is less than two. This includes most granites from the eastern, central, and southwestern United States, southwestern England, the Fennoscandian (Baltic Shield) area, western and central France, Spain, and many other areas. Granites in which plagioclase greatly exceeds alkali feldspar are common in large regions of the western United States and are thought to be characteristic of the great series of batholiths stretching from Alaska and British Columbia southward through Idaho and California into Mexico. Granites with a great excess of alkali feldspar over plagioclase are known from New England; they occur in smaller bodies at numerous sites in British Paleogene and Neogene rocks and in the Oslo region of Norway, but their most extensive development is in northern Nigeria.

Rocks containing less than 20 percent quartz are almost never named granite, and rocks containing more than 20 percent (by volume) of dark, or ferromagnesian, minerals are also seldom called granite. The minor essential minerals of granite may include muscovite, biotite, amphibole, or pyroxene. Biotite may occur in granite of any type and is usually present, though sometimes in very small amounts. The sodic-amphiboles and pyroxenes (riebeckite, arfvedsonite, aegirine) are characteristic of the alkali granites. If neither feldspar is in great excess, neither amphibole nor pyroxene is likely to be an essential constituent; the other minerals will then ordinarily be either biotite or muscovite, or both.

There are two major source regions for producing molten granite: igneous and sedimentary protoliths (source rocks). These result in I-type granitoids, derived from igneous protoliths and containing moderate amounts of Al_2O_3 and high amounts of Na_2O, and S-type granitoids, derived from sedimentary protoliths and containing high amounts of Al_2O_3 and relatively low amounts of Na_2O. Amphibole and pyroxene are more common in I-type granitoids, while S-type granitoids may have garnet, cordierite, and sillimanite. Both types of granitoids may also contain biotite and muscovite.

Classification of Volcanic and Hypabyssal Rocks

Owing to the aphanitic texture of volcanic and hypabyssal rocks, their modes cannot be readily determined; consequently, a chemical classification is widely accepted and employed by most petrologists. One popular scheme is based on the use of both chemical components and normative mineralogy. Because most lay people have little access to analytic facilities that yield igneous rock compositions, only an outline will be presented here in order to provide an appreciation for the classification scheme.

The first major division is based on the alkali (soda + potash) and silica contents, which yield two groups, the subalkaline and alkaline rocks. The subalkaline rocks have two divisions based mainly on the iron content, with the iron-rich group called the tholeiitic series and the iron-poor group called calc-alkalic. The former group is most commonly found along the oceanic ridges and on the ocean floor; the latter group is characteristic of the volcanic regions of the continental margins (convergent, or destructive, plate boundaries; see below Forms of occurrence: Distribution of igneous rocks on Earth's surface). In some magmatic arcs (groups of islands arranged in a curved pattern), notably Japan, both the tholeiitic and calc-alkalic series occur. This is the case, for example, in the volcanoes of northeastern Honshu, the largest of Japan's four main islands, and both series may be found within the same volcano. The alkaline rocks frequently occur on oceanic islands (usually formed during the late stages of magma consolidation after tholeiitic eruptions) and in continental rifts (extensive fractures). Based on the relative proportions of soda and potash, the calc-alkalic series is subdivided into the sodic and potassic series.

Chemically the subalkaline rocks are saturated with respect to silica; consequently, they have normative minerals such as orthopyroxene [$Mg(Fe)_2Si_2O_6$] and quartz but lack nepheline and olivine (in the presence of quartz). This chemical property also is reflected in the mode of the basic members that have two pyroxenes, orthopyroxene and augite [$Ca(Mg, Fe)Si_2O_6$], and perhaps quartz. Plagioclase is common in phenocrysts, but it can also occur in holocrystalline rocks in the microcrystalline matrix along with the pyroxenes and an iron–titanium oxide phase. In addition to the differences in iron content between the tholeiitic and calc-alkalic series, the latter has a higher alumina content (16 to 20 percent), and the range in silica content is larger (48 to 75 percent compared to 45 to 63 percent for the former). Hornblende and biotite phenocrysts are common in the calc-alkalic andesites and dacites but are lacking in the tholeiites except as alteration products. The dacites and rhyolites commonly have phenocrysts of plagioclase, alkali feldspar (usually sanidine), and quartz in a glassy matrix. Hornblende and plagioclase phenocrysts are more widespread in dacites than in rhyolites, which have more biotite and alkali feldspar. When occurring near volcanic vents, (openings from which volcanic materials are brought to Earth's surface), basalts and andesites of both series are found as tuffs or agglomerates; otherwise, they typically occur as flows. Dacite and rhyolite occur as flows near vents but are most commonly found as tuffs composed of fragmented pieces of glass, phenocrysts, and rock.

The alkaline rocks typically are chemically undersaturated with respect to silica; hence they lack normative orthopyroxene (i.e., they have only one pyroxene, the calcium-rich augite) and quartz but have normative nepheline. Microscopic examination of the alkali olivine basalts usually reveals phenocrysts with an abundance of olivine,

ALKALINE ROCK

Various rocks in which the chemical content of the alkalies (potassium oxide and sodium oxide) is great enough for alkaline minerals to form are called alkaline rocks. Such minerals may be unusually sodium rich, with a relatively high ratio of alkalies to silica (SiO_2), as in the feldspathoids. Other alkaline minerals have a high ratio of alkalies to alumina (Al_2O_3), as in aegirine pyroxene and the sodic amphibole riebeckite.

English-speaking petrologists have followed Alfred Harker, who divided igneous rocks of Cenozoic age (that is, those laid down between about 65.5 million years ago and the present day) into calc-alkaline and alkaline suites. Alkaline rocks include many with unusual names, but the more common alkali-basalt, syenite, and phonolite are included in the group. The most common and widely distributed rocks of the world—e.g., granite, granodiorite, andesite, and basalt—do not contain the alkaline minerals. Alkaline rocks are generally considered to be abnormal types, and there have been many intensive studies of their origin, yielding a number of theories, each of which may be valid for a specific case.

one pyroxene (augite, which is usually titanium-rich), and plagioclase. Nepheline may be seen in the matrix. Trachytes typically are leucocratic with an abundance of feldspars aligned roughly parallel to the direction of the lava flow.

ORIGIN AND DISTRIBUTION

Magmas are chemically complex fluid systems. The viscosity of a magma greatly affects how they flow, as well as the behaviour of the crystals and other materials within magmas and the explosivity of the volcanic eruptions that release them. Magma solidifies as its temperature declines, but the chemical reactions that cause crystallization can proceed along different chemical pathways. The viscosity of magmas and various aspects of the crystallization process are also affected by the presence of water and other volatile substances.

ORIGIN OF MAGMAS

Basaltic magmas that form Earth's oceanic crust are generated in the asthenosphere at a depth of about 70 km (43 miles). The mantle rocks located at depths from about 70 to 200 km (43 to 124 miles) are believed to exist at temperatures slightly above their melting point, and possibly 1 or 2 percent of the rocks occur in the molten state. As a result, the asthenosphere behaves plastically, and upon penetrating this zone seismic waves experience a slight drop in velocity; this shell came to be known as the low velocity zone. Only after the acceptance of the plate tectonic theory has this zone become known as the asthenosphere. The most common mantle rock within the asthenosphere is peridotite, which is composed predominantly of magnesium-rich olivine, along with lesser amounts of chromium diopside and enstatite and an even smaller quantity of garnet. Peridotite may undergo partial melting to produce magmas with different compositions.

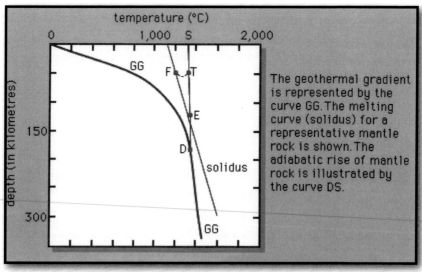

The geothermal gradient is represented by the curve GG. The melting curve (solidus) for a representative mantle rock is shown. The adiabatic rise of mantle rock is illustrated by the curve DS.

A proposed temperature distribution within the Earth. Copyright Encyclopædia Britannica, Inc.; rendering for this edition by Rosen Educational Services

Theories on the generation of basaltic magma mainly attribute its origin to the derivation of heat from within peridotite rather than by some outside source such as the radioactive decay of uranium, thorium, and potassium, which are only of minor consequence. Because of the difference in composition between basalt and peridotite, only a small amount of heat is needed to produce about 3 to at most 25 percent melt.

Granitic, or rhyolitic, magmas and andesitic magmas are generated at convergent plate boundaries where the oceanic lithosphere (the outer layer of Earth composed of the crust and upper mantle) is subducted so that its edge is positioned below the edge of the continental plate or another oceanic plate. Heat will be added to the subducting lithosphere as it moves slowly into the hotter depths of the mantle. The andesitic magma is believed to be generated in the wedge of mantle rock below the crust and

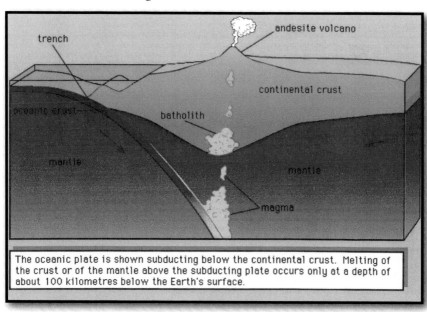

Collision of a continental plate with an oceanic plate. Copyright Encyclopædia Britannica, Inc.; rendering for this edition by Rosen Educational Services

above the subducted plate or within the subducted plate itself. The former requires the partial melting of a "wet" peridotite. Experiments conducted at pressures simulating mantle conditions have demonstrated that peridotite will produce andesitic melts during partial melting under hydrous conditions. The latter theory suggests that the subducted basaltic crust is partially melted and may be combined with some subducted oceanic sediments to form andesites. A third theory involves the mixing of basaltic magma that was generated in the mantle with granitic or rhyolitic magma or with crustal rocks. The silicic magmas can be formed by a combination of two processes; the presence of water under pressure lowers the melting temperature by as much as 200 °C (392 °F) and thereby expedites magma generation. At a convergent plate boundary, the lower continental crust is heated to a temperature near its melting point by being pushed downward into hotter regions of the mantle. Basaltic or andesitic magma generated below the crust may accumulate near the Moho, which is a discontinuity that separates Earth's crust from its mantle. As the magma cools, it crystallizes and releases its latent heat of crystallization. This evolved heat is transferred to the lower crustal rocks along with the simple heat released by cooling. If the lower crustal rocks contain some water, their melting temperatures would be lowered and the heating provided by the above processes would possibly be sufficient to partially melt the crustal rocks producing rhyolitic magma.

NATURE OF MAGMAS

Magmas can be thought of as mutual solutions, or melts, of rock-forming components that are variously present as simple ions, as complex ions and ionic groups, and as molecules. The most abundant of the simple ions in common magmas are such singly and doubly charged cations as Na^+, K^+, Ca^{2+}, Mg^{2+}, and Fe^{2+}. Because these ions can move about rather freely in the system, they occupy no fixed positions with respect to other ions that are present. In contrast, the smaller and more highly charged cations, notably Si^{4+}, Al^{3+}, and (to a lesser degree) Fe^{3+}, are surrounded or screened by O^{2-} ions and other anions (negative ions) to form parts of relatively stable complex ions such as $(SiO_4)^{4-}$, $(AlO_4)^{5-}$, and $(FeO_6)^{9-}$. Simple anions, including F^-, Cl^-, O^{2-}, and $(OH)^-$, ordinarily are present in much smaller amounts. Water, hydrochloric acid (HCl), hydrogen fluoride (HF), carbon dioxide (CO_2), and other volatile molecular substances occur as well, generally in equilibrium with ionic forms such as $(OH)^-$, Cl^-, F^-, and $(CO_3)^{2-}$.

Because the bond that unites silicon and oxygen is a remarkably strong one, $(SiO_4)^{4-}$ ions are stable in magmas even at exceedingly high temperatures. They also tend to join with one another, or polymerize, to form more complex anionic groups, a tendency that is especially great in the more silicic magmas. The joining is accomplished by a sharing of oxygen ions between adjacent silicon ions to form Si-O-Si bridges like those in many silicate and aluminosilicate minerals; in the simplest such case, $(Si_2O_7)^{6-}$ ions are the result. Because the $(AlO_4)^{5-}$ ions also have a strong tendency to polymerize, most of the large ionic groups in magmas probably contain both silicon and aluminum ions. These groups, which resemble the frameworks of many rock-forming minerals but are geometrically less regular, significantly affect the viscosity and crystallization of magmas.

The viscosity of magmas, which spans an enormous range of values, affects their flow behaviour, the movements of crystals and inclusions of foreign matter within them, the diffusion of materials through them, the growth of crystals from them, and the explosivity of eruptions (when aided by growth of gas bubbles near the surface). Lava flows are thin and rapid for low-viscosity magmas, but thick and slow for viscous flows. Fluid magma promotes the growth of large crystals such as the ones found in pegmatites, but crystal growth is prevented in viscous magmas, which usually are quenched as glass. Highly explosive eruptions such as occurred at Mount St. Helens commonly result from gas bubbles nucleating, growing, and rising in a highly viscous magma. It can be demonstrated thermodynamically that the overpressure (excess rock pressure) developed in growing and rising bubbles is inversely proportional to their radii. In fluid magmas, gas bubbles grow large in size and rise quickly, which causes their pressures to be expended; hence, only a spectacular fountaining of hot lava is observed at the surface. In contrast, a viscous magma prevents the growth of bubbles, so that they will rise slowly while retaining excess pressure; as a result, the associated volcano erupts violently. Energies equivalent to the amount produced by several nuclear bombs are released in such explosions. Viscosity increases greatly with decreasing temperature and less markedly with increasing pressure. It also can be governed in part by the amount and distribution of any solid materials or bubbles of gas present, which both tend to increase viscosity. Finally, it varies considerably among magmas of differing gross composition, mainly because of the differences in the degree of Si-O and Al-O polymerization. Thus, highly silicic magmas generally are more viscous than mafic ones by several orders of magnitude, a difference reflected by contrasts in the eruptive behaviour of rhyolitic and basaltic lavas. Basaltic magmas at 1,100 °C (about 2,000 °F) can be at least 100,000 times more viscous than water at room temperature, whereas rhyolitic magmas at 800 °C (about 1,475 °F) are at least 10 million times more viscous than room-temperature water. The presence of volatile constituents can markedly increase the fluidity of magmas, even those that are rich in SiO_2. This effect has been attributed to the breaking of Si-O-Si bridges through substitution of ions such as F^- and $(OH)^-$ for shared O^{2-} ions in elements of the polymerized groups.

A typical magma can be broadly viewed as an assemblage of relatively large and rather closely packed oxygen ions, among which some cations have considerable mobility; others, such as Si^{4+} and Al^{3+}, tend to occupy positions that are more fixed. The entire system is a dynamic one, however, and even the largest of the Si-O and Al-O ion groups are constantly changing form and position as bonds are broken and new ones are established. If the magma quickly loses thermal energy and cools to a glass, these internal movements are sharply restricted, and the various constituents become essentially frozen in position. If cooling is slower, the contained complex ions and polymerized ion groups have time to assume more regular arrangements and to be stabilized by cations of appropriate size, charge, and other properties. Crystalline solids are thereby formed. Their regular internal structure is relatively conserving of space, and so they have somewhat higher specific gravities than the magma from which they were nourished.

CRYSTALLIZATION FROM MAGMAS

The crystallization of magmas may occur discontinuously at fixed temperatures at constant pressures, or they may occur continuously when temperatures or pressures change. One example of a discontinuous reaction (the olivine-liquid-pyroxene reaction) is the forsterite-cristobalite system, whereas one example of a continuous reaction (the plagioclase-liquid reaction) is the albite-anorthite system. The progress of both reactions and their ultimate convergence with one another can be plotted together in a Y-shaped graph called Bowen's reaction series. Daughter magmas may also occur as a result of reactions between the parent magma and the wall rocks that surround it.

THE FORSTERITE-CRISTOBALITE SYSTEM

Because magmas are multicomponent solutions, they do not crystallize at a single temperature at a given pressure like water at 0 °C (32 °F) and 1 standard atmosphere of pressure. Rather, they crystallize over a wide range of temperatures beginning at liquidus temperatures (that is, the line on a phase diagram depicting the equilibrium between liquid, solid, and gaseous phases in a mixture) for basaltic magmas as high as 1,150 °C (about 2,100 °F) and ending as a complete solid at a low solidus temperature of about 800 °C (about 1,475 °F). (The solidus temperature corresponds to a line on a phase diagram showing where the complete crystallization of a given substance occurs.) During their crystallization at constant pressure, common minerals that make up basaltic magma (e.g., olivine) become unstable at some temperature and react with the liquid to form a more stable phase. In the case of olivine, this phase is pyroxene. This reaction relationship is best illustrated with the use of a phase diagram of a portion of the olivine Mg_2SiO_4 (forsterite) + SiO_2 (cristobalite, a high-temperature form of quartz) binary system at one atmosphere.

Consider a mixture X of two minerals in the proportions 28 percent cristobalite and 72 percent forsterite. At a temperature of 1,601 °C (2,914 °F), this mixture is entirely liquid. At temperatures below 1,557 °C (2,835 °F), forsterite (Fo) and enstatite (En) are stable, but between 1,557 and 1,600 °C, forsterite and the liquid whose composition is represented by L are in equilibrium. At a temperature of 1,570 °C (2,858 °F), there is about 7 percent forsterite and 93 percent liquid. As the liquid X cools, it intersects the liquidus freezing curve at a temperature of 1,600 °C, where forsterite begins to crystallize. As the temperature drops further, the liquid follows the liquidus down toward R, the peritectic point (incongruent melting point in a binary system), while it continually crystallizes more forsterite. It should be noted that the liquid composition is becoming enriched in silica, until at R, it has more silica than enstatite. At this point the forsterite reacts with the liquid to yield two moles of $MgSiO_3$ (enstatite) for every mole of Mg_2SiO_4 that combines with one mole of SiO_2 removed from the liquid R. This can be written as a chemical equation: $Mg_2SiO_4 + SiO_2 \rightleftharpoons 2MgSiO_3$. Because SiO_2 is removed from the liquid R, a proportionate amount of enstatite must be crystallized from the liquid to keep its composition at point R. In the case of the starting composition X, which is depleted in SiO_2 relative to enstatite, the peritectic liquid, R, will be consumed by the reaction prior to the forsterite, and the resultant mixture will consist of forsterite and enstatite. However, in the case in which the starting composition is Y, which is enriched in silica relative to enstatite, the forsterite will be depleted before the liquid, and the reaction will yield the liquid and enstatite. Only in the case where the starting composition matches that of enstatite will the liquid and the forsterite be consumed at the same time, leaving only enstatite. The starting composition X represents the most common crystallization behaviour for saturated tholeiitic basaltic magmas; consequently, these magmas will experience a reaction between the liquid and the olivine, forsterite, at some point during their crystallization. This means that the liquid will be consumed by the reaction with forsterite and crystallization will cease. If, however, forsterite can be removed physically from the liquid before the reaction can occur, the reaction will be prevented and the peritectic liquid will remain to crystallize the pyroxene, enstatite, and move down toward the eutectic temperature where cristobalite and enstatite will crystallize.

THE ALBITE-ANORTHITE SYSTEM

Most of the common minerals found in igneous rocks are solid-solution phases. These include olivine, pyroxene, amphibole, biotite, and plagioclase feldspars. Crystallization behaviour is illustrated best by using the $NaAlSi_3O_8$ (albite or Ab)–$CaAl_2Si_2O_8$ (anorthite or An) plagioclase system.

Consider a liquid of composition L (60 percent An + 40 percent Ab) which is at an initial temperature of

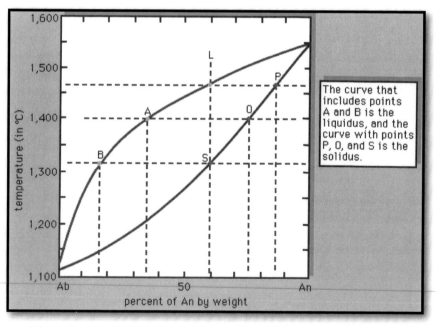

Phase diagram of the albite (Ab)–anorthite (An) system at one atmosphere of pressure. After N. Bowen, "Melting Phenomena of the Plagioclase Feldspars," American Journal of Science, *vol. 34 (1913). Copyright Encyclopædia Britannica, Inc.; rendering for this edition by Rosen Educational Services*

1,500 °C (about 2,730 °F). On cooling it will begin crystallizing plagioclase with 85 percent An at the liquidus temperature of about 1,470 °C (about 2,680 °F). As cooling continues further, the liquid will move down the liquidus while simultaneously reacting continuously with the early-formed plagioclase to convert it to a homogeneous plagioclase that is more albitic and in equilibrium with the liquid. For example, at 1,400 °C (about 2,550 °F), about 65 percent plagioclase with about 73 percent An has crystallized from the liquid, which is now at about 36 percent An and 64 percent Ab. Finally, when the temperature of about 1,330 °C (about 2,425 °F) is reached, the last small amount of the liquid of composition 20 percent An + 80 percent Ab is consumed in the reaction and a homogeneous plagioclase of 60 percent An + 40 percent Ab remains.

Now consider the case in which the liquid is prevented from reacting with the early-formed plagioclase. This may be achieved by physically removing the plagioclase immediately after its formation or by cooling the liquid faster than the reaction process can consume the plagioclase. The liquid could theoretically reach the pure Ab composition at 1,100 °C (about 2,000 °F), where it will disappear into the crystallizing albite. A whole range of plagioclase compositions from An_{84} to An_{00} will be preserved in the cooling process.

Bowen's Reaction Series

These two examples illustrate two principal reactions that occur during crystallization of common magmas, one discontinuous (the olivine-liquid-pyroxene reaction) and the other continuous (the plagioclase-liquid reaction). This was recognized first by the American petrologist Norman L. Bowen; in his honour, the mineral series has since been called the Bowen's reaction series.

A Y-shaped diagram can be constructed linking the two principal reactions. The left branch of the Y-shaped arrangement consists of the discontinuous series that begins with olivine at the highest temperature and progresses through pyroxene, amphibole, and biotite as the temperature decreases. This series is discontinuous because the reaction occurs at a fixed temperature at constant pressure wherein the early-formed mineral is converted to a more stable crystal. Each mineral in the series displays a different silicate structure that exhibits increased polymerization as the temperature drops; olivine belongs to the island silicate structure type; pyroxene, the chain; amphibole, the double chain; and biotite, the sheet. On the other hand, the right branch is the continuous reaction series in which plagioclase is continuously reacting with the liquid to form a more albitic phase as the temperature decreases. In both cases, the liquid is consumed in the reaction. When the two reaction series converge at a low temperature, minerals that will not react with the remaining liquid approach eutectic crystallization. Potash feldspar, muscovite, and quartz are crystallized. The phases that are crystallized first are the common minerals that compose basalt or gabbro, like bytownite or labradorite with pyroxene and minor amounts of olivine. Andesite or diorite minerals, such as andesine with either pyroxene or amphibole, crystallize next and are followed by orthoclase and quartz, which are the essential constituents of rhyolite or granite. A basaltic liquid at the top of the Υ can descend to the bottom of the series to crystallize quartz only if the earlier reactions are prevented. As demonstrated above, complete reactions between early-formed minerals and the liquid depletes the supply of the liquid, thereby curtailing the progression down the series. One

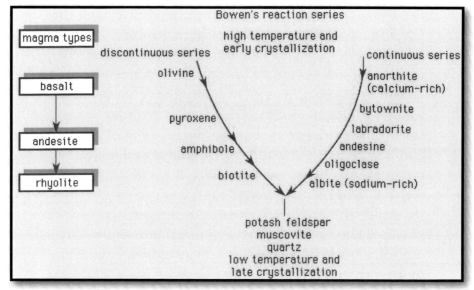

Bowen's reaction series showing the sequence of minerals that would be formed and removed during fractional crystallization of a melt. The magmas relating to the crystallizing minerals are shown on the left. Copyright Encyclopædia Britannica, Inc.; rendering for this edition by Rosen Educational Services

means by which basaltic magma can be transformed to rocks lower in the series is by fractional crystallization. In this process, the early-formed minerals are removed from the liquid by gravity (such minerals as olivine and pyroxene are denser than the liquid from which they crystallized), and so unreacted liquid remains later in the series.

ASSIMILATION

Another method of creating different daughter magmas from a parent is by having the latter react with its wall rocks. Consider a magma that is crystallizing pyroxene and labradorite. If the magma tears from its wall minerals, say, olivine and anorthite, which are formed earlier than pyroxene and labradorite in the series, they will react with the liquid to form these same minerals with which the magma is in equilibrium. The heat for driving this reaction comes directly from the magma itself. More pyroxene and labradorite will crystallize during the reaction and will release their latent heats of crystallization. On the other hand, if a mineral (quartz, for example) formed at a later stage than pyroxene or labradorite falls from the rock wall into the magma, the latent heat provided by further crystallization of pyroxene and labradorite will cause it to dissolve. This situation will occur only if the quartz from the wall rock is at a lower temperature than the magma. It will cause the magma to transfer its heat to the quartz in a cooling process. The cooling of the magma will necessarily be accompanied by the crystallization of the minerals already present. In both cases, the composition of the parent magma will be changed by the xenolithic (foreign rock) contamination. The contaminant need not belong to the reaction series in order for it to cause reactions or dissolution. In most cases, the end result will be a shift from the original composition of the parent magma toward that of the contaminant. This process in which wall rocks are incorporated into the magma is called assimilation. Because assimilation is accompanied by crystallization, it is likely that both fractional crystallization and assimilation will take place simultaneously. This combined process, referred to as AFC for assimilation–fractional crystallization, has been proposed as the mechanism by which andesites are produced from basalts.

Volatile Constituents and Late Magmatic Processes

Water and most other volatile substances profoundly influence the properties and behaviour of magmas in which they are dissolved. They reduce viscosity, lower temperatures of crystallization by tens to hundreds of degrees, and participate directly in the formation of minerals that contain essential hydroxyl (OH) or elements such as the halogens. They also increase rates of crystallization and reaction, especially when they are present as a fluid phase distinct from the magma. In general, however, they have only a limited influence on the sequence of magmatic crystallization, except in the latest stages of the reaction series.

The relatively low confining pressures in volcanic environments permit ready escape of volatile constituents, which nonetheless leave their imprint in the form of special mineral assemblages and a variety of textural and structural features among the volcanic rocks. Under the higher pressures of plutonic environments, these constituents tend to be maintained in magmatic solution and to be increasingly concentrated as crystallization progresses with falling temperature. Few members of the reaction series require them as compositional contributors; water, for example, is not thus used until amphiboles or micas begin to form, and even then the amounts removed from the melt rarely are large. Escape of volatiles from the system can occur "osmotically" if the enclosing rocks are pervious to them but not to the magma, but in general they are fractionated in favour of the residual melt until their concentration reaches the limit of solubility under the prevailing conditions of temperature and effective confining pressure. When this happens, normally at a very late stage of magmatic crystallization, they are exsolved from the melt as a separate fluid phase that under most circumstances is a supercritical gas. This process has been referred to as resurgent boiling, a somewhat misleading term because the exsolved fluid is not necessarily expelled from the system.

Coexistence of residual magma and a volatile-rich fluid (generally aqueous) promotes the partitioning and segregation of constituents, as well as the growth of very large crystals. The exsolved fluid, with its very low viscosity, not only can move readily through open spaces in the nearly solid igneous rock and in adjacent rocks but also serves as a medium through which various substances can diffuse rapidly in response to concentration gradients. Thus, it plays an important role in the formation of such special rock types as the pegmatites and lamprophyres, special features such as miaroles and plumose mineral aggregates, and many kinds of ore deposits whose constituents are derived from the original magma.

Most plutonic systems remain at elevated temperatures for long periods of time after all magma has been used up, and during these periods hydrothermal conditions normally obtain. These depend upon the continued presence of a typically aqueous fluid that further facilitates crystallization and exchanges of materials. It speeds up exsolution within homogeneous solid phases and devitrification of any glass that may be present, and it is a potent agent in the alteration, leaching, and replacement of minerals. Rock textures thereby are modified, especially along boundaries between original mineral grains, and details of composition also can be much changed. In some instances the bulk chemistry of the rock is markedly affected.

The hydrothermal alterations favour development of phases such as albite, carbonates, chlorites, clay minerals, epidotes, iron oxides, micas, silica minerals, talc, and zeolites, and many of them are accompanied by gross changes in volume.

FORMS OF OCCURRENCE

Igneous rocks can be divided into two categories: extrusive igneous rocks and intrusive igneous rocks. Extrusive rocks are the products of magma that has cooled and hardened on Earth's surface, whereas intrusive igneous rocks result from the crystallization of magma within Earth itself. On Earth's surface, igneous rocks tend to be concentrated near the boundaries of tectonic plates and in regions characterized by flood basalts.

EXTRUSIVE IGNEOUS ROCKS

Extrusive igneous rocks are the products of volcanic activity. They appear at the surface as molten lava that spreads in sheets and hardens, or they are made up of fragments of magma ejected from vents by violent gaseous explosions. Large-scale extrusive features include stratovolcanoes (composite cones), shield volcanoes, lava domes, and cinder cones. Smaller extrusive features include lava flows known as pahoehoe and aa.

OBSIDIAN

Obsidian is a natural glass of volcanic origin that is formed by the rapid cooling of viscous lava. Obsidian is extremely rich in silica (about 65 to 80 percent), is low in water, and has a chemical composition similar to rhyolite. Obsidian has a glassy lustre and is slightly harder than window glass. Though obsidian is typically jet-black in colour, the presence of hematite (iron oxide) produces red and brown varieties, and the inclusion of tiny gas bubbles may create a golden sheen. Other types with dark bands or mottling in gray, green, or yellow are also known.

Obsidian generally contains less than 1 percent water by weight. Under high pressure at depth, rhyolitic lavas may contain up to 10 percent water, which helps to keep them fluid even at a

The natural glass obsidian, an extrusive igneous rock, is formed by cooling lava. Shutterstock.com

low temperature. Eruption to the surface, where pressure is low, permits rapid escape of this volatile water and increases the viscosity of the melt. Increased viscosity impedes crystallization, and the lava solidifies as a glass.

Different obsidians are composed of a variety of crystalline materials. Their abundant, closely spaced crystallites (microscopic embryonic crystal growths) are so numerous that the glass is opaque except on thin edges. Many samples of obsidian contain spherical clusters of radially arranged, needlelike crystals called spherulites. Microlites (tiny polarizing crystals) of feldspar and phenocrysts (large, well-formed crystals) of quartz may also be present.

Most obsidian is associated with volcanic rocks and forms the upper portion of rhyolitic lava flows. It occurs less abundantly as thin edges of dikes and sills. The obsidians of Mount Hekla in Iceland, the Eolie Islands off the coast of Italy, and Obsidian Cliff in Yellowstone National Park, Wyoming, U.S., are all well-known occurrences.

Obsidian was used by American Indians and many other peoples for weapons, implements, tools, and ornaments and by the ancient Aztecs and Greeks for mirrors. Because of its conchoidal fracture (smooth curved surfaces and sharp edges), the sharpest stone artifacts were fashioned from obsidian; some of these—mostly arrowheads—have been dated by means of the hydration rinds that form on their exposed surfaces through time. Obsidian in attractive and variegated colours is sometimes used as a semiprecious stone.

INTRUSIVE IGNEOUS ROCKS

Erosion of volcanoes will immediately expose shallow intrusive bodies such as volcanic necks and diatremes. A volcanic neck is the "throat" of a volcano and consists of a pipelike conduit filled with hypabyssal rocks. Ship Rock in New Mexico and Devil's Tower in Wyoming are remnants of volcanic necks, which were exposed after the surrounding sedimentary rocks were eroded away. Many craterlike depressions may be filled with angular fragments of country rock (breccia) and juvenile pyroclastic debris. When eroded, such a depression exposes a vertical

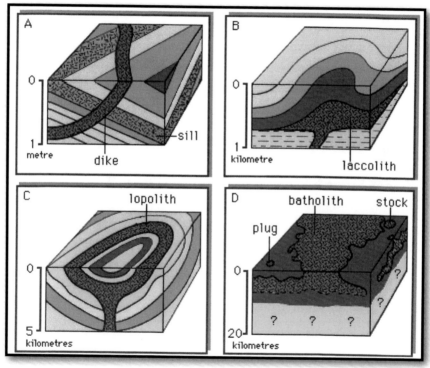

Forms of intrusive igneous rock bodies in hypothetical sections of Earth strata. Note the change of scale from A through D. Copyright Encyclopædia Britannica, Inc.; rendering for this edition by Rosen Educational Services

funnel-shaped pipe that resembles a volcanic neck with the exception of the brecciated filling. These pipes are dubbed diatremes. Many diatremes are formed by explosion resulting from the rapid expansion of gas—carbon dioxide and water vapour. These gases are released by the rising magma owing to the decrease in pressure as it nears the surface. Some diatremes contain kimberlite, a peridotite that contains a hydrous mineral called phlogopite. Kimberlite may contain diamonds.

Dikes are usually tabular bodies that may radiate from the central vent of a volcano or from a volcanic neck. Not all dikes are associated with volcanoes, but they can be distinguished by their discordant relationship with the structure of the country rock that they cut across. Many dikes are only a few metres wide, but large ones, such as the dike that feeds the Muskox intrusion in the Northwest Territories of Canada, reach widths of more than 150 metres (about 500 feet). Related to dikes are features that maintain a concordant relationship with the structure of the country rocks. Magmas may force their way between layers of country rock and solidify parallel to them to form sills. On the west bank of the Hudson River opposite New York City, the 300-metre- (984-foot-) thick Palisades sill is exposed and can be traced for 80 km (about 50 miles). A laccolith also is concordant with country rock, but it is distinguished from a sill by having a flat floor with a domed (mushroom-shaped) roof. Laccoliths were first described in the Henry Mountains of Utah, where they may measure up to 200 metres (about 660 feet) thick with basal diameters exceeding 3 km (about 2 miles). Rocks of intermediate silica content generally make up these domed intrusions. In contrast, lopoliths are saucer-shaped bodies with a concave upward roof and floor and are commonly composed of mafic rocks. Lopoliths are huge in size; the Bushveld intrusive complex in South Africa, for example, has an area of about 66,000 square km (about 25,500 square miles) and an exposed thickness of 8 km (5 miles). The Muskox intrusion, mentioned above, is another large lopolith, which is estimated to be about 80 km long and 11 km (about 7 miles) wide (roof rocks covering part of the intrusion prevent an exact measurement). These lopoliths are commonly layered with igneous minerals and rocks; in the Bushveld intrusion, one layer about 1 metre thick consisting of almost pure chromite (an ore of chromium) extends for tens of kilometres. Large irregularly shaped plutons are called either stocks or batholiths, depending on their sizes. Plutons larger than 100 square km (about 39 square miles) in area are termed batholiths, while those of lesser size are called stocks. It may be possible, however, that some stocks are the visible portions of batholiths that have not been exposed by erosion. Batholiths (from the Greek word *bathos*, meaning depth) are deep-seated crustal intrusions, whereas stocks may be formed at shallow depths only a few kilometres below the surface. Rocks ranging from quartz diorite to granite are commonly found in batholiths. Large batholiths in North America include the Sierra Nevada, the Idaho, and the Coast Range, which is about 600 km (about 375 miles) long and 200 km (about 125 miles) wide and extends from the Alaskan border through British Columbia to Washington state. Many pulses of intrusions contribute to the formation of these large bodies; for example, eight episodes of activity have been recognized in the Sierra Nevada batholith. They are formed, therefore, by the coalescence of many smaller batholiths and stocks.

Distribution of Igneous Rocks on Earth's Surface

Igneous rocks occur widely. They are the products of activities that take place at divergent and convergent boundaries between Earth's tectonic plates. Igneous rocks also form far from plate boundaries as a result of hot spot activity (which produce flood basalts) and rising basaltic magma that intrudes between layers of rock. Igneous rocks also occur on the Moon and on other celestial bodies.

Divergent Plate Boundaries

Most of the igneous activity on Earth is restricted to a narrow zone that is related intimately with the motions of the lithospheric plates. Indeed, the composition of the magma, the types of volcanism, and the characteristics of intrusions are governed to a large extent by plate tectonics. The magmatism at divergent plate boundaries along the crests of the oceanic rises and ridges is mostly unseen except in places where the volcanic activity occurs subaerially (e.g., Iceland, which sits on the Mid-Atlantic Ridge). Along these divergent boundaries, the erupted basalts have such a restricted compositional range that they are referred to as mid-ocean-ridge basalt (MORB). They are subalkaline tholeiites that contain olivine in the norm and less than 0.25 percent potash. The chemistry suggests that MORB was generated from a mantle that was depleted of volatile elements (e.g., lanthanum [La], cerium [Ce], sodium, and potassium) in a previous partial melting process. A wide rift valley marks the crest of most of the oceanic ridges and rises. The valley is bounded by faults created by the divergent forces and is floored in its centre by a fracture zone (a mass of rock with many small breakages). These faults and

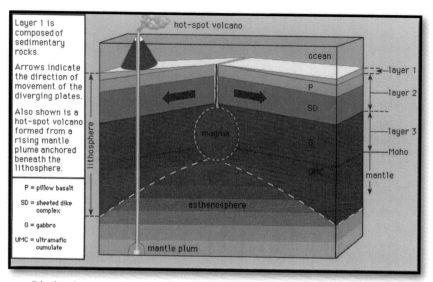

Layer 1 is composed of sedimentary rocks.

Arrows indicate the direction of movement of the diverging plates.

Also shown is a hot-spot volcano formed from a rising mantle plume anchored beneath the lithosphere.

P = pillow basalt

SD = sheeted dike complex

G = gabbro

UMC = ultramafic cumulate

Idealized cross section of a divergent plate boundary showing the structure of the oceanic lithosphere. Copyright Encyclopædia Britannica, Inc.; rendering for this edition by Rosen Educational Services

fractures are the conduits for the MORB magmas that flood the valley, build volcanoes, and produce dikes by filling the conduits. Layer 2 of the oceanic crust results from these magmatic activities. As the plates diverge, MORB becomes the ocean floor on which oceanic sediments (layer 1) are deposited. This makes MORB the most abundant rock on Earth's surface.

Below the collection of lavas and dikes in layer 2 are found gabbro and diorite. They represent the plutonic rocks formed as a result of differentiation of the MORB magma that fed the volcanic activity along the rift. (Differentiation is the process in which more than one rock type is derived from a single parent magma.) These coarse-grained intrusives account for about 4 to 5 km (2.5 to 3 miles) of layer 3, which rests on a sequence of layered ultramafic rocks. The rocks were formed by the gravitative accumulation of mafic minerals from the original MORB magma that filled a large chamber below the ridge axis. Below this layered sequence is mantle rock that is highly deformed and depleted (of elements such as lanthanum, cerium, sodium, and potassium that have been removed by repeated partial melting). Because seismic waves cannot distinguish between layered ultramafic rocks, which are not true mantle rocks, and ultramafic mantle rocks, the Moho actually is positioned between layer 3 and the layered ultramafics. The sequences consisting of layer 1 (limestone and chert sedimentary rocks), layer 2 of MORB lavas and dikes, and layer 3 of gabbro and diorite and the ultramafic rocks are known as ophiolites. Many geologists believe that ophiolites formed at oceanic ridges were emplaced by tectonic forces at convergent plate boundaries and then became exposed in highly deformed orogenic (mountain) belts. In fact, the same sequences of rocks were first reported in the Alps and were considered deep-seated intrusions. Some geologists still argue that all ophiolites were not formed at divergent plate boundaries.

Away from the axis of divergence, the composition of the volcanic rocks becomes more diverse. Most of the magmatism is related to hot spots, which are hot rising plumes of mantle rock that are anchored beneath the moving lithospheric plates. The Hawaiian Islands owe their existence to the magmatism associated with a hot spot that currently is located just southeast of the large island of Hawaii. This mantle plume not only provides magma for the eruptions at Kilauea Volcano but also is responsible for the submarine volcano named Loihi that will eventually become a new island. Most of the islands are built on a tholeiite basalt base, but the caps of the volcanoes are alkali basalts. The final episodes of volcanic activity on an island are extremely

A lava flow from Kilauea, Hawaii. Kilauea is the world's largest active volcano. ©www.istockphoto.com / Ashok Rodrigues

undersaturated; nephelinites and olivine melilite nephelinites are common products. The alkali basalts have differentiated to more silica-rich compositions, with hawaiites, mugearites, and trachytes being erupted in minor amounts. The two active volcanoes on Hawaii, Mauna Loa and Kilauea, are still erupting tholeiite basalts. Tholeiites on all the islands far from the ocean ridge crests are different from MORB in that they are enriched in lanthanum, cerium, sodium, and potassium. Early in Earth's history, a high-magnesium, high-temperature mafic magma called komatiite erupted from hot spots. Since most komatiites are found only in Archean regions, they are thought to be evidence for Earth being hotter than when it was initially formed. The youngest komatiite was recently discovered on the island of Gorgona, Colom.

CONVERGENT PLATE BOUNDARIES

Igneous rocks associated with convergent plate boundaries have the greatest diversity. In this case, granite batholiths underlie the great composite volcanoes and consist of rocks ranging from basalt through andesite to dacite and rhyolite. These boundaries are destructive and consume the subducting oceanic lithosphere formed at the divergent centres. The rocks generated, however, are added on (accreted) to the continent. Oceanic trenches outline the junction of the colliding plates, but the igneous activity takes place on the overriding plate along a line at least about 100 km (about 60 miles) above the subducting plate. In other words, almost no volcanism occurs between this 100-km line (called the volcanic front) and the trench. The horizontal distance between the trench and the volcanic front depends on the angle of subduction; the steeper the angle, the shorter the distance. Volcanism occurs from this volcanic axis inland for a few hundred kilometres. The dominant rock constituting the composite volcanoes is andesite, but in some younger island arcs basalt tends to be more common, and in older volcanic areas dacite or rhyolite becomes prominent. Two different series of rocks are found in some volcanic chains. In Japan a tholeiitic series and a calc-alkalic series sometimes erupt from the same volcano. The former is characterized by lower magnesium, potassium, nickel, chromium, uranium, and thorium and a higher iron:magnesium ratio. Mineralogically, the tholeiitic series characteristically contains pigeonite (a low-calcium monoclinic pyroxene) in the groundmass of the basalts and andesites. The calc-alkalic series lacks pigeonite but instead has hypersthene. Most of the composite volcanoes of the Cascades Range in Oregon and Washington in the northwestern United States are characteristically calc-alkalic. In some volcanic arcs in areas farthest from the trench, a potassic series is found. In Japan the volcanoes within the Sea of Japan and farthest from the Japan Trench have alkali basalt compositions. Recent discoveries in modern convergent margins have identified igneous rocks within the oceanic trench sediments. These occur in regions where a mid-ocean ridge is being subducted. This creates higher heat flow and different types of igneous rocks, termed trondhjemite-tonalite-dacite (TTD) suites and alkaline, mafic, and felsic types.

In older areas of convergence, the composite volcanoes have been eroded, exposing the deeper plutonic granite batholiths that extend the entire length of the convergent boundaries. The batholiths are predominantly granodiorite, but gabbro through granite occur as well. It seems anomalous to find diorite, the plutonic equivalent of andesite, in low abundance since andesite is the dominant rock type of the volcanoes that were above these batholiths. Two basic types of granite have been recognized. The more common variety is located closer to the trench, has hornblende as its mafic mineral, is enriched in sodium and calcium, and has mantle chemical signatures; it is called I-type granite. The other type, called S-type granite, has muscovite and biotite and is depleted in sodium but enriched in aluminum such that corundum occurs in the norm and isotopic signatures. This suggests that such granites were formed by partial fusion of sedimentary rocks.

FLOOD BASALTS

On the continental plates at areas away from active convergence, the magmatism is confined to rift valleys and local hot spots. The volume of magma produced is minor in comparison to that generated at oceanic rises and at convergent plate boundaries. Flood basalts are the most common form of occurrence. They span the rock record from the Precambrian to the Neogene Period (from about 4.6 billion to 2.6 million years ago) and are found worldwide. The 1.1-billion-year-old Keweenawan flood basalts in the Lake Superior region of northern Michigan may have formed in a rift that failed. The rifting of Pangaea that began during Jurassic time (approximately 200 million to 146 million years ago) generated flood basalt eruptions all along the newly opened Atlantic Ocean. Two voluminous eruptions associated with the opening of the South Atlantic produced the Paraná basalt in Brazil and the Karoo (or Karroo) in South Africa. The Deccan basalts in India were formed in the rift valleys associated with the breakup of Gondwana during the Cretaceous Period (approximately 146 million to 65.5 million years ago). Chemically, the most abundant basalts are supersaturated tholeiites with normative quartz, but olivine tholeiites and alkali basalts also are found. Feeder dike swarms (groups consisting of many parallel dikes) and sills are common in flood basalt plateaus. Alkaline rocks, such as those found in the East African Rift System, occur as well but are less abundant. This rift system stretches southward from the Red Sea–Gulf of Aden to Lake Victoria. Undersaturated basalts are most common in these rifts. During one eruption, a magma composed mostly of sodium carbonate issued from a volcanic vent that had been erupting alkali basalts.

OTHER TERRESTRIAL OCCURRENCES

Other diverse and unusual igneous rocks are found in the stable continental areas far from plate boundaries. These include the large layered basaltic intrusions—namely, the Stillwater Complex in Montana, the Muskox intrusion in the Northwest Territories of Canada, the Bushveld Complex in South Africa, and the Skaergaard intrusion in eastern Greenland. Tholeiitic magma underwent a fractional crystallization process that deposited layers of ultramafic rocks overlain by gabbroic and anorthositic layers. The end products of this fractionation are quartz- and feldspar-bearing rocks with a peculiar texture (known as graphic intergrowth) in which quartz and feldspar are intimately intergrown with each other. These rocks are called granophyres. Such layered intrusions have some economic importance; some of them contain thick (a few metres) layers of chromite, which is the source of chromium and also platinum. Two other rare occurrences in cratonic (stable) areas of Earth's crust are the kimberlites and carbonatites. Both are of economic value because they yield diamonds and niobium, respectively. Kimberlites are mica peridotites that are found in pipes. The stable interiors of South Africa and Siberia have widespread occurrences, but these pipes also are found in North America, Australia, Brazil, and India. In North America, near Murfreesboro, Ark., individuals can pay a fee to search for diamonds in the Prairie Creek kimberlite pipe located in the Crater of Diamonds State Park. Not all kimberlites contain diamonds. When diamonds do occur, they constitute less than one part per million of the rock. Carbonatites are igneous rocks rich in carbonate (containing at least 50 percent) that commonly occur in ring complexes in association with other silica-poor rocks such as nepheline syenites. In North America, carbonatites have been found in dozens of localities in northern Ontario and western Quebec.

EXTRATERRESTRIAL OCCURRENCES

The dominant igneous rock on Earth's surface is basalt. It appears that such is also the case on Earth's close neighbours. The lunar maria are covered with basalt lava flows. These lunar basalts have a mineralogy similar to that of terrestrial basalts, but chemically they have no water, a lower amount of alkalis and alumina, and a higher iron oxide and chromium content. On the lunar highlands, plagioclase-rich rocks are most common; these include anorthosites, gabbros, troctolites (olivine-plagioclase rock), and minor basalt. It appears that basalt is common on Mars as well. The large shield volcano Olympus Mons must have been formed from eruptions of fluid basalt flows. The X-ray fluorescence analyses performed by the Vikings 1 and 2 landers showed that the rocks are basaltic. In contrast, compositions of meteorites that originated from Mars include both basalts and ultramafic rocks such as dunite, clinopyroxenite, and iherzolite. The Mars Pathfinder and Rover show that andesite may also be present, but that result is still debated. Venus apparently has volcanic features with granitic to basaltic compositions.

CHAPTER 3
SEDIMENTARY ROCK

S edimentary rock is formed at or near Earth's surface by the accumulation and lithification of sediment (detrital rock) or by the precipitation from solution at normal surface temperatures (chemical rock). Sedimentary rocks are the most common rocks exposed on Earth's surface but are only a minor constituent of the entire crust, which is dominated by igneous and metamorphic rocks.

Sedimentary rocks are produced by the weathering of preexisting rocks and the subsequent transportation and deposition of the weathering products. Weathering refers to the various processes of physical disintegration and chemical decomposition that occur when rocks at Earth's surface are exposed to the atmosphere (mainly in the form of rainfall) and the hydrosphere. These processes produce soil, unconsolidated rock detritus, and components dissolved in groundwater and runoff. Erosion is the process by which weathering products are transported away from the weathering site, either as solid material or as dissolved components, eventually to be deposited as sediment. Any unconsolidated deposit of solid weathered material constitutes sediment. It can form as the result of deposition of grains from moving bodies of water or wind, from the melting of glacial ice, and from the downslope slumping (sliding) of rock and soil masses in response to gravity, as well as by precipitation of the dissolved products of weathering under the conditions of low temperature and pressure that prevail at or near Earth's surface.

Sedimentary rocks are the lithified equivalents of sediments. They typically are produced by cementing, compacting, and otherwise solidifying preexisting unconsolidated sediments. Some varieties of sedimentary rock, however, are precipitated directly into their solid sedimentary form and exhibit no intervening existence as sediment. Organic reefs and bedded evaporites are examples of such rocks. Because the processes of physical (mechanical) weathering and chemical weathering are significantly different, they generate markedly distinct products and two fundamentally different kinds of sediment and sedimentary rock: (1) terrigenous clastic sedimentary rocks and (2) allochemical and orthochemical sedimentary rocks.

Clastic terrigenous sedimentary rocks consist of rock and mineral grains, or clasts, of varying size, ranging from clay-, silt-, and sand-size up to pebble-, cobble-, and boulder-size materials. These clasts are transported by gravity, mudflows, running water, glaciers, and wind and eventually are deposited in various settings (e.g., in desert dunes, on alluvial fans, across continental shelves, and in river deltas). Because the agents of transportation commonly sort out discrete particles by clast size, terrigenous clastic sedimentary rocks are further subdivided on the basis of average clast diameter. Coarse pebbles, cobbles, and boulder-size gravels lithify to form conglomerate and breccia; sand becomes sandstone; and silt and clay form siltstone, claystone, mudrock, and shale.

Chemical sedimentary rocks form by chemical and organic reprecipitation of the dissolved products of chemical weathering that are removed from the weathering site. Allochemical sedimentary rocks, such as many limestones and cherts, consist of solid precipitated nondetrital fragments (allochems) that undergo a brief history of transport and abrasion prior to deposition as nonterrigenous clasts. Examples are calcareous or siliceous shell fragments and oöids, which are concentrically layered spherical grains of calcium carbonate. Orthochemical sedimentary rocks, on

Colorful Bryce Canyon in Utah provides a spectacular example of sedimentary rocks. Natural spires such Thor's Hammer, seen here, are known as hoodoos and are formed by rain- and wind-eroded limestone. Shutterstock.com

BANDED-IRON
FORMATION (BIF)

BIF is a chemically precipitated sediment, typically thin bedded or laminated, consisting of 15 percent or more iron of sedimentary origin and layers of chert, chalcedony, jasper, or quartz. Such formations occur on all the continents and usually are older than 1.7 billion years. They also are highly metamorphosed. Most BIFs contain iron oxides—hematite with secondary magnetite, goethite, and limonite—and are commonly used as low-grade iron ore (e.g., as in the Lake Superior region of North America). Because BIFs apparently have not formed since Precambrian time, special conditions are thought to have existed at the time of their formation. Considerable controversy exists over BIF origin, and a number of theories have been proposed. Their formation has been variously ascribed to volcanic activity; rhythmic deposition from iron and silica solutions due to seasonal variations; oxidation of iron-rich sediments contemporaneous with deposition; and precipitation from solution as a result of special oxidation-reduction conditions.

the other hand, consist of dissolved constituents that are directly precipitated as solid sedimentary rock and thus do not undergo transportation. Orthochemical sedimentary rocks include some limestones, bedded evaporite deposits of halite, gypsum, and anhydrite, and banded iron formations.

Sediments and sedimentary rocks are confined to Earth's crust, which is the thin, light outer solid skin of Earth ranging in thickness from 40–100 km (25–62 miles) in the continental blocks to 4–10 km (2.5–6 miles) in the ocean basins. Igneous and metamorphic rocks constitute the bulk of the crust. The total volume of sediment and sedimentary rocks can be either directly measured using exposed rock sequences, drill-hole data, and seismic profiles or indirectly estimated by comparing the chemistry of major sedimentary rock types to the overall chemistry of the crust from which they are weathered. Both methods indicate that Earth's sediment-sedimentary rock shell forms only about 5 percent by volume of the terrestrial crust, which in turn accounts for less than 1 percent of Earth's total volume. On the other hand, the area of outcrop and exposure of sediment and sedimentary rock comprises 75 percent of the land surface and well over 90 percent of the ocean basins and continental margins. In other words, 80–90 percent of Earth's surface area is mantled with sediment or sedimentary rocks rather than with igneous or metamorphic varieties. The sediment-sedimentary rock shell forms only a thin superficial layer. The mean shell thickness in continental areas is 1.8 km (about 1 mile); the sediment shell in the ocean basins is roughly 0.3 km (0.2 mile). Rearranging this shell as a globally encircling layer (and depending on the raw estimates incorporated into the model), the shell thickness would be roughly 1–3 km (0.6–2 miles).

Despite the relatively insignificant volume of the sedimentary rock shell, not only are most rocks exposed at the terrestrial surface of the sedimentary variety, but many of the significant events in Earth history are most accurately dated and documented by analyzing and interpreting the sedimentary rock record instead of the more voluminous igneous and metamorphic rock record. When properly understood and interpreted, sedimentary rocks provide information on ancient geography, termed paleogeography. A map of the distribution of sediments that formed in shallow oceans along alluvial fans bordering rising mountains or in deep, subsiding ocean trenches will indicate past relationships between seas and landmasses. An accurate interpretion of paleogeography and depositional settings allows conclusions to be made about the evolution of mountain systems, continental blocks, and ocean basins, as well as about the origin and evolution of the atmosphere and hydrosphere. Sedimentary rocks contain the fossil record of ancient life-forms that enables the documentation of the evolutionary advancement from simple to complex organisms in the plant and animal kingdoms. Also, the study of the various folds or bends and breaks or faults in the strata of sedimentary rocks permits the structural geology or history of deformation to be ascertained.

Finally, it is appropriate to underscore the economic importance of sedimentary rocks as they contain essentially the world's entire store of oil and natural gas, coal, phosphates, salt deposits, groundwater, and other natural resources.

Several subdisciplines of geology deal specifically with the analysis, interpretation, and origin of sediments and sedimentary rocks. Sedimentary petrology is the study of their occurrence, composition, texture, and other overall characteristics, while sedimentology emphasizes the processes by which sediments are transported and deposited. Sedimentary petrography involves the classification and study of sedimentary rocks using the petrographic microscope. Stratigraphy covers all aspects of sedimentary rocks, particularly from the perspective of their age and regional relationships as well as the correlation of sedimentary rocks in one region with sedimentary rock sequences elsewhere.

CLASSIFICATION SYSTEMS

In general, geologists have attempted to classify sedimentary rocks on a natural basis, but some schemes have genetic implications (i.e., knowledge of origin of a particular rock type is assumed), and many classifications reflect the philosophy, training, and experience of those who propound them. No scheme has found universal acceptance, and discussion here will centre on some proposals.

TERMS DESIGNATING COMPOSITION AND PHYSICAL CHARACTERISTICS

Detrital rocks
Rudites (coarse)
conglomerates (rounded clasts)
breccias (angular clasts)
basal, or transgression
fanglomerates (in alluvial fans)
tillites (glacially transported)
Arenites (medium-grained)
sandstone
arkose (feldspar-rich)
graywacke (sandstone with mud matrix)
quartzite (orthoquartzite)
Lutites (fine-grained)
siltstone
shale
mudstone or claystone
argillite
loess (transported and deposited by wind)
Nondetrital rocks
Precipitates
chemical precipitates (rocks formed by precipitation from seawater or fresh water)
evaporites (products of evaporation from saline brines)
duricrust rocks (hardened surface or mean-surface layer of any composition)
Organic
zoogenic (made up of hard parts of animals; e.g., crinoidal limestone)
phytogenic (made up of plant remains; e.g., algal limestone)

The book *Rocks and Rock Minerals* by Louis V. Pirsson was first published in 1908, and it has enjoyed various revisions. Sedimentary rocks are classified there rather simplistically according to physical characteristics and composition into detrital and nondetrital rocks.

Numerous other attempts have been made to classify sedimentary rocks. The most significant advance occurred in 1948 with the publication in the *Journal of Geology* of three definitive articles by the American geologists Francis J. Pettijohn, Robert R. Shrock, and Paul D. Krynine. Their classifications provide the basis for all modern discussion of the subject. The nomenclature associated with several schemes of classifying clastic and nonclastic rocks will be discussed throughout this chapter.

For the purposes of the present discussion, three major categories of sedimentary rocks are recognized: (1) terrigenous clastic sedimentary rocks, (2) carbonates (limestone and dolomite), and (3) noncarbonate chemical sedimentary rocks. Terrigenous clastic sedimentary rocks are composed of the detrital fragments of preexisting rocks and minerals and are conventionally considered to be equivalent to clastic sedimentary rocks in general. Because most of the clasts are rich in silica, they are also referred to as siliciclastic sedimentary rocks. Siliciclastics are further subdivided on the basis of clast diameter into conglomerate and breccia, sandstone, siltstone, and finer-than-silt-sized mudrock (shale, claystone, and mudstone). The carbonates, limestones and dolomites, consist of the minerals aragonite, calcite, and dolomite. They are chemical sedimentary rocks in the sense that they possess at least in part a crystalline, interlocking mosaic of precipitated carbonate mineral grains. However, because individual grains such as fossil shell fragments exist for some period of time as sedimentary clasts, similar to transported quartz or feldspar clasts, most carbonates bear some textural affinities to the terrigenous clastic sedimentary rocks. The noncarbonate chemical sedimentary rocks include several rock types that are uncommon in the sedimentary rock record but remain important either from an economic point of view or because their deposition requires unusual settings. Specific varieties described in this chapter include siliceous rocks (cherts), phosphate rocks (phosphorites), evaporites, iron-rich sedimentary rocks (iron formations and ironstones), and organic-rich (carbonaceous) deposits in sedimentary rocks (coal, oil shale, and petroleum).

Despite the diversity of sedimentary rocks, direct measurement of the relative abundance of the specific types based on the study of exposed sequences suggests that only three varieties account for the bulk of all sedimentary rocks: mudrock, 47 percent; sandstone, 31 percent; and carbonate, 22 percent. Another method, which involves comparing the chemical composition of major sedimentary rock types with the chemistry of Earth's continental crust, yields somewhat different numbers: mudrock, 79 percent; sandstone, 13 percent; and carbonate, 8 percent. Most sedimentary petrologists concede that the sedimentary rock record preserved and exposed within the continental blocks is selectively biased in favour of shallow-water carbonates and sandstones. Mudrocks are preferentially transported to the ocean basins. Consequently, indirect estimates based on chemical arguments are probably more accurate.

Terrigenous Clastic Rocks

A prominent physical feature of terrigenous clastic rocks is texture—that is, the size, shape, and arrangement of the constituent grains. These rocks have a fragmental texture: discrete grains are in tangential contact with one another. Terrigenous clastic sedimentary rocks are further subdivided on the basis of the mean grain diameter that characterizes most fragments, using the generally accepted size limits. Granules, pebbles, cobbles, boulders, and blocks constitute the coarse clastic sediments; sand-size (arenaceous) clasts are considered medium clastic sediments; and fine clastics sediments consist of silt- and clay-size materials.

The simplest way of classifying coarse clastic sedimentary rocks is to name the rock and include a brief description of its particular characteristics. Conglomerates and breccias differ from one another only in clast angularity. The former consist of abraded, somewhat rounded, coarse clasts, whereas the latter contain angular, coarse clasts. Thus, a pebble conglomerate is a coarse clastic sedimentary rock whose discrete particles are rounded and range from 4 to 64 mm (0.2 to 2.5 inches) in diameter. A more precise description reveals the rock types of the mineral fragments that compose the conglomerate—for example, a granite-gneiss pebble conglomerate.

Sandstones have long intrigued geologists because they are well exposed, are abundant in the geologic record, and provide an enormous amount of information about depositional setting and origin. Many classification schemes have been developed for sandstones, only the most popular of which are reviewed below. Most schemes emphasize the relative abundance of sand-size quartz, feldspar, and rock fragment components, as well as the nature of the material housed between this sand-size "framework" fraction.

Fine clastics are commonly, but rather simplistically, referred to as mudrocks. Mudrocks actually can include any clastic sedimentary rock in which the bulk of the clasts have diameters finer than $\frac{1}{16}$ mm (0.0025 inch). Varieties include siltstone (average grain size between

$\frac{1}{16}$ and $\frac{1}{256}$ mm [0.0025 and 0.00015 inch]) and claystone (discrete particles are mostly finer than $\frac{1}{256}$ mm [0.00015 inch]). Mud is a mixture of silt- and clay-size material, and mudrock is its indurated product. Shale is any fine clastic sedimentary rock that exhibits fissility, which is the ability to break into thin slabs along narrowly spaced planes parallel to the layers of stratification. Despite the great abundance of the fine clastics, disagreement exists as to what classification schemes are most useful for them, and an understanding of their origin is hindered by analytical complexities.

CARBONATE ROCKS: LIMESTONES AND DOLOMITES

Limestones and dolostones (dolomites) make up the bulk of the nonterrigenous sedimentary rocks. Limestones are for the most part primary carbonate rocks. They consist of 50 percent or more calcite and aragonite (both $CaCO_3$). Dolomites are mainly produced by the secondary alteration or replacement of limestones; i.e., the mineral dolomite [$CaMg(CO_3)_2$] replaces the calcite and aragonite minerals in limestones during diagenesis. A number of different classification schemes have been proposed for carbonates, and the many categories of limestones and dolomites in the geologic record represent a large variety of depositional settings.

NONCARBONATE CHEMICAL SEDIMENTARY ROCKS

Noncarbonate chemical sedimentary rocks differ in many respects from carbonate sedimentary rocks and terrigenous clastic sedimentary rocks, and there is no single classification that has been universally accepted. This is a reflection of the great variation in mineral composition, texture, and other properties of these rock types. Such

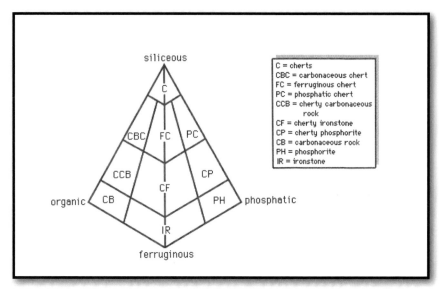

Common noncarbonate, nonclastic sedimentary rocks. Copyright Encyclopædia Britannica, Inc.; rendering for this edition by Rosen Educational Services

rocks as ironstones and banded iron formations (limonite, goethite, hematite, siderite, and chamosite), phosphorites, evaporites (rock salt, gypsum, and other salts), siliceous rocks (cherts), and organic-rich (carbonaceous) deposits of oil, natural gas, and coal in sedimentary rocks occur in much less abundance than carbonates and siliciclastic sedimentary rocks, although they may form thick and widespread deposits. Classification schemes that incorporate all types of noncarbonate chemical sedimentary rocks do not exist because no triangular or tetrahedral scheme can accommodate all of them.

TEXTURE

Texture refers to the physical makeup of rock—namely, the size, shape, and arrangement (packing and orientation) of the discrete grains or particles of a sedimentary rock. Two main natural textural groupings exist for sedimentary rocks: clastic (or fragmental) and nonclastic (essentially crystalline). Noncarbonate chemical sedimentary rocks in large part exhibit crystalline texture, with individual mineral grains forming an interlocking arrangement. Depositional setting is an insignificant factor in both determining crystal size and altering crystalline texture. The size of crystals is controlled to a greater degree by the rate of precipitation, and their texture is modified by postdepositional recrystallization (reflecting the diagenetic environment). As a result, little attention is paid to crystalline textures other than providing a simple description of it (for example, coarsely crystalline versus finely crystalline). Also, even though carbonate rocks commonly include allochems that behave as clasts, they too are commonly diagenetically altered. Consequently, only cursory efforts are made to texturally characterize limestones and dolomites. Therefore, the following discussion deals in detail only with the textural techniques applied to terrigenous (siliciclastic) sedimentary rocks.

GRAIN SIZE

Particle size is an important textural parameter of clastic rocks because it supplies information on the conditions of transportation, sorting, and deposition of the sediment and provides some clues to the history of events that occurred at the depositional site prior to final induration. Determining the sizes of the discrete particles that constitute a sedimentary rock can be difficult, particularly if the rock is firmly indurated. Various methods of measuring grain-size distribution have been devised; likewise several different grade-size schemes exist.

The size of particulate materials that make up sediments and sedimentary rocks are measured by weighing the proportions that accumulate in a series of wire mesh screen sieves, by visually counting grains with a petrographic microscope, or by determining the rate at which particles of varying diameter accumulate in a water-filled glass cylinder (known as a settling tube).

The millimetre and phi unit grade scales and terminology are the standard ones used for sediments and sedimentary rocks. In the millimetre scale, each size grade differs from its predecessor by the constant ratio of 1:2; each size class has a specific class name used to refer to the particles included within it. This millimetre, or Udden-Wentworth, scale is a geometric grain-size scale since there is a constant ratio between class limits. Such a scheme is well suited for the description of sediments because it gives equal significance to size ratios, whether they relate to gravel, sand, silt, or clay. The phi scale is a useful, logarithmic-based modification of the Udden-Wentworth scale. Grain-size diameters in millimetres are converted to phi units using the conversion formula: phi $(\phi) = - \log_2 S$, where ϕ is size expressed in phi units and S is the grain size in millimetres. Phi values for grains coarser than 1 mm (0.04 inch) are negative, while those for grains finer than 1 mm are positive.

After the grain-size distribution for a given sediment or sedimentary rock has been determined by sieving, microscopic analysis, or use of a settling tube, it can be characterized using standard statistical measures in either of two ways: (1) visual inspection of various types of graphs that plot overall percent abundance versus grain-size diameter (e.g., histograms or bar diagrams, size frequency and cumulative size frequency curves, and probability curves that compare the actual grain-size distribution to a normal straight-line Gaussian distribution) or (2) arithmetic calculations made using diameter values in either millimetres or phi units that are read off the graphic plots and inserted into standard formulas. For siliciclastic sedimentary rocks, the following standard statistical measures are conventionally described for grain-size distributions: (1) mode, the most frequently occurring particle size or size class, (2) median, the midpoint size of any grain-size distribution, (3) mean, an estimate of the arithmetic average particle size, (4) sorting or standard deviation, a measure of the range, scatter, or variation in grain size, (5) skewness, the degree of symmetry or asymmetry of the grain-size distribution, which is in turn a function of the coincidence or noncoincidence of mean, median, and mode, and (6) kurtosis (peakedness) of a grain-size distribution, which compares sorting in the central portion of the population with that in the tails.

Analysis of grain-size distribution is conducted with the disputed assumption that particular transporting agents and depositional settings (e.g., river delta deposits versus shallow marine longshore-bar sands) impose a distinctive textural "fingerprint" on the sediments they produce. Despite continuing efforts, the success of the various graphic and arithmetic approaches in characterizing grain-size distributions is debatable, as is their reliability in pinpointing ancient depositional settings. The grain-size distribution of sediments in many settings commonly appears to be inherited or to exhibit as much variation within a single environment as between different ones.

PARTICLE SHAPE

Three different but related properties determine particle shape: form, roundness, and surface texture. Particle form is the overall shape of particles, typically defined in terms of the relative lengths of the longest, shortest, and intermediate axes. Particles can be spherical, prismatic, or bladelike. Roundness or angularity is a measure of the smoothness of particles. Surface texture refers to the presence or absence of small, variously shaped markings (pits, polish, scratches) that may occur on grain surfaces.

Each of these attributes of particle shape is traditionally measured in a standard fashion for the purpose of identifying the transporting agent and the depositional environment. Form is determined either by painstakingly measuring individual particles in three dimensions or by Fourier shape analysis, which uses harmonics analysis and computer digitizing to provide a precise description of particles in two dimensions. Form alone has limited usefulness in inferring depositional setting but more accurately reflects the mineralogy of the grains involved. Roundness is characterized by visually comparing grains to standard silhouette profiles. It is largely the result of abrasion history, which is controlled by the depositional agent and environment. For example, windblown and surf zone sands are well-rounded, while glacial sands and turbidity current deposits are angular. Particle roundness or angularity also reflects mineralogy (soft minerals are abraded more readily than hard minerals), clast size (coarse particles become rounded more rapidly than do fine ones), and transport distance (sands become more abraded and hence rounder as the distance traveled increases). Particle surfaces can be visually examined for pitting, markings, and polish through the use of a microscope or hand lens, or in some cases, a scanning electron microscope (SEM). Certain surface textures have been genetically linked to specific depositional agents; for example, classic V-shaped percussion marks identify quartz grains of the beach and nearshore zones.

FABRIC

The fabric of a sedimentary rock controls the rock's porosity and permeability and therefore its ability to hold and/or transmit fluids such as oil and water. The orientation, or lack thereof, of the crystals or grains that make up a sedimentary rock constitutes one aspect of fabric. Genetically, there are two principal varieties of oriented fabrics: primary (or depositional) and secondary (or deformational). Primary fabrics are produced while the sediment is accumulating. For example, river currents and some submarine gravity flows generate sediments whose flaky and prismatic constituent particles have long or short axes parallel with one another to produce an oriented fabric. Secondary fabrics result from a rotation of the constituent elements under stress or from the growth of new elements during diagenesis. Fabrics in coarse clastic sedimentary rocks like conglomerates and sandstones can be determined by measuring and plotting dimensional directions, such as the long axes of pebbles or sand grains. In mudrocks, fabrics can be ascertained by studying the platelike arrangement of mica and clay minerals.

In addition to orientation, a factor known as packing contributes to a rock's fabric. Packing refers to the distribution of grains and intergranular spaces (either empty or filled with cement or fine-grained matrix) in a sedimentary rock. It is controlled by grain size and shape and by the degree of compaction of a sedimentary rock; in turn it determines the rock's bulk density. A description of packing is generally based on the analysis of thin sections of a sedimentary rock using a petrographic microscope. Particular attention is paid to the number of grain-to-grain contacts (packing proximity) and to comparisons between the sum of the lengths of grains to the total length of a traverse across a thin section (packing density).

MINERALOGICAL AND GEOCHEMICAL COMPOSITION

Minerals that make up sedimentary rocks are of two principal types—namely, detrital and authigenic. Detrital minerals, such as grains of quartz and feldspar, survive weathering and are transported to the depositional site as clasts. Authigenic minerals, such as calcite, halite, and gypsum, form in situ within the depositional site in response to geochemical processes. The chemical compounds that constitute them ultimately are generated by chemical weathering and are transported from the weathering site to the point of precipitation primarily in solution. Clay minerals are abundant in sedimentary rocks, particularly mudrocks, and some are detrital. They may have been produced at the weathering site by the partial decomposition of minerals like feldspar. They are transported as clasts, however, and thus can be regarded simply as fine- to very fine-textured detrital particles. Other clay minerals

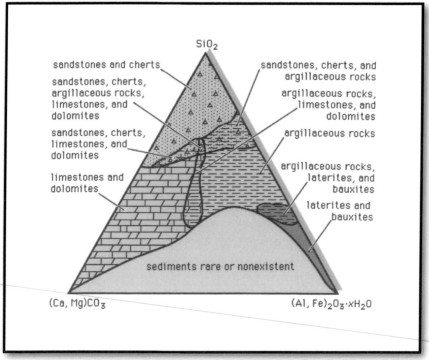

Chemical composition of sedimentary rocks. Copyright Encyclopædia Britannica, Inc.; rendering for this edition by Rosen Educational Services

form authigenically at the site of deposition. Some of the important clay minerals are kaolinite, halloysite, montmorillonite, illite, vermiculite, and chlorite.

The mean chemical composition of the major varieties of sedimentary rocks exhibits wide variation. Significant contrasts in overall composition among sandstones, carbonates, and mudrocks reflect fundamental differences not only in the mechanisms by which detrital minerals of different sizes are transported and deposited but also in the chemical conditions that permit precipitation of various authigenic minerals.

Diagenesis includes all physicochemical, biochemical, and physical processes (short of metamorphism) that modify sediments in the time between their deposition and their analysis. Lithification, the process by which sediment is converted into solid sedimentary rock, is one result of diagenesis. Many diagenetic processes such as cementation, recrystallization, and dolomitization are essentially geochemical processes; others such as compaction are fundamentally physical processes. All diagenetic changes occur at the low temperatures and pressures characteristic of surface and near-surface environments. These changes can take place almost immediately after sediment formation, or they can occur hundreds or even millions of years later.

SEDIMENTARY STRUCTURES

Sedimentary structures are the larger, generally three-dimensional physical features of sedimentary rocks; they are best seen in outcrop or in large hand specimens rather than through a microscope. Sedimentary structures include features such as bedding, ripple marks, fossil tracks and trails, and mud cracks. They conventionally are subdivided into categories based on mode of genesis. Structures that are produced at the same time as the sedimentary rock in which they occur are called primary sedimentary structures. Examples include bedding or stratification, graded bedding, and cross-bedding. Sedimentary structures that are produced shortly after deposition and as a result of compaction and desiccation are called penecontemporaneous sedimentary structures. Examples include mud cracks and load casts. Still other sedimentary structures such as concretions, vein fillings, and stylolites form well after deposition and penecontemporaneous modification; these are known as secondary structures. Finally, others such as stromatolites and organic burrows and tracks, though they may in fact be primary, penecontemporaneous, or even secondary, may be grouped as a fourth category—organic sedimentary structures.

Considerable attention is paid to the sedimentary structures exhibited by any sedimentary rock. Primary sedimentary structures are particularly useful because their abundance and size suggest the probable transporting and depositional agents. Certain varieties of primary sedimentary structures like cross-bedding and ripple marks display orientations that are consistently related to the direction of current movement. Such structures are referred to as directional sedimentary structures because they can be used to infer the ancient paleocurrent pattern or dispersal system by which a sedimentary rock unit was deposited. Other sedimentary structures are stratigraphic "top and bottom" indicators. For example, the progressive upward decrease in clastic grain size diameters, known as graded bedding, would allow a geologist to determine which way is stratigraphically "up"—i.e., toward the younger beds in a dipping sedimentary bed. The suite (repeated sequence) of sedimentary structures in any single stratigraphic unit is another attribute by which that unit may be physically differentiated from others in the region.

External Stratification

Stratification (or bedding) is expressed by rock layers (units) of a general tabular or lenticular form that differ in rock type or other characteristics from the material with which they are interstratified (sometimes stated as interbedded, or interlayered). These beds, or strata, are of varying thickness and areal extent. The term stratum identifies a single bed, or unit, normally greater than 1 cm (0.4 inch) in thickness and visibly separable from superjacent (overlying) and subjacent (underlying) beds. "Strata" refers to two or more beds, and the term lamina is sometimes applied to a unit less than 1 cm in thickness. Thus, lamination consists of thin units in bedded, or layered, sequence in a natural rock succession, whereas stratification consists of bedded layers, or strata, in a geologic sequence of interleaved sedimentary rocks.

For most stratified sedimentary rocks, the arrangement of layers is one of unequal thickness, ranging from very thin laminae to discrete beds that measure a few to many metres in thickness. The terms thick and thin as applied to bedding, or stratification, are relative, reflecting the training of a particular geologist as well as experience with a specific stratigraphic section or sections.

Bedding Types and Bedding-Plane Features

It is common to discover a rhythmic pattern in a pile of stratified sedimentary rocks represented by a repetitive sequence of rock types. In most instances of such cyclic sedimentation, the bedding, or stratification, is horizontal or essentially so; that is, the transporting, sorting, and depositing agents of wind, running water, and lake and ocean currents and waves accumulated the laminae and strata in a flat-lying or horizontal arrangement. They are termed well-bedded, a type of primary stratification.

Primary stratification in sediments and sedimentary rocks can be cross-bedded (cross-stratified), graded, and imbricate and can also display climbing laminae, ripples, and beds.

Graded bedding simply identifies strata that grade upward from coarse-textured clastic sediment at their base to finer-textured materials at the top. The stratification may be sharply marked so that one layer is set off visibly from those above and beneath it. More commonly, however, the layers are blended. This variety of bedding results from a check in the velocity of the transporting agent, and thus coarse-textured sediment (gravel, for

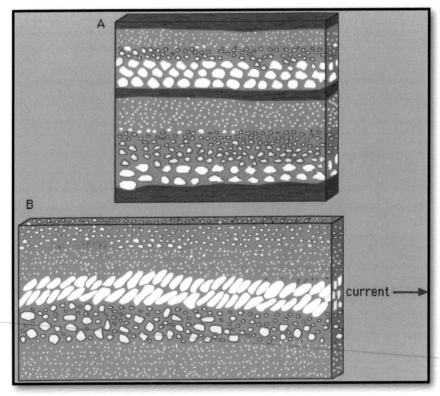

(A) Graded bedding. (B) Imbricate bedding. Copyright Encyclopædia Britannica, Inc.; rendering for this edition by Rosen Educational Services

example) is deposited first, followed upward by pebbles, granules, sand, silt, and clay. It is commonly associated with submarine density currents.

Imbricate bedding is a shingle structure in a deposit of flattened or disk-shaped pebbles or cobbles. That is to say, elongated and commonly flattened pebbles and cobbles in gravelly sediment are deposited so that they overlap one another like roofing shingles. Imbricate bedding forms where high-velocity currents move over a streambed or where strong currents and waves break over a gradually sloping beach, thereby forming beach shingle.

Growth structures in sedimentary rocks are in situ features that accumulate largely as the result of organic buildups within otherwise horizontal or nearly flat-lying strata. Reefs and stromatolites are two common varieties of such growth structures.

Upper surfaces of beds commonly display primary sedimentary features that are classified as bedding-plane structures. A three-dimensional view may be obtained if some of these can be seen from the side as well as from the top of a pile of strata. They include such features as ripples (ripple marks), climbing ripples, rills, pits, mud cracks, trails and tracks, salt and ice casts and molds, and others. Bedding-plane markings and irregularities can be allocated to one of three classes: (1) those on the base of a bed (load and current structures and organic markings), (2) those within a bed (parting lineation), and (3) those on top of a bed (ripple marks, pits, impressions, mud cracks, tracks and trails of organisms, and others).

DEFORMATION STRUCTURES

In addition to sedimentary structures that are normally associated with bedding planes, there are other such structures that result from deformation during or shortly after sedimentation but before induration of the sediment into rock. These are nontectonic features—i.e., they are not bends and folds brought about by metamorphism or other such causes. Deformation structures can be grouped into several classes, as follows: (1) founder and load structures, (2) convoluted structures, (3) slump structures, (4) injection structures, such as sandstone dikes or sills, and (5) organic structures.

Structures found on the bottom of a bed are called sole markings, because they formed on the "sole" of the bed. Sole marks are commonly formed on sandstone and limestone beds that rest upon shale beds. They are termed casts, because they are fillings of depressions that formed on the surface of the underlying mud. They originate (1) by unequal loading upon the soft and plastic wet mud, (2) by the action of currents across the upper mud surface, or (3) by the activities of organisms on this surface. Load casts form as the result of downsinking of sandstone or limestone into the mud beneath. Current marks can form by the action of water currents on upper surfaces of the beds or by "tools" (such as wood and fossils) that are transported by currents over soft sediment.

SEDIMENTARY ENVIRONMENTS

The sedimentary environment is the specific depositional setting of a particular sedimentary rock and is unique in terms of physical, chemical, and biological characteristics. The physical features of a sedimentary environment include water depth and the velocity and persistence of currents. Chemical characteristics of an environment include the salinity (proportion of dissolved salts), acidity or basicity (pH), oxidation potential (Eh), pressure, and temperature. The biological characteristics are mainly the assemblage of fauna and flora that populate the setting.

These conditions, combined with the nature of the transporting agent and the source area, largely determine the properties of the sediments deposited within the environment. A number of ways of classifying depositional environments exist, but most modern schemes employ a geomorphologic approach. That is to say, an environment is defined in terms of a distinct geomorphic unit or landform, modern examples of which are readily visible for comparative purposes—e.g., a river delta, an alluvial fan, a submarine fan, or the abyssal floor of an ocean basin.

Individual environments are further grouped into (1) marine environments, which include the nearshore, shallow littoral zone and the offshore, deep littoral zone, as well as deepwater realms, (2) mixed marine and nonmarine settings such as the beach and supratidal zones, and (3) nonmarine settings like lacustrine and various alluvial settings. Each environment is associated with a set of criteria that constitutes its distinguishing features.

SEDIMENTARY FACIES

Sedimentary facies are the physical, chemical, and biological aspects of a sedimentary bed and the lateral change within sequences of beds of the same geologic age. Sedimentary rocks can be formed only where sediments are deposited long enough to become compacted and cemented into hard beds or strata. Sedimentation commonly occurs in areas where the sediment lies undisturbed for many years in sedimentary basins. Whereas some such basins are small, others occupy thousands of square kilometres and usually have within them several different local depositional environments. Physical, chemical, and biological factors influence these environments, and the conditions that they produce largely determine the nature of the sediments that accumulate. Several different local (sedimentary) environments may thus exist side by side within a basin as conditions change laterally; the sedimentary rocks that ultimately are produced there can be related to these depositional environments. These different but contemporaneous and juxtaposed sedimentary rocks are known as sedimentary facies, a term that was first used by the Swiss geologist Amanz Gressly in 1838.

Sedimentary facies are either terrigenous, resulting from the accumulation of particles eroded from older rocks and transported to the depositional site; biogenic, representing accumulations of whole or fragmented shells and other hard parts of organisms; or chemical, representing inorganic precipitation of material from solution. As conditions change with time, so different depositional sites may change their shapes and characteristics. Each facies thus has a three-dimensional configuration and may in time shift its position.

There are several ways of describing or designating sedimentary facies. By noting the prime physical (or lithological) characteristics, one is able to recognize lithofacies. The biological (or more correctly, paleontological) attributes—the fossils—define biofacies. Both are the direct result of the depositional history of the basin. By ascribing modes of origin to different facies (i.e., interpreting the lithofacies or biofacies) one can visualize a genetic system of facies. It is also common to speak of alluvial facies, bar facies, or reef facies, using the environment as a criterion. This may lead to confusion when revisions of interpretation have to be made because of new or more accurate information about the rocks themselves.

Just as there are regular associations of different local environments in modern sedimentary basins, associations of facies also are known to follow similar patterns in the stratigraphic column. A common example of the latter is that of regular lithofacies and biofacies successions being formed between the edge, or shoreline, of a water-filled basin and the deeper water at its middle. Coarse sediment gives way to finer sediment in the deepening water. Changes in sea level as time passes are a common cause of successive changes in the stratigraphic column. As sea level rises and the sea spreads across what was land, shallow-water sediments are laid down in the newest area to receive such material while areas that were shallow are now deeper and receive finer, or otherwise different, sediments. As the sea advances inland, the belts of sedimentation follow and the retreat of the sea causes the belts to move back offshore.

Johannes Walther, a German geologist, noted in 1894 that the vertical facies sequence in a sedimentary basin undergoing expansion and deepening so that the sea transgresses the land surface (or the reverse, a regression) is the same as the horizontal sequence. This has enabled geologists, knowing the pattern of facies at the surface, to predict accurately what may also be found at depth within a sedimentary basin. It is clear, however, that Walther's observation only applies where there is no major break (i.e., an erosional interval) in the continuity of the succession.

SEDIMENTARY ROCK TYPES

Sedimentary rocks come in a variety of different forms. They include conglomerates, sandstones, mudrocks, and limestones, as well as siliceous rocks, phosphorites, and evaporites. Most sedimentary rocks contain some amount of iron, but certain sedimentary rocks, such as banded iron formation (BIF) and ironstone, are rich in the element. Other rocks, such as coal and shale, contain organic accumulations of tissues and other parts that did not undergo the process of decomposition.

CONGLOMERATES AND BRECCIAS

Conglomerates and breccias are sedimentary rocks composed of coarse fragments of preexisting rocks held together either by cement or by a finer-grained clastic matrix. Both contain significant amounts (at least 10 percent) of coarser-than-sand-size clasts. Breccias are consolidated rubble; their clasts are angular or subangular. Conglomerates are consolidated gravel whose clasts are subrounded to rounded. Sometimes the term rudite (or rudaceous) is used to collectively refer to both breccias and conglomerates.

Classification Schemes

A number of classification schemes have been proposed to further subdivide conglomerates and breccias. One scheme is purely descriptive, partitioning these coarse clastic sedimentary rocks on the basis of grain size (e.g., boulder breccia versus cobble conglomerate) or composition or both (chert pebble breccia versus limestone cobble conglomerate). Yet another scheme differentiates individual conglomerates and breccias according to depositional agency and environmental setting (alluvial fan conglomerate as opposed to beach conglomerate). The best classification systems incorporate objective physical characteristics of both composition and texture as well as mode of genesis. Conglomerates and breccias belong to four genetic categories: (1) epiclastic, produced by the physical disintegration (weathering) of preexisting rocks, (2) pyroclastic, produced by the explosive activity of volcanoes, (3) cataclastic, formed by local earth movements (fault breccias) or solution phenomena (collapse breccias), and (4) meteoritic, produced by the impact of extraterrestrial bodies on Earth's surface. In a strict sense, epiclastic conglomerates and breccias are the only true sedimentary rocks, because they alone are produced by weathering.

Epiclastic Conglomerates and Breccias

There are two principal types of epiclastic conglomerates and breccias: intraformational, derived penecontemporaneously by eroding, transporting, and depositing material from within the depositional basin itself; and interformational, derived from source rocks that lie outside the area in which the deposit occurs. Epiclastic conglomerates and breccias together probably make up no more than 1 or 2 percent of the conventional sedimentary rock record.

Intraformational conglomerates and breccias are widespread in the geologic record but are volumetrically unimportant. They occur as laterally continuous bands or horizons within sequences of shallow-water marine or nonmarine deposits. Their origin is commonly related to the existence of brief episodes of strong bottom-hugging currents capable of ripping up recently deposited, unconsolidated sediment. For example, shallow marine limestone deposits commonly have thin bands of boulder-, cobble-, and pebble-size carbonate clasts (edgewise conglomerate or breccia beds) that are generated when storm waves erode and redeposit carbonate mud layers. Likewise, high-velocity river currents that accompany torrential rains give rise to shale pebble conglomerates and breccias within sequences of floodplain alluvium. Other intraformational conglomerates and breccias mix shallow- and deep-water sedimentary rock clasts encased in a finer-grained matrix of deeper-water material. Such deposits accumulate as depositional aprons that flank the scarps (steep slopes) bounding shallow-water platformal areas such as the modern Great Bahama and Little Bahama banks off Florida in the southeastern United States.

Interformational conglomerates and breccias, the coarse clastic sedimentary rocks derived by the weathering of preexisting rocks outside the depositional basin, are most important from the points of view of both volume and geologic significance. They can be subdivided into two specific categories: (1) clast-supported conglomerates (and breccias) and (2) matrix-supported conglomerates.

Clast-Supported Conglomerates

These rocks contain less than 15 percent matrix—i.e., material composed of clasts finer than granule size (2-mm [0.08-inch] diameter or less). They typically exhibit an intact fabric that has a clast-supported framework such that the individual granules, pebbles, cobbles, and boulders touch each other. The space between framework components either is empty or is filled with chemical cement, finer-than-granule clasts, or both. Clast-supported conglomerates may be composed of large clasts of a single rock or mineral type (oligomictic orthoconglomerates), or they may contain a variety of rock and mineral clast types (petromictic orthoconglomerates). If the clasts are all of quartz, then it is called a quartzose conglomerate.

Clast-supported conglomerates (and orthobreccias) are deposited by highly turbulent water. For example, beach deposits commonly contain lenses and bands of oligomictic orthoconglomerate, composed mainly (95 percent or more) of stable, resistant, coarse clasts of vein quartz, quartzite, quartz sandstone, and chert. Such deposits are typically generated in the upper reaches of winter storm beaches where strong surf can sift, winnow, and abrade coarse pebbles and boulders. The most indestructible components are thereby consolidated as conglomeratic lenses that are interfingered with finer-grained, quartz-rich beach sandstones. Petromictic conglomerates and breccias, on the other hand, reflect the existence of high-relief (mountainous) source areas. Topographically high source areas signify tectonic mobility in the form of active folding or faulting or both. The existence of petromictic conglomerates and breccias in the geologic record is therefore significant: their presence and age not only pinpoint the timing and location of mountain building accompanied by sharp uplift and the possibility of regionally significant fault scarps but also can be used to infer the past distribution of physiographic features such as mountain fronts, continental block margins, continental shelf-continental slope boundaries, and the distribution of oceanic trenches and volcanic island arcs. Deep marine conglomerates may be called resedimented conglomerates. These were retransported from seashore areas by turbidity currents.

Bedding (layering and stratification) in clast-supported conglomerates, if apparent at all, is typically thick and lenticular. Graded bedding, in which size decreases from bottom to top, is common: because agitated waters rarely subside at once, declining transport power causes a gradual upward decrease in maximum clast size. Relative to the bedding, the pebbles in sandy conglomerates tend to lie flat, with their smallest dimension positioned vertically and the greatest aligned roughly parallel to the current. In closely packed orthoconglomerates, however, there is often a distinct imbrication; i.e., flat pebbles overlap in the same direction like roof shingles. Imbrication is upstream on riverbeds and seaward on beaches.

Clast-supported conglomerates are quite important economically because they hold enormous water reserves that are easily released through wells. This feature is attributable to their high porosity and permeability. Porosity is the volume percentage of "void" (actually fluid- or air-filled) space in a rock, whereas permeability is defined as the rate of flow of water at a given pressure gradient through a unit volume. The interconnectedness of voids in conglomerates contributes to their permeability. Also, because the chief resistance to flow is generally due to friction and capillary effects, the overall coarse grain size makes conglomerates even more permeable. The high degree of porosity and permeability causes conglomerates to generate excellent surface drainage, so they are to be avoided as dam and reservoir sites.

Matrix-Supported Conglomerates

Matrix-supported conglomerates, also called diamictites, exhibit a disrupted, matrix-supported fabric; they contain 15 percent or more (sometimes as much as 80 percent) sand-size and finer clastic matrix. The coarse detrital clasts "float" in a finer-grained detrital matrix. They actually are mudrocks in which there is a sprinkling of granules, pebbles, cobbles, or boulders, or some combination of them. Accordingly, they are sometimes referred to as conglomerate mudstones or pebbly mudstones.

Although matrix-supported conglomerates originate in a variety of ways, they are not deposited by normal currents of moving water. Some are produced by submarine landslides, massive slumping, or dense, sediment-laden, gravity-driven turbidity flows. Matrix-supported conglomerates that can be definitively related to such mechanisms are called tilloids. Tilloids commonly make up olistostromes, which are large masses of coarse blocks chaotically mixed within a muddy matrix. The terms till (when unconsolidated) and tillite (when lithified) are used for diamictites that appear to have been directly deposited by moving sheets of glacial ice. Tillites typically consist of poorly sorted angular and subangular, polished and striated blocks of rock floating in an unstratified clay matrix. The clasts may exhibit a weak but distinct alignment of their long axes approximately parallel to the direction of ice flow. Tillites are notoriously heterogeneous in composition: clasts appear to be randomly mixed together without respect to size or compositional stability. These clasts are derived mainly from the underlying bedrock. Extremely coarse, far-traveled blocks and boulders are called erratics.

Other rarer diamictites, known as laminated pebbly (or cobbly or bouldery) mudstones, consist of delicately laminated mudrocks in which scattered coarser clasts occur. Laminations within the muddy component are broken and bent. They are located beneath and adjacent to the larger clasts but gently overlap or arch over them, suggesting that the coarse clasts are dropstones (i.e., ice-rafted blocks released as floating masses of ice melt).

SANDSTONES

Sandstones are siliciclastic sedimentary rocks that consist mainly of sand-size grains (clast diameters from 2 to $\frac{1}{16}$ mm [0.08 to 0.0025 inch]) either bonded together by interstitial chemical cement or lithified into a cohesive rock by the compaction of the sand-size framework component together with any interstitial primary (detrital) and secondary (authigenic) finer-grained matrix component. They grade, on the one hand, into the coarser-grained siliciclastic conglomerates and breccias described above, and, on the other hand, into siltstones and the various finer-grained mudrocks described below. Like their coarser analogues — namely, conglomerates and breccias — sand-size (also called arenaceous) sedimentary rocks are not exclusively generated by the physical disintegration of preexisting rocks. Varieties of limestone that contain abundant sand-size allochems such as oöids and fossil fragments are, in at least a textural sense, types of sandstones, although they are not terrigenous siliciclastic rocks. Such rocks, called micrites when lithified or carbonate sands when unconsolidated, are more properly discussed as limestones. Also, pyroclastic sandstones or tuffs formed by lithifying explosively produced volcanic ash deposits can be excluded from this discussion because their origin is unrelated to weathering.

Sandstones are significant for a variety of reasons. Volumetrically they constitute between 10 and 20 percent of Earth's sedimentary rock record. They are resistant to erosion and therefore greatly influence the landscape. When they are folded, they create the backbone of mountain ranges like the Appalachians of eastern North America, the Carpathians of east-central Europe, the Pennines of northern England, and the Apennine Range of Italy; when flat-lying, they form broad plains and plateaus like the Colorado and Allegheny plateaus. Sandstones are economically important as major reservoirs for both petroleum and water, as building materials, and as valuable sources of metallic ores. Most significantly, they are the single most useful sedimentary rock type for deciphering Earth history. Sandstone mineralogy is the best indicator of sedimentary provenance: the nature of a sedimentary rock source area, its composition, relief, and location. Sandstone textures and sedimentary structures also are reliable indexes of the transportational agents and depositional setting.

Sandstone Components and Colour

There are three basic components of sandstones: (1) detrital grains, mainly transported, sand-size minerals such as quartz and feldspar, (2) a detrital matrix of clay or mud, which is absent in "clean" sandstones, and (3) a cement that is chemically precipitated in crystalline form from solution and that serves to fill up original pore spaces.

The colour of a sandstone depends on its detrital grains and bonding material. An abundance of potassium feldspar often gives a pink colour; this is true of many feldspathic arenites, which are feldspar-rich sandstones. Fine-grained, dark-coloured rock fragments, such as pieces of slate, chert, or andesite, however, give a salt-and-pepper appearance to a sandstone. Iron oxide cement imparts tones of yellow, orange, brown, or red, whereas calcite cement imparts a gray colour. A sandstone consisting almost wholly of quartz grains cemented by quartz may be glassy and white. A chloritic clay matrix results in a greenish black colour and extreme hardness; such rocks are wackes.

ULURU AND THE OLGAS

Ayers Rock, Northern Territory, Australia. Paul Steel/Photo Index

Uluru, which is also commonly known as Ayers Rock, is a giant monolith, one of the tors (isolated masses of weathered rock) in south-western Northern Territory, Australia. It is perhaps the world's largest monolith. The Aboriginals of the region call it Uluru. Composed of arkosic sandstone, which changes colour according to the position of the sun, the rock is most impressive at sunset, when it is coloured a fiery orange-red by the sun's rays.

Rising 335 metres (1,100 feet) above the surrounding desert plain, Uluru/Ayers Rock is oval in shape, 3.6 km (2.2 miles) long by 2 km (1.5 miles) wide. Its lower slopes have become fluted by the erosion of weaker rock layers, while the top is scored with gullies and basins that produce giant cataracts after infrequent rainstorms. Shallow caves at the base of the rock, which is within Uluru–Kata Tjuta National Park (established in 1958 as Ayers Rock–Mount Olga National Park), are sacred to several Aboriginal tribes and contain carvings and paintings. Sighted in 1872 by Ernest Giles, the rock was named for former South Australian premier Sir Henry Ayers. In 1985 official ownership of Uluru/Ayers Rock was given to the Aboriginals, who thereupon leased the rock and the national park to the government for 99 years.

The national park is one of Australia's best-known tourist destinations. Visitors arrive at the rock via Alice Springs, 450 km (280 miles)

northeast by road. The buildings of the tourist resort near Uluru/Ayers Rock are coloured to blend in with the surrounding desert. Hiking around the base of the rock is a popular activity, as is climbing up the rock itself. However, the local Aboriginal people have sought to ban climbing on it. The rock and the surrounding park were named a World Heritage site in 1987, and the park was redesignated in 1994 for its cultural significance.

The Olga Rocks (Aboriginal: Kaja Tjuta) are a group of tors (isolated weathered rocks) in southwestern Northern Territory, Australia. The Olgas are a circular grouping of some 36 red conglomerate domes rising from the desert plains north of the Musgrave Ranges. They occupy an area of 11 square miles (28 square km) within Uluru–Kata Tjuta National Park (established in 1958 as Ayers Rock–Mount Olga National Park) and culminate at Mount Olga, 460 metres (1,500 feet) above the plain and 1,069 metres (3,507 feet) above sea level. Mount Olga is the most westerly of Australia's three giant tors; the others are Uluru/Ayers Rock and Mount Conner (Artilla). They were visited and named in 1872 after Queen Olga of Württemberg by the explorer Ernest Giles. Their Aboriginal name, Kata Tjuta, means "many heads." The rocks offer visitors a constantly changing array of colour as the sun moves overhead and illuminates the luxurious vegetation in deep clefts between the domes.

FORMATION OF SANDSTONES TODAY

Sandstones occur in strata of all geologic ages. Much scientific understanding of the depositional environment of ancient sandstones comes from detailed study of sand bodies forming at the present time. One of the clues to origin is the overall shape of the entire sand deposit. Inland desert sands today cover vast areas as a uniform blanket; some ancient sandstones in beds a few hundred metres thick but 1,600 km (about 1,000 miles) or more in lateral extent, such as the Nubian Sandstone of North Africa, of Mesozoic age (about 245 to 66.4 million years old), also may have formed as blankets of desert sand.

Deposits from alluvial fans form thick, fault-bounded prisms. River sands today form shoestring-shaped bodies, tens of metres thick, a few hundred metres wide, up to 60 km (about 37 miles) or more long, and usually oriented perpendicularly to the shoreline. In meandering back and forth, a river may construct a wide swath of sand deposits, mostly accumulating on meander-point bars. Beaches, coastal dunes, and barrier bars also form "shoestring" sands, but these are parallel to the shore. Deltaic sands show a fanlike pattern of radial, thick, finger-shaped sand bodies interbedded with muddy sediments. Submarine sand bodies are diverse, reflecting the complexities of underwater topography and currents. They may form great ribbons parallel with the current; huge submarine "dunes" or "sand waves" aligned perpendicularly to the current; or irregular shoals, bars, and sheets. Some sands are deposited in deep water by the action of density currents, which flow down submarine slopes by reason of their high sediment concentrations and, hence, are called turbidity currents. These characteristically form thin beds interbedded with shales; sandstone beds often are graded from coarse grains at the base to fine grains at the top of the bed and commonly have a clay matrix.

BEDDING STRUCTURE

One of the most fruitful methods of deciphering the environment of deposition and direction of transport of ancient sandstones is detailed field study of the sedimentary structures.

Bedding in sandstones, expressed by layers of clays, micas, heavy minerals, pebbles, or fossils, may be tens of feet thick, but it can range downward to paper-thin laminations. Flagstone breaks in smooth, even layers a few centimetres thick and is used in paving. Thin, nearly horizontal lamination is characteristic of many ancient beach sandstones. Bedding surfaces of sandstones may be marked by ripples (almost always of subaqueous origin), by tracks and trails of organisms, and by elongated grains that are oriented by current flow (fossils, plant fragments, or even elongated sand grains). Sand-grain orientation tends to parallel direction of the current; river-channel trends in fluvial sediments, wave-backwash direction in beach sands, and wind direction in eolian sediments are examples of such orientation.

A great variety of markings, such as flutes and scour and fill grooves, can be found on the undersides of some sandstone beds. These markings are caused by swift currents during deposition; they are particularly abundant in sandstones deposited by turbidity currents.

Within the major beds, cross-bedding is common. This structure is developed by the migration of small ripples, sand waves, tidal-channel large-scale ripples, or dunes and consists of sets of beds that are inclined to the main horizontal bedding planes. Almost all sedimentary environments produce characteristic types of cross-beds; as one example, the lee faces of sand dunes (side not facing the wind) may bear cross-beds as much as 33 metres (108 feet) high and dipping 35°.

Some sandstones contain series of graded beds. The grains at the base of a graded bed are coarse and gradually become finer upward, at which point there is a sharp change to the coarse basal layer of the overlying bed. Among the many mechanisms that can cause these changes in grain size are turbidity currents, but in general they can be caused by any cyclically repeated waning current.

After the sand is deposited, it may slide downslope or subside into soft underlying clays. This shifting gives rise to contorted or slumped bedding on a scale of centimetres to tens of metres. Generally these are characteristic of unstable areas of rapid deposition.

Local cementation may result in concretions of calcite, pyrite, barite, and other minerals. These can range from sand crystals or barite roses to spheroidal or discoidal concretions tens of metres across.

The fossil content also is a useful guide to the depositional environment of sandstones. Desert sandstones usually lack fossils. River-channel and deltaic sandstones may contain fossil wood, plant fragments, fossil footprints, or vertebrate remains. Beach and shallow marine sands contain mollusks, arthropods, crinoids, and other marine creatures, though marine sandstones are much less fossiliferous than marine limestones. Deepwater sands are frequently devoid of skeletal fossils, although tracks and trails may be common. The fossils are not actually structures, of course, but the living organisms were able to produce them. Burrowing by organisms, for example, may cause small-scale structures, such as eyes and pods or tubules of sand.

Texture

The texture of a sandstone is the sum of such attributes as the clay matrix, the size and sorting of the detrital grains, and the roundness of these particles. To evaluate this property, a scale of textural maturity that involved four textural stages was devised in 1951. These stages are described as follows.

Immature sandstones contain a clay matrix, and the sand-size grains are usually angular and poorly sorted. This means that a wide range of sand sizes is present. Such sandstones are characteristic of environments in which sediment is dumped and is not thereafter worked upon by waves or currents. These environments include stagnant areas of sluggish currents such as lagoons or bay bottoms or undisturbed seafloor below the zone of wave or current action. Immature sands also form where sediments are rapidly deposited in subaerial environments, such as river floodplains, swamps, alluvial fans, or glacial margins. Submature sandstones are created by the removal of the clay matrix by current action. The sand grains are, however, still poorly sorted in these rocks. Submature sandstones are common as river-channel sands, tidal-channel sands, and shallow submarine sands swept by unidirectional currents. Mature sandstones are clay-free, and the sand grains are subangular, but they are well sorted—that is, of nearly uniform particle size. Typically, these sandstones form in environments of current reversal and continual washing, such as beaches. Supermature sandstones are those that are clay-free and well sorted and, in addition, in which the grains are well rounded. These sandstones probably formed primarily as desert dunes, where intense eolian abrasion over a very long period of time may wear sand grains to nearly spherical shapes.

The methodology used for detailed study of siliciclastic sedimentary rock textures, particularly grain-size distribution and grain shape (angularity and sphericity) has been described earlier. The information that results from textural analyses is especially useful in identifying sandstone depositional environments. Dune sands in all parts of the world, for example, tend to be fine-sand-size (clast diameters from $\frac{1}{4}$ to $\frac{1}{8}$ mm [0.01 to 0.005 inch]) because sand of that dimension is most easily moved by winds. Desert (eolian) sandstones also tend to be bimodal or polymodal—i.e., having two (or more) abundant grain-size classes separated by intervening, less prevalent size classes. Dune and beach sands exhibit the best sorting; river and shallow marine sands are less well sorted. River-floodplain, deltaic, and turbidity-current sand deposits show much poorer sorting. Skewness (the symmetry or asymmetry of a grain-size distribution) also varies as a function of depositional setting. Beach sands are commonly negatively skewed (they have a tail of more poorly sorted coarse grains), whereas dune and river sands tend to be positively skewed (a tail of more poorly sorted fine grains).

Careful analysis of grain roundness and grain shape also can aid in distinguishing the high-abrasion environments of beach and especially dune sands from those of fluvial or marine sands. Rounding takes place much more rapidly in sands subjected to wind action than in water-laid sands. In general, coarser sand grains are better rounded than finer grains because the coarser ones hit bottom more frequently and also hit with greater impact during transport. Sand grains may also have polished, frosted, pitted, or otherwise characteristic surfaces. These depend on the grain size, the agent of transport, and the amount of chemical attack. For example, polish can occur on medium-grained beach sands and fine-grained desert sands and can also be produced chemically by weathering processes.

CLASSIFICATION OF SANDSTONES

There are many different systems of classifying sandstones, but the most commonly used schemes incorporate both texture (the presence and amount of either interstitial matrix—i.e., clasts with diameters finer than 0.03 mm [about 0.001 inch]—or chemical cement) and mineralogy (the relative amount of quartz and the relative abundance of rock fragments to feldspar grains). Although not intended to have tectonic significance, the relative proportions of quartz, feldspar, and fragments are good indicators of an area's tectonic regime. It is possible to discriminate between stable cratons (rich in quartz and feldspar), orogens (rich in quartz and fragments), and magmatic arcs (rich in feldspar and fragments).

Sandstones are first subdivided into two major textural groups, arenites and wackes. Arenites consist of a sand-size framework component surrounded by pore spaces that are either empty (in the case of arenite sands) or filled with crystalline chemical cement (in the case of arenites). Wackes consist of a sand-size framework component floating in a finer-grained pasty matrix of grains finer than 0.03 mm whose overall abundance exceeds 15 percent by volume.

Both arenites and wackes can be further subdivided into three specific sandstone families based on the relative proportions of three major framework grain types: quartz, feldspar, and rock fragments. For example, quartz arenites are rocks whose sand grains consist of at least 95 percent quartz. If the sand grains consist of more than 25 percent feldspar (and feldspar grains are in excess of rock fragments), the rock is termed arkosic arenite or "arkose," although such sandstones are also somewhat loosely referred to as feldspathic sandstones. In subarkosic arenite (or subarkose), feldspar sand grains likewise exceed rock fragments but range in abundance from 5 to 15 percent. Lithic arenites have rock fragments that exceed feldspar grains; the abundance of rock fragments is greater than 25 percent. Sublithic arenites likewise contain more rock fragments than feldspar, but the amount of rock fragments is lower, ranging from 5 to 25 percent. Lithic arenites can be further subdivided according to the nature of the rock fragments. This classification scheme also recognizes three major types of wackes or graywackes that are roughly analogous with the three major arenite groups: quartz wacke, feldspathic wacke (with the subvariety arkosic wacke), and lithic wacke. The three major arenite sandstone families are separately described in the following sections, but the varieties of wacke can be conveniently considered together as a single group.

Quartz Arenites

Quartz arenites are usually white, but they may be any other colour; cementation by hematite, for example, makes them red. They are usually well sorted and well rounded (supermature) and often represent ancient dune, beach, or shallow marine deposits. Characteristically, they are ripple-marked or cross-bedded and occur as widespread thin blanket sands. On chemical analysis, some are found to contain more than 99 percent SiO_2 (quartz). Most commonly they are cemented with quartz, but calcite and iron oxide frequently serve as cements as well.

This type of sandstone is widespread in stable areas of continents surrounding the craton, such as central North America (St. Peter Sandstone of Ordovician age [about 505 to 438 million years old]), central Australia, or the Russian Platform, and are particularly common in Paleozoic strata (that formed from 570 to 245 million years ago). Quartz arenites have formed in the past when large areas of subcontinental dimensions were tectonically stable (not subject to uplift or deformation) and of low relief, so that extensive weathering could take place, accompanied by prolonged abrasion and sorting. This process eliminated all the unstable or readily decomposed minerals such as feldspar or rock fragments and concentrated pure quartz together with trace amounts of zircon, tourmaline, and various other resistant heavy minerals.

Quartz arenites have also accumulated to thicknesses of hundreds and even thousands of metres on the continental shelf areas produced as passive continental margins develop during the early stages of continental rifting and the opening of an ocean basin. These thick, continental margin deposits form only if source areas are sufficiently stable to permit beach abrasion and intense chemical weathering capable of destroying rock fragments and feldspars. Subsequent ocean basin closure and continental collision deforms the continental shelf and rise assemblages, incorporating clean quartz arenite units into the resulting folded and faulted mountain system, typically as major ridges. Examples include the Cambrian Chilhowee Group and Silurian Tuscarora Sandstone and Clinch Sandstone formations in the Appalachian Mountains of eastern North America and the Flathead Sandstone and Tapeats Sandstone of the Rocky Mountains in the western part of the continent.

Arkosic Sandstones

Arkosic sandstones are of two types. The most common of these is a mixture of quartz, potash feldspar, and granitic rock fragments. Chemically, these rocks are 60–70 percent silica (or silicon dioxide) and 10–15 percent aluminum oxide (Al_2O_3), with significant amounts of potassium (K), sodium (Na), and other elements. This type of arkosic sandstone, or arkose, can form wherever block faulting of granitic rocks occurs, given rates of uplift, erosion, and deposition that are so great that chemical weathering is outweighed and feldspar can survive in a relatively unaltered state. These rocks are usually reddish, generally immature, very poorly sorted, and frequently interbedded with arkose conglomerate; alluvial fans or fluvial aprons are the main depositional environments. The Triassic Newark Group of Connecticut is a classic example of this type of arkosic sandstone.

Arkoses also form under desert (or rarely, Arctic) conditions in which the rate of chemical decomposition of the parent granite or gneiss is very slow. These arkoses are generally well sorted and rounded (supermature) and show other desert features, such as eolian cross-beds, associated gypsum, and other evaporitic minerals. The Precambrian Torridonian Arkose of Great Britain is thought to be of desert origin. Basal sands deposited on a granitic-gneissic craton also are usually arkosic. Subarkose sandstones (e.g., Millstone Grit from the Carboniferous of England) have a feldspar content that is diminished by more extensive weathering or abrasion or by dilution from nonigneous source rocks.

Lithic Arenites

Lithic arenites occur in several subvarieties, but they are normally gray or of salt-and-pepper appearance because of the inclusion of dark-coloured rock fragments. Most commonly, fragments of metamorphic rocks such as slate, phyllite, or schist predominate, producing phyllarenite. If volcanic rock fragments such as andesite and basalt are most abundant, the rock is termed a volcanic arenite. If chert and carbonate rock fragments are predominant, the name chert or calclithite is applied.

Lithic arenites are usually rich in mica and texturally immature; the silicon dioxide content is 60–70 percent; aluminum oxide is 15 percent; and potassium, sodium, iron (Fe), calcium (Ca), and magnesium (Mg) are present in lesser amounts. Lithic arenites are very common in the geologic record, are widespread geographically, and are of all ages. They generally were formed as the result of rapid uplift, intense erosion, and high rates of deposition. Many of the classic postorogenic clastic wedge systems found in the major mountain systems of the world contain abundant lithic arenites. In the Appalachians, these include the Ordovician Juniata Formation of the Taconic clastic wedge, the Devonian Catskill Formation of the Acadian clastic wedge, and the Pocono and Mauch Chunk formations of the Alleghenian clastic wedge. Most lithic arenites are deposited as fluvial apron, deltaic, coastal plain, and shallow marine sandstones, interbedded with great thicknesses of shale and frequently with beds of coal or limestone. If they are deposited in an oxidizing environment such as a well-drained river system, they are reddish (e.g., the Catskill Formation of the northeastern United States and the Devonian Old Red Sandstone of England).

Wackes

Wacke, or graywacke, is the name applied to generally dark-coloured, very strongly bonded sandstones that consist of a heterogeneous mixture of rock fragments, feldspar, and quartz of sand size, together with appreciable amounts of mud matrix. Almost all wackes originated in the sea, and many were deposited in deep water by turbidity currents.

Wackes typically are poorly sorted, and the grain sizes present range over three orders of magnitude—e.g., from 2 to 2,000 micrometres (8×10^{-5} to 8×10^{-2} inch). Commonly, the coarsest part of a wacke bed is its base, where pebbles may be abundant. Shale fragments, which represent lumps of mud eroded from bottom sediments by the depositing current, may be concentrated elsewhere in the bed.

Many wackes contain much mud, typically 15–40 percent, and this increases as the mean grain size of the rock decreases. The particles forming the rock are typically angular. This, and the presence of the interstitial mud matrix, has led to these rocks being called "microbreccias." The fabric and texture indicate that the sediments were carried only a short distance and were subject to very little reworking by currents after deposition.

The most widespread internal structure of wackes is graded bedding, although some sequences display it poorly. Sets of cross strata more than 3 cm (1.2 inches) thick are rare, but thinner sets are very common. Parallel lamination is widespread, and convolute bedding is usually present. These internal structures are arranged within wacke beds in a regular sequence. They appear to result from the action of a single current flow and are related to changes in the hydraulics of the depositing current. In some beds, the upper part of the sequence of structures is missing, presumably because of erosion or nondeposition. In others, the lower part is missing. This has been attributed to change in the hydraulic properties of the depositing current as it moves away from its source and its velocity decreases to the point at which the first sediment deposited is laminated, rather than massive and graded as is the case closer to the source.

The most typical external structures of wacke beds are sole markings, which occur on their undersurfaces. Flute and groove molds are the most characteristic, but many other structures have been recorded.

The upper surfaces of wacke beds are less well characterized by sedimentary structures. The most typical are current lineation and various worm tracks, particularly of the highly sinuous form *Nereites*. Apart from these trace fossils, wackes are usually sparsely fossiliferous. Where fossils occur they are generally free-floating organisms (graptolites, foraminiferans) that have settled to the bottom, or bottom-living (benthic), shallow-water organisms displaced into deeper water as part of the sediment mass.

Wackes are chemically homogeneous and are generally rich in aluminum oxide (Al_2O_3), ferrous oxide (FeO) + ferric oxide (Fe_2O_3), magnesium oxide (MgO), and soda (Na_2O). The abundance of soda relative to potash (K_2O) (reflecting a typically high sodium plagioclase feldspar content) and dominance of ferrous oxide over ferric oxide (reflecting large amounts of chlorite in the matrix) chemically distinguishes wackes from the three arenite families. The bulk composition of most wackes mimics that of their source owing to a lack of chemical differentiation by weathering and sorting. The matrix component, which is by definition any clasts 30 micrometres or finer, allows wackes to be differentiated from the other major sandstones. To be characterized as a wacke, its matrix component must equal or exceed 15 percent; in some cases more than 50 percent matrix has been reported. The origin of the matrix component, however, is controversial. Even though laboratory studies demonstrate that gravity-driven, bottom-hugging turbidity currents deposit sand-size grains together with mud-size clasts, modern deep-sea fan and abyssal plain sands (turbidites) have a matrix component that seldom exceeds 10 percent. A large portion of the matrix in ancient wackes must therefore be secondary, derived either from the disaggregation of feldspar and fine-grained lithic fragments like shale, phyllite, and volcanic rocks or from the postdepositional infiltration of clay- and silt-size clasts from overlying beds.

Wackes are widespread in the geologic record and occur throughout geologic history. They typically are not found in association with sedimentary rocks that accumulate upon stable continental blocks and are instead confined either to intensely deformed mountain systems or to their modern analogues: ocean trenches, the continental slope and rise, and abyssal plain areas. Many, perhaps most, wackes are redeposited marine sands derived from source areas in which weathering, erosion, and deposition are too rapid to permit chemical differentiation and the breakdown of unstable components. Wackes of Archean age (those formed from 3.8 to 2.5 billion years ago) constitute the dominant sandstone type in the classic greenstone belts of the Precambrian shields (large areas of basement rocks in a craton that formed 3.8 billion to 570 million years ago around which younger sedimentary rocks have been deposited). They probably accumulated in rapidly subsiding trenches and ocean basins that surrounded primitive continental blocks. Proterozoic wackes (those formed from about 2.5 billion to 570 million years ago) are dominantly trench and ocean basin deposits, as are wackes of Phanerozoic age (those formed from 570 million years ago to the present day). They represent the accumulation of sand-size prisms of material that today are deposited both within ocean trenches (e.g., the modern trenches off Indonesia) and as submarine fan aprons (e.g., the Astoria Fan off the Pacific coast of Washington and Oregon in the United States) developed at the base of the continental slope at the mouths of submarine canyons. More distal carpets of wacke sand can extend for thousands of square kilometres across oceanic abyssal plains. Classic examples of the continental margin and ocean basin deposits include the late Precambrian Ocoee Supergroup and Ordovician Martinsburg Formation of the Appalachians, the Jurassic and Cretaceous Franciscan Formation of the Pacific Coast Ranges of California, much of the Alpine flysch of Switzerland and France, and many of the famous turbidite sands found in the Italian Apennines.

The feature common to all modern depositional sites is that they adjoin landmasses in areas of high submarine relief. The landmass may be a continent bordered by either a passive, aseismic margin (for example, the eastern margin of North America) or a seismically active margin such as that found along the western coast of both North and South America. The landmass can also be an active volcanic arc such as the Aleutian Islands chain or the Japan islands arc. The critical factor is the close proximity of topographically high and emergent clastic source areas and steeply sloped submarine depositional slopes, basins, or trenches.

MUDROCKS

In terms of volume, mudrocks are by far the most important variety of sedimentary rock, probably constituting nearly 80 percent of Earth's sedimentary rock column. Despite this abundance, the literature on mudrocks does not match in extent or detail that dealing with sandstones, carbonate rocks, and the various rarer sedimentary rock varieties like evaporite and phosphorite.

This paradox reflects the difficulties inherent both in analyzing such rocks, owing to their poor exposure and fine grain size, and in interpreting any data obtained from their analysis because of the effects of diagenesis. Mudrocks include all siliciclastic sedimentary rocks composed of silt- and clay-size particles: siltstone ($\frac{1}{16}$ mm to $\frac{1}{256}$ mm [0.0025 inch to 0.00015 inch] diameters), claystone (less than $\frac{1}{256}$ mm), and mudstone (a mix of silt and clay). Shale refers specifically to mudrocks that regularly exhibit lamination or fissility or both. Mudrocks are also loosely referred to as both lutites and pelites and as argillaceous sedimentary rocks.

Though mudrocks are composed mainly of detritus weathered from preexisting rocks, many contain large amounts of chemically precipitated cement (either calcium carbonate or silica), as well as abundant organic material. Mudrocks produced from the alteration of volcanic lava flows and ash beds to clay and zeolite minerals are called bentonites.

GENERAL PROPERTIES OF SHALES

The properties of shales are largely determined by the fine grain size of the constituent minerals. The accumulation of fine clastic detritus generally requires a sedimentary environment of low mechanical energy (one in which wave and current actions are minimal), although some fine material may be trapped by plants or deposited as weakly coherent pellets in more agitated environments. The properties of the clay mineral constituents of lutites are particularly important, even when they do not make up the bulk of a rock.

The mineralogy of shales is highly variable. In addition to clay minerals (60 percent), the average shale contains quartz and other forms of silica, notably amorphous silica and cristobalite (30 percent), feldspars (5 percent), and the carbonate minerals calcite and dolomite (5 percent).

Iron oxides and organic matter (about 0.5 and 1 percent, respectively) are also important. Older calculations greatly underestimated clay minerals because of incorrect assignment of potassium to feldspar minerals. The most abundant clay mineral is illite; montmorillonite and mixed-layer illite-montmorillonite are next in abundance, followed by kaolinite, chlorite, chlorite-montmorillonite, and vermiculite. The quartz-to-feldspar ratio generally mirrors that of associated sands. In pelagic (deep-sea) sediments, however, feldspar may be derived from local volcanic sources, whereas quartz may be introduced from the continents by wind, upsetting simple patterns. A large number of accessory minerals occur in shales. Some of these are detrital, but diagenetic or in situ varieties (e.g., pyrite, siderite, and various phosphates) and volcanically derived varieties (e.g., zeolites, zircon, and biotite) have been noted.

ORIGIN OF SHALES

The formation of fine-grained sediments generally requires weak transporting currents and a quiet depositional basin. Water is the common transporting medium, but ice-rafted glacial flour (silt produced by glacial grinding) is a major component in high-latitude oceanic muds, and windblown dust is prominent, particularly in the open ocean at low and intermediate latitudes. Shale environments thus include the deep ocean; the continental slope and rise; the deeper and more protected parts of shelves, shallow seas, and bays; coastal lagoons; interdistributory regions of deltas, swamps, and lakes (including arid basin playas); and river floodplains. The deep-sea muds are very fine, but an orderly sequence from coarse sediments in high-energy nearshore environments to fine sediments at greater depths is rarely found. Sediments at the outer edges of present-day continental shelves are commonly sands, relict deposits of shallower Pleistocene (from about

2.6 million to 11,700 years ago) glacial conditions, whereas muds are currently being deposited in many parts of the inner shelf. The nearshore deposition of clay minerals is enhanced by the tendency of riverborne dispersed platelets to flocculate in saline waters (salinity greater than about four parts per thousand) and to be deposited just beyond the agitated estuarine environment as aggregates hydraulically equivalent to coarser particles. Differential flocculation leads to clay-mineral segregation, with illite and kaolinite near shore and montmorillonite farther out to sea. Advance of silty and sandy delta-slope deposits over clays also leads to complex grain-size patterns.

Shales may be deposited in environments of periodic agitation. Sediments deposited on submarine slopes are frequently mechanically unstable and may be redistributed by slumping and turbidity currents to form thick accumulations (possible present-day eugeosynclinal equivalents) on the lower continental slope and rise. Part of the shale in many wacke-shale alternations may be of turbidite origin. Fine sediment can be deposited in marshes and on tidal flats. Trapping by marsh plants and binding of muds in fecal pellets are important. Because of electrochemical interactions among fine particles, muds plastered on a tidal flat by an advancing tide are difficult to reerode on the ebb. This may lead, as in the present-day Waddenzee, in the Netherlands, to a size increase from nearshore tidal flat muds to lag sands seaward. Fine floodplain sediments may dry out to coherent shale pellets, and these, on reerosion, can be redistributed as sands and gravels.

SHALES OF ECONOMIC VALUE

Black shales are often of economic importance as sources of petroleum products and metals, and this importance will probably increase in the future. The lacustrine Eocene

Green River Shales of Colorado, Wyoming, and Utah are potentially rich petroleum sources and are undergoing exploratory extraction. Bituminous layers of the Early Permian Irati Shales of Brazil are similarly important. These shales contain the remains of the marine reptile *Mesosaurus*, also found in South Africa, and played a prominent part in the development of the concepts of continental drift. The widespread thin Chattanooga Shale (Devonian-Mississippian) of the eastern United States has been exploited for its high (up to 250 parts per million) uranium content. The Kupferschiefer of the Permian (286 to 245 million years old) is a bituminous shale rich in metallic sulfides of primary sedimentary or early diagenetic origin; it covers a large area of central Europe as a band generally less than one metre thick, and in eastern Germany and in Poland there is sufficient enrichment in copper, lead, and zinc for its exploitation as an ore.

LIMESTONES AND DOLOMITES

Limestones and dolomites are collectively referred to as carbonates because they consist predominantly of the carbonate minerals calcite ($CaCO_3$) and dolomite ($CaMg[CO_3]_2$). Almost all dolomites are believed to be produced by recrystallization of preexisting limestones, although the exact details of this dolomitization process

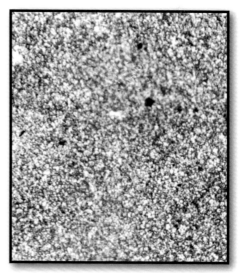

Photomicrograph showing micritic limestone from the Triassic Period (magnified 18×). Courtesy of A. Bosellini

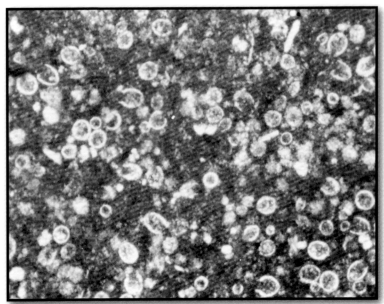

Photomicrograph showing micritic limestone from the Triassic Period (magnified 18×). Courtesy of A. Bosellini

Photomicrograph showing skeletal oolitic limestone, with clean calcite cement, from the Lower Triassic Period (magnified 18×). Courtesy of A. Bosellini

continue to be debated. Consequently, the following discussion initially deals with limestones and dolomites as a single rock type and subsequently considers the complex process by which some limestones become dolomite.

Carbonates are by far the only volumetrically important nonsiliciclastic sedimentary rock type. Most are marine, and thick sequences of carbonate rocks occur in all the continental blocks, a surviving record of the transgressions and regressions of shallow marine (epeiric) seas that repeatedly blanketed the stable continental cratonic areas from time to time mainly during the late Precambrian, Paleozoic, and Mesozoic eras. Modern marine carbonate sediments, whose formation is favoured by warm, shallow water, are presently being deposited in a broad band straddling the Equator. The texture, sedimentary structures, composition, and organic content of carbonates provide numerous insights into the environment of deposition and regional paleogeography. Many important oil reservoirs of the world, especially those of the Middle East, occur in carbonate rocks.

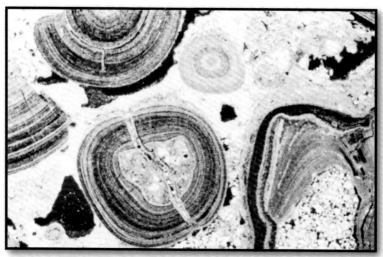

Photomicrograph showing pisolitic dolomite from the Upper Triassic Period (magnified 5×). Courtesy of A. Bosellini

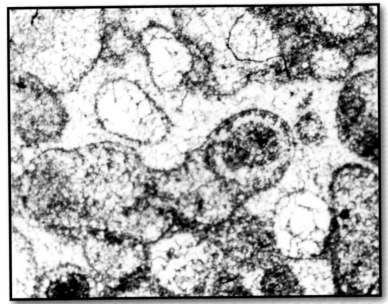

Photomicrograph showing recrystallized lump limestone from the Permian Period (magnified 18×). Courtesy of A. Bosellini

Photomicrograph showing diagenetic dolomite from the Middle Triassic Period growing at the expense of existing micritic material (magnified 15×). Courtesy of A. Bosellini

MINERALOGY

Though ancient limestones and dolomites are composed of calcite and dolomite, respectively, other calcite group minerals such as magnesite ($MgCO_3$), rhodochrosite ($MnCO_3$), and siderite ($FeCO_3$) occur in limited amounts in restricted environments. Modern carbonate sediments are composed almost entirely of metastable aragonite ($CaCO_3$) and magnesium-rich calcite, both of which readily recrystallize during diagenesis to form calcite. Carbonate rocks commonly grade naturally into siliciclastic sedimentary rocks as the proportion of terrigenous grains of varying size and mineralogy increases. Such mixtures are the consequence of the infringement of a dominantly siliciclastic depositional setting (e.g., a quartz arenitic beach area) into, for example, a lagoon or tidal flat in which carbonate mud accumulates.

TEXTURAL COMPONENTS

Carbonate minerals present in ancient limestones and dolomites occur in one of three textural forms: (1) discrete silt to sand to coarser carbonate grains, or allochems, such as oöids or skeletal fragments, (2) mud-size interstitial calcium carbonate matrix called microcrystalline calcite or micrite, and (3) interlocking, 0.02- to 0.1-mm- [0.0008- to 0.0004-inch-] diameter crystals of clear interstitial calcium carbonate cement or spar. In a rather simplistic sense, these three carbonate rock textural components are comparable, respectively, to the three possible constituents in a sandstone: (1) the coarser rock and mineral grains, (2) interstitial matrix, and (3) interstitial chemical cement.

Several types of allochems exist: oöids, skeletal grains, carbonate clasts, and pellets. Oöids (also known as oölites or oöliths) are sand-size spheres of calcium carbonate mud concentrically laminated about some sort of nucleus grain, perhaps a fossil fragment or a silt-size detrital quartz grain. Oöids develop today on shallow shelf areas where strong bottom currents can wash the various kinds of material that form oöid nuclei back and forth in well-agitated, warm water that is supersaturated with calcium carbonate. The concentric layers of aragonite (in modern oöids) is produced by blue-green algae that affix themselves to the grain nucleus. Skeletal fragments, also known as bioclasts, can be whole fossils or broken fragments of organisms, depending on current and wave strength as well as depositional depth. The content and texture of the bioclast component in any carbonate will vary noticeably as a function of both age (due to evolution) and depositional setting (because of subsequent abrasion and transport as well as ecology). Carbonate clasts include fragments weathered from carbonate source rocks outside the depositional basin (lithoclasts) as well as fragments of carbonate sediment eroded from within the basin almost immediately after it was deposited (intraclasts). Silt- to sand-size particles of microcrystalline calcite or aragonite that lack the internal structure of oöids or bioclasts generally are called pellets or peloids. Most are fecal pellets generated by mud-ingesting organisms. Pellets can be cemented together into irregularly shaped composite grains dubbed lumpstones or grapestones.

Microcrystalline carbonate mud (micrite) and sparry carbonate cement (sparite) are collectively referred to as orthochemical carbonate because, in contrast to allochems, neither exhibits a history of transport and deposition as clastic material. Micrite can occur either as matrix that fills or partly fills the interstitial pores between allochems or as the main component of a carbonate rock. It originates mainly as the result of organic activity: algae generate tiny needles of aragonite within their tissues, and after their death such needles fall to the depositional surface as unconsolidated mud, which soon recrystallizes to calcite. Some micrite is produced by inorganic precipitation of aragonite; grain-to-grain collision and the resulting abrasion of allochems also can generate modest amounts of micrite. Most of the coarser and clearer crystals of sparry calcite that fill interstitial pores as cement represent either recrystallized micrite or essentially a direct inorganic precipitate.

A number of carbonate classification schemes have been developed, but most modern ones subdivide and name carbonate rock types on the basis of the kinds of allochems present and the nature of the interstitial pore filling, whether it is micrite or spar. The most widely used scheme of this type is the descriptive classification devised by the American petrologist Robert L. Folk.

Origin of Limestones

Limestones originate mainly through the lithification of loose carbonate sediments. Modern carbonate sediments are generated in a variety of environments: continental, marine, and transitional, but most are marine. The present-day Bahama banks is the best known modern carbonate setting. It is a broad submarine shelf covered by shallow, warm seawater. The Bahama shelf, or carbonate platform, mimics the setting that repeatedly prevailed across the stable cratonic areas of the major continental blocks during late Precambrian, Paleozoic, and Mesozoic time and serves as a model for explaining the various limestone types that make up such ancient carbonate successions.

The edge of the shelf is marked by a topographically sharp escarpment flanked by coarse, angular limestone breccia. Submarine channels etched into the escarpment serve as waterways down which shallow-water carbonate sediment can be transported by turbidity currents capable of redistributing them as apronlike deposits on the oceanic abyssal plain. In many areas, the fringe of the Bahama banks is marked by wave-resistant reef rocks (sometimes classified as boundstone). Abrasion of these reefs by wave activity generates abundant skeletal debris. Variations in depth and current strength control the relative amounts of micrite and sparite, the prevalence of specific organisms and their productivity, and the likelihood of generating oöids, pellets, and carbonate rock fragments. Micrite and micritic allochemical sediments accumulate in deep-water, low-energy, protected areas like lagoons and tidal flats and on the leeward side of major islands. In high-energy, shallow-water locales such as beaches, coastal dunes, and tidal channels, currents winnow out any micrite, and these become the sites of sparry allochemical sediment deposition. Pinpointing the exact depositional setting for an ancient carbonate deposit requires detailed analysis of its texture, composition, sedimentary structures, geometry, fossil content, and stratigraphic relationships with modern carbonate depositional sites.

In addition to the ancient analogues of the modern carbonate deposits described above are freshwater limestones (marls) and limestone muds (or calcilutites) of deep-water abyssal plains. Freshwater limestones of limited extent represent a spectrum of small-scale settings developed within and along the margins of lacustrine basins. Deep-water abyssal plain limestones are quite restricted in volume and age in the geologic record for a number of reasons. First of all, abyssal plain sequences are less likely to be incorporated into the orogenic belts that develop as continental margins are compressed during ocean basin closure. Second, pelagic calcareous oozes are the obvious modern analogues of ancient abyssal plain calcilutites. These oozes are produced by aragonite-secreting plankton that float near the surface (such as foraminiferans and coccoliths), which upon their death leave their shells, or tests, to settle slowly to the ocean bottom and accumulate. The development of such deep-sea deposits is therefore obviously dependent on the existence of calcium-secreting planktonic organisms, and these did not evolve until Mesozoic time. Finally, calcareous ooze accumulation is severely restricted both by latitude (being largely confined to a band extending 30° to 40° north and south of the Equator) and abyssal plain depth (approximately 2,000 metres [about 6,500 feet]). Below a depth of about 4,500 metres (about 14,800 feet), which is the carbonate compensation depth (CCD), the pressure and temperature of seawater produces a rate of dissolution in excess of the rate of pelagic test accumulation.

BIOGENIC OOZE

Biogenic ooze, which is also called biogenic sediment, is the term for any pelagic sediment that contains more than 30 percent skeletal material. These sediments can be made up of either carbonate (or calcareous) ooze or siliceous ooze. The skeletal material in carbonate oozes is calcium carbonate usually in the form of the mineral calcite but sometimes aragonite. The most common contributors to the skeletal debris are such microorganisms as foraminiferans and coccoliths, microscopic carbonate plates that coat certain species of marine algae and protozoa. Siliceous oozes are composed of opal (amorphous, hydrated silica) that forms the skeleton of various microorganisms, including diatoms, radiolarians, siliceous sponges, and silicoflagellates. The distribution of biogenic oozes depends mainly on the supply of skeletal material, dissolution of the skeletons, and dilution by other sediment types, such as turbidites or clays.

Primary productivity, the production of organic substances through photosynthesis and chemosynthesis, in the ocean surface waters controls the supply of material to a large extent. Productivity is high at the Equator and in zones of coastal upwelling and also where oceanic divergences occur near Antarctica. Productivity is lowest in the central areas of the oceans (the gyres) in both hemispheres.

Siliceous oozes are more reliable indicators of high productivity than carbonate oozes. This is because silica dissolves quickly in surface waters and carbonate dissolves in deep water; hence, high surface productivity is required to supply siliceous skeletons to the ocean floor. Carbonate oozes dominate the deep Atlantic seafloor, while siliceous oozes are most common in the Pacific; the floor of the Indian Ocean is covered by a combination of the two.

Carbonate oozes cover about half of the world's seafloor. They are present chiefly above a depth of 4,500 metres (about 14,800 feet); below that they dissolve quickly. This depth is named the Calcite Compensation Depth (or CCD). It represents the level at which the rate of carbonate accumulation equals the rate of carbonate dissolution. In the Atlantic basin the CCD is 500 metres (about 1,600 feet) deeper than in the Pacific basin, reflecting both a high rate of supply and low rate of dissolution in comparison to the Pacific. The input of carbonate to the ocean is through rivers and deep-sea hydrothermal vents. Variation in input, productivity, and dissolution rates in the geologic past have caused the CCD to vary over 2,000 metres (about 6,600 feet). The CCD intersects the flanks of the world's oceanic ridges, and as a result these are mostly blanketed by carbonate oozes.

Siliceous oozes predominate in two places in the oceans: around Antarctica and a few degrees of latitude north and south of the Equator. At high latitudes the oozes include mostly the shells of diatoms. South of the Antarctic Convergence diatom oozes dominate the seafloor sediment cover and mix with glacial marine sediments closer to the continent. Seventy-five percent of all the oceans' silica supply is being deposited in the area surrounding Antarctica. Radiolarian oozes are more common near the Equator in the Pacific. Here, both siliceous oozes and calcareous oozes occur, but carbonate deposition dominates the region immediately near the Equator. Siliceous oozes bracket the carbonate belt and blend with pelagic clays farther north and south. Because siliceous skeletons dissolve so quickly in seawater, only the more robust skeletal remains are found in the siliceous oozes. Thus, fossils of this kind are not completely representative of the organisms living in the waters above.

Dolomite is produced by dolomitization, a diagenetic process in which the calcium carbonate minerals aragonite and calcite are recrystallized and converted into the mineral dolomite. Dolomitization can obscure or even obliterate all or part of the original limestone textures and structures; in the case where such original features survive, carbonate nomenclature and interpretation can still be applied to the rock with emphasis on the effects of alteration.

The exact processes by which limestones are dolomitized are not thoroughly understood, but dolomites occur widely in the geologic record. The relative proportion of dolomite to limestone progressively increases with age in carbonate rocks. This secular trend probably either reflects the earlier existence of geochemical settings that were more favourable to dolomitization or is the logical result of the fact that the likelihood for a limestone to undergo dolomitization increases proportionally with its age.

Geochemists have been unable to precipitate normal dolomite under the conditions of temperature and pressure that exist in nature; temperatures within the 200 °C (392 °F) range are required to support precipitation. A few modern, so-called primary marine dolomite localities have been studied, but close investigation of these areas suggests that even these penecontemporaneous dolomites are produced by altering calcite or aragonite almost immediately after their initial precipitation. Dolomites generated by later alteration of older limestones are known as diagenetic dolomites.

The study of the few reported penecontemporaneous dolomite sites allows some conclusions to be formed regarding the dolomitization process. These modern dolomites develop mainly under conditions of high salinity (hypersalinity), which commonly exist in arid regions across supratidal mud flats as well as on the flat, saline plains and playa lake beds known as sabkhas. In highly saline environments, the ratio of dissolved magnesium ions to dissolved calcium ions progressively increases above the norm for seawater (5:1) as a result of the selective formation of calcium-rich evaporite minerals like gypsum and anhydrite. These magnesium-rich brines then tend to be flushed downward owing to their high density; the entire process is named evaporative reflux. Penecontemporaneous dolomites would result from the positioning of sabkhas and arid supratidal flats in a site that is in immediate contact with carbonate sediment; diagenetic dolomites would logically result when such dolomite-producing settings overlie older limestone deposits. The presence of fissures or highly permeable zones serving as channelways for downward percolation of dolomitizing fluids would also promote the alteration. Other studies have emphasized a possible role in dolomitization for dense brackish (salty) fluids formed when seawater and meteoric waters (those precipitated from the atmosphere as rain or snow) are produced along coastal zones.

SILICEOUS ROCKS

Those siliceous rocks composed of an exceptionally high amount of crystalline siliceous material, mainly the mineral quartz (especially microcrystalline quartz and fibrous chalcedony) and amorphous opal, are most commonly known as chert. A wide variety of rock names are applied to cherty rocks reflecting their colour (flint is dark chert;

jasper is usually red; prase is green) and geographic origin (novaculite of Arkansas, U.S.; silexite of France). The term chert is applied here to all fine-grained siliceous sediments and sedimentary rocks of chemical, biochemical, and organic origin.

TYPES OF CHERTS

Two major varieties of chert deposits exist—namely, bedded chert and nodular chert. Bedded cherts occur in individual bands or layers ranging in thickness from one to several centimetres or even tens of metres. They are intimately associated with volcanic rocks, commonly submarine volcanic flows as well as deep-water mudrocks. Classic examples include the Miocene Monterey Formation of the Coast Ranges of California, the Permian Rex Chert of Utah and Wyoming, the Arkansas Novaculite of the Ouachita Mountains, and the Mesozoic chert deposits of the Franciscan Formation of California. Nodular cherts occur as small to large (millimetres to centimetres) knotlike and fistlike clusters of quartz, chalcedony, and opal concentrated along or parallel with bedding planes in shallow-water marine carbonate rocks as well as pelagic limestones. Individual nodules may be ovoid or semispherical in shape; masses of chert typically form a network.

ORIGIN OF CHERTS

Many bedded cherts are composed almost entirely of the remains of silica-secreting organisms like diatoms and radiolarians. Such deposits are produced by compacting and recrystallizing the organically produced siliceous ooze deposits that accumulate on the present-day abyssal ocean floor. The modern oozes gather in latitudes where high organic productivity of floating planktonic radiolarians and diatoms takes place in the warm surface waters. As individual organisms die, their shells settle slowly to the abyssal floor and accumulate as unconsolidated siliceous ooze. Siliceous oozes are particularly prominent across areas of the ocean floor located far from continental blocks, where the rate of terrigenous sediment supply is low, and in deeper parts of the abyssal plain lying below the carbonate compensation depth, where the accumulation of calcareous oozes cannot occur. Some bedded cherts might not be of organic origin. They instead may be produced by precipitating silica gels derived from the same magma chambers from which the submarine basalts (pillow lava) that are intimately associated with bedded cherts are precipitated.

The origin of nodular cherts has long been debated, but most are produced by the secondary replacement of the carbonate minerals and fossils within shallow marine shelf deposits. Evidence of secondary origin includes relict structures of allochems such as skeletal fragments and oöids preserved entirely within chert nodules. Silica can be mobilized from elsewhere within a rock and transported in solution under proper conditions of temperature and geochemistry. Likely sources of silica found scattered within shallow-water shelf carbonates include siliceous sponge spicules, radiolarians or diatom shells, and windblown sand grains. The details of the process and the possible role of microscopic organisms like bacteria in dissolving, mobilizing, and reconcentrating the silica remains uncertain.

Finally, geysers and hot springs such as those of the Yellowstone National Park area of northwestern Wyoming, U.S., are also sites of chert deposition. Encrustations of silica, known as sinter or geyserite, are volumetrically unimpressive but nevertheless are curiosities. The geyser and hot springs activity at Yellowstone is probably typical, with a subterranean body of magma as the source of silica-rich hydrothermal solutions rising periodically near or to the surface.

Phosphorites

Many sedimentary rocks contain phosphate in the form of scattered bones composed of the mineral apatite (calcium phosphate), but rocks composed predominantly of phosphate are rare. Nevertheless, three principal types exist: (1) regionally extensive, crystalline nodular, and bedded phosphorites, (2) localized concentrations of phosphate-rich clastic deposits (bone beds), and (3) guano deposits.

Evaporites

Evaporites are layered crystalline sedimentary rocks that form from brines generated in areas where the amount of water lost by evaporation exceeds the total amount of water from rainfall and influx via rivers and streams. The mineralogy of evaporite rocks is complex, with almost 100 varieties possible, but less than a dozen species are volumetrically important. Minerals in evaporite rocks include carbonates (especially calcite, dolomite, magnesite, and aragonite), sulfates (anhydrite and gypsum), and chlorides (particularly halite, sylvite, and carnallite), as well as various borates, silicates, nitrates, and sulfocarbonates. Evaporite deposits occur in both marine and nonmarine sedimentary successions.

Though restricted in area, modern evaporites contribute to genetic models for explaining ancient evaporite deposits. Modern evaporites are limited to arid regions (those of high temperature and low rates of precipitation), for example, on the floors of semidry ephemeral playa lakes in the Great Basin of Nevada and California, across the coastal salt flats (sabkhas) of the Middle East, and in salt pans, estuaries, and lagoons around the Gulf of Suez. Ancient evaporates occur widely in the Phanerozoic geologic record, particularly in those of Cambrian (from 570 to 505 million years ago), Permian (from 286 to 245 million years ago), and Triassic (from 245 to 208 million years ago) age, but are rare in sedimentary sequences of Precambrian age. They tend to be closely associated with shallow marine shelf carbonates and fine (typically rich in iron oxide) mudrocks. Because evaporite sedimentation requires a specific climate and basin setting, their presence in time and space clearly constrains inferences of paleoclimatology and paleogeography. Evaporite beds tend to concentrate and facilitate major thrust fault horizons, so their presence is of particular interest to structural geologists. Evaporites also have economic significance as a source of salts and fertilizer.

All evaporite deposits result from the precipitation of brines generated by evaporation. Laboratory experiments can accurately trace the evolution of brines as various evaporite minerals crystallize. Normal seawater has a salinity of 3.5 percent (or 35,000 parts per million), with the most important dissolved constituents being sodium and chlorine. When seawater volume is reduced to one-fifth of the original, evaporite precipitation commences in an orderly fashion, with the more insoluble components (gypsum and anhydrite) forming first. When the solution reaches one-tenth the volume of the original, more soluble minerals like sylvite and halite form. Natural evaporite sequences show vertical changes in mineralogy that crudely correspond to the orderly appearance of mineralogy as a function of solubility but are less systematic.

NONMARINE ENVIRONMENT

Evaporite deposition in the nonmarine environment occurs in closed lakes—i.e., those without outlet—in arid and semiarid regions. Such lakes form in closed interior basins or shallow depressions on land where drainage is internal and runoff does not reach the sea. If water depths are shallow or, more typically, somewhat ephemeral, the term playa or playa lake is commonly used.

Water inflow into closed lakes consists principally of precipitation and surface runoff, both of which are small in amount and variable in occurrence in arid regions. Groundwater flow and discharge from springs may provide additional water input, but evaporation rates are always in excess of precipitation and surface runoff. Sporadic or seasonal storms may give rise to a sudden surge of water inflow. Because closed lakes lack outlets, they can respond to such circumstances only by deepening and expanding. Subsequent evaporation will reduce the volume of water present to prestorm or normal amount; fluctuation of closed lake levels therefore characterizes the environment.

Such changing lake levels and water volumes lead to fluctuating salinity values. Variations in salinity effect equilibrium relations between the resulting brines and lead to much solution and subsequent reprecipitation of evaporites in the nonmarine environment. As a result of these complexities as well as the distinctive nature of dissolved constituents in closed lake settings, nonmarine evaporite deposits contain many minerals that are uncommon in marine evaporites—e.g., borax, epsomite, trona, and mirabilite.

SHALLOW MARINE ENVIRONMENT

Evaporite deposition in the shallow marine environment (sometimes termed the salina) occurs in desert coastal areas, particularly along the margins of such semi-restricted water bodies as the Red Sea, Persian Gulf, and Gulf of California. Restriction is, in general, one of the critical requirements for evaporite deposition, because free and unlimited mixing with the open sea would allow the bodies of water to easily overcome the high evaporation rates of arid areas and dilute these waters to near-normal salinity. This semi-restriction cannot, in fact, prevent a large amount of dilution by mixing; coastal physiography is the principal factor involved in brine production. Shallow-water evaporites, almost exclusively gypsum, anhydrite, and halite, typically interfinger with tidal flat limestone and dolomite and fine-grained mudrock.

DEEP-BASIN ENVIRONMENT

Most of the thick, laterally extensive evaporite deposits appear to have been produced in deep, isolated basins that developed during episodes of global aridity. The most crucial requirement for evaporite production is aridity; water must be evaporated more rapidly than it can be replenished by precipitation and inflow. In addition, the evaporite basin must somehow be isolated or at least partially isolated from the open ocean so that brines produced through evaporation are prevented from returning there. Restricting brines to such an isolated basin over a period of time enables them to be concentrated to the point where evaporite mineral precipitation occurs. Periodic breaching of the barrier, due either to crustal downwarping or to global sea-level changes, refills the basin from time to time, thereby replenishing the volume of seawater

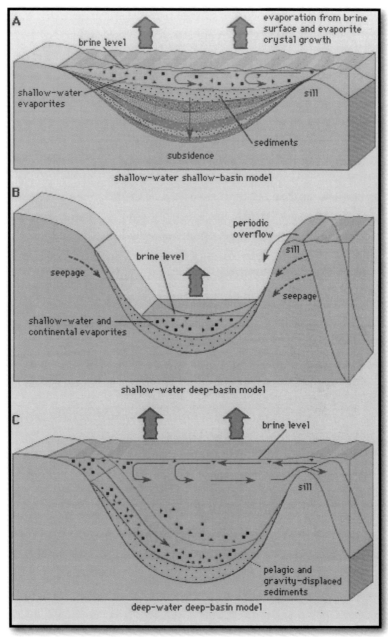

Three models for deposition of marine evaporites in basins of restricted water circulation. Copyright Encyclopædia Britannica, Inc.; rendering for this edition by Rosen Educational Services

to be evaporated and making possible the inordinately thick, regionally extensive evaporite sequences visible in the geologic record.

Debate continues over the exact mechanisms for generating thick evaporite deposits. Three possible models for restricting "barred" evaporite basins have been developed. They differ in detail, and none has garnered a consensus of support. The deep-water, deep-basin model accounts for replenishment of the basin across the barrier or sill, with slow, continual buildup of thick evaporites made possible by the seaward escape of brine that allows a constant brine concentration to be maintained. The shallow-water, shallow-basin model produces thick evaporites by continual subsidence of the basin floor. The shallow-water, deep-basin model shows the brine level in the basin beneath the level of the sea as a result of evaporation; brines are replenished by groundwater recharge from the open ocean.

Iron-Rich Sedimentary Rocks

Almost all sedimentary rocks are iron-bearing in the sense that mudrocks, sandstones, and carbonates typically have an iron content of several percent. Nevertheless, sedimentary rocks in which the proportion of iron exceeds 15 percent are separately categorized as iron-rich. Two major types of iron-rich sedimentary rocks are recognized: (1) iron formation, or banded iron formation (BIF)— regionally extensive, locally thick sequences composed of alternating thin (millimetre to centimetre thick) layers of mainly crystalline-textured iron-rich minerals and chert— and (2) ironstone—noncherty, essentially clastic-textured, iron-rich minerals of local extent.

Banded iron formations are predominantly Precambrian in age; most are 1.8 to 2.2 billion years old; none are younger than Cambrian age. The most important iron-bearing minerals in iron formations are hematite, magnetite, and greenalite. These deposits constitute the world's major source of iron ore. Classic examples are found in the Mesabi Range of Minnesota, U.S., and the Kiruna ores of Sweden.

Ironstones are principally of Phanerozoic age, mainly Early Paleozoic (roughly 440 to 570 million years old) and Jurassic (about 144 to 208 million years old), but can be as old as Middle Precambrian age (about 1.6 to 3 billion years old). They appear to be restricted to basins no larger than 150 km (93 miles) in any direction. Major iron minerals are goethite, hematite, and chamosite.

ORIGIN OF BANDED IRON FORMATION

The origin of banded iron formation is not clearly understood. Banded iron formation units are typically 50 to 600 metres (about 165 to 1,970 feet) thick. Their complex mineralogy includes various iron oxides, iron carbonates, iron silicates, and iron sulfides. The essentially crystalline texture of these minerals together with the definitive crystalline texture of the laminated chert bands with which the iron mineral layers alternate is perplexing. At present, iron is not easily dissolved, nor can it be readily transported in solution and subsequently precipitated as crystalline-textured, iron-rich minerals, because of the presence of free atmospheric oxygen. Many sedimentary petrologists consequently conclude that banded iron formation deposition is a uniquely Precambrian occurrence made possible by, and supporting the existence of, an earlier anaerobic Earth atmosphere (one lacking free oxygen) quite unlike that in existence today. Controversy also continues over the ultimate source of iron (weathering as opposed to magmatic iron escaping from Earth's interior) and over the possible role of microorganisms such as bacteria and algae in the precipitation of the iron.

The origin of ironstones also is not well understood, but most appear to be derived from the erosion and redeposition of lateritic (iron-rich, red) soils. Ironstones occur as thin (a few tens of metres at most) units interbedded with shallow marine and transitional carbonates, mudrocks, and sandstones. They generally have an oölitic texture. Cross-bedding, ripple marks, and small scour and fill channels are abundant. Slight uplift and erosion of reddish soils developed in coastal regions drained by rivers that transport and deposit such material in deltas and embayments along the coast is compatible with the features and fossils found in deposits of this sort. Classical ironstone deposits include the Ordovician Wabana Formation of Newfoundland and the Silurian Clinton Group of the central and southern Appalachians.

ORGANIC-RICH SEDIMENTARY DEPOSITS

Coal, oil shale, and petroleum are not sedimentary rocks per se; they represent accumulations of undecayed organic tissue that can either make up the bulk of the material (e.g., coal), or be disseminated in the pores within mudrocks, sandstones, and carbonates (e.g., oil shale and petroleum). Much of the undecomposed organic matter in sediment and sedimentary rocks is humus, plant matter that accumulates in soil. Other important organic constituents include peat, humic organic matter that collects in bogs and swamps where oxidation and bacterial decay is incomplete, and sapropel, fine-grained organic material—mainly the soft organic tissue of phytoplankton and zooplankton, along with bits and pieces of higher plants—that amass subaqueously in lakes and oceans.

Organic-rich sedimentary rock deposits are collectively referred to as fossil fuels because they consist of the undecayed organic tissue of plants and animals preserved in depositional settings characterized by a lack of free oxygen. Fossil fuels constitute the major sources of energy in the industrial world, and their unequal distribution in time (exclusively Phanerozoic) and space (more than half of the proved petroleum reserves are in the Persian Gulf region of the Middle East) has a significant effect on the world's political and economic stability.

FOSSIL FUELS

Fossil fuels constitute a class of materials of biological origin that occur within Earth's crust that can be used as a source of energy.

Fossil fuels include coal, petroleum, natural gas, oil shales, bitumens, tar sands, and heavy oils. All contain carbon and were formed as a result of geologic processes acting on the remains of organic matter produced by photosynthesis, a process that began in the Archean Eon more than 3 billion years ago. Most carbonaceous material occurring before the Devonian Period (approximately 415 million years ago) was derived from algae and bacteria.

All fossil fuels can be burned in air or with oxygen derived from air to provide heat. This heat may be employed directly, as in the case of home furnaces, or utilized to produce steam to drive generators that can supply electricity. In still other cases—for example, gas turbines used in jet aircraft—the heat yielded by burning a fossil fuel serves to increase both the pressure and the temperature of the combustion products to furnish motive power.

Since the late 18th century, fossil fuels have been consumed at an ever-increasing rate. Today they supply nearly 90 percent of all the energy consumed by the industrially developed countries of the world. Although new deposits continue to be discovered, the reserves of the principal fossil fuels remaining in Earth are limited. The amounts of fossil fuels that can be recovered economically are difficult to estimate, largely because of changing rates of consumption and future value as well as technological developments. For example, using current technology, a typical coal bed must be no less than about 60 cm (2 feet) thick and buried no more than about 2,000 m (6,600 feet) to be mined economically. However, advances in technology may make it possible in the future to mine thinner beds at greater depths at reasonable cost, increasing the amount of recoverable coal. Estimates of remaining petroleum resources are equally difficult. As recoverable supplies of conventional (light-to-medium) oil become depleted, it is expected that heavy oil, and oil extracted from tar sands and oil shales, will be exploited as sources of liquid petroleum on a wide scale.

Coal

Coals are the most abundant organic-rich sedimentary rock. They consist of undecayed organic matter that either accumulated in place or was transported from elsewhere to the depositional site. The most important organic component in coal is humus. The grade or rank of coal is determined by the percentage of carbon present. The term peat is used for the uncompacted plant matter that accumulates in bogs and brackish swamps. With increasing compaction and carbon content, peat can be transformed into the various kinds of coal: initially brown coal or lignite, then soft or bituminous coal, and finally, with metamorphism, hard or anthracite coal. In the geologic record, coal occurs in beds, called seams, which are blanketlike coal deposits a few centimetres to metres or hundreds of metres thick.

Many coal seams occur within cyclothems, rhythmic successions of sandstone, mudrock, and limestone in which nonmarine units are regularly and systematically overlain by an underclay, the coal seam itself, and then various marine lithologies. The nonmarine units are thought to constitute the floor of ancient forests and swamps developed in low-lying coastal regions; the underclay is a preserved relict of the soil in which the coal-producing vegetation was rooted; and the marine units overlying the coal record the rapid transgression of the sea inland that killed the vegetation by drowning it and preventing its decomposition by rapid burial. The exact mechanism responsible for generating the rapid episodes of marine transgression and regression necessary to generate coal-bearing cyclothems is not definitively known. A combination of episodic upwarping and downwarping of the continental blocks or global (eustatic) changes in sea level or both, coupled with normal changes in the rate of sediment supply that occurs along coasts traversed by major laterally meandering river systems, may have been the cause.

In any case, coal is a rare, though widely distributed, lithology. Extensive coal deposits overall occur mainly in rocks of Devonian age (those from 408 to 360 million years old) and younger because their existence is clearly contingent on the evolution of land plants. Nevertheless, small, scattered coal deposits as old as early Proterozoic have been described. Coal-bearing cyclothem deposits are especially abundant in the middle and late Paleozoic sequences of the Appalachians and central United States and in the Carboniferous of Great Britain, probably because during this time interval global climates were warm and humid and large portions of the continental blocks were low-lying platforms located only slightly above sea level.

Oil Shale

Mudrock containing high amounts of organic matter in the form of kerogen is known as oil shale or kerogen shale. Kerogen is altered, undecayed, fatty organic matter, mainly sapropel, and is very fine-grained. It can be generated in place or transported. The most famous oil shale deposit in the world, located in the United States, is the Green River Formation of Utah, Wyoming, and Colorado of Eocene age (i.e., formed 57.8 to 36.6 million years ago). This vast deposit contains fossils and sedimentary structures, suggesting rapid deposition and burial of unoxidized organic matter in shallow lakes or marine embayments. The quantity of oil entrapped in the Green River Formation is significant. The cost of extracting the oil trapped in the mudrock by heating the oil shale, however, far exceeds the cost of extracting equivalent quantities of oil, natural gas, or coal. Also, the refractory process not only requires extensive strip mining and immense volumes of water but also results in a volume expansion of the original oil shale. Despite these considerable economic and technical problems, oil shales potentially represent a significant future energy resource.

OIL AND NATURAL GAS

Natural gas refers collectively to the various gaseous hydrocarbons generated below Earth's surface and trapped in the pores of sedimentary rocks. Major natural gas varieties include methane, ethane, propane, and butane. These natural gases are commonly, though not invariably, intimately associated with the various liquid hydrocarbons—mainly liquid paraffins, naphthenes, and aromatics—that collectively constitute oil.

Hydrocarbons can also exist in a semisolid or solid state such as asphalt, asphaltites, mineral waxes, and pyrobitumens. Bitumens can occur as seepages, impregnations filling the pore space of sediments (e.g., tar sands of the Canadian Rocky Mountains), and in veins or dikes. Asphaltites occur primarily in dikes and veins that cross sedimentary rocks such as gilsonite deposits in the Green River Formation of Utah. These natural bitumens probably form from the loss of volatiles, oxidation, and biological degradation resulting from oil seepage to the surface. Solid hydrocarbons are of interest to geologists as their presence is a good indicator of petroleum below the surface in that region. Also, solid hydrocarbons have commercial value.

The exact process by which oil and natural gas are produced is not precisely known, despite the extensive efforts made to determine the mode of petroleum genesis. Crude oil is thought to form from undecomposed organic matter, principally single-celled floating phytoplankton and zooplankton that settle to the bottom of marine basins and are rapidly buried within sequences of mudrock and limestone. Natural gas and oil are generated from such source rocks only after heating and compaction. Typical petroleum formation (maturation) temperatures do not exceed 100 °C (212 °F), meaning that the depth of burial of source rocks cannot be greater than a few kilometres. After their formation, oil and natural gas migrate from source rocks to reservoir rocks composed of sedimentary rocks largely as a consequence of the lower density of the hydrocarbon fluids and gases. Good reservoir rocks, by implication, must possess high porosity and permeability. A high proportion of open pore spaces enhances the capacity of a reservoir to store the migrating petroleum; the interconnectedness of the pores facilitates the withdrawal of the petroleum once the reservoir rock is penetrated by drill holes.

SECULAR TRENDS IN THE SEDIMENTARY ROCK RECORD

Reexamination of the sedimentary rock record preserved within the continental blocks suggests systematic changes through time in the relative proportions of the major sedimentary rock types deposited. These changes can be linked to the evolution of the atmosphere and hydrosphere and to the changing global tectonic setting.

Carbonates and quartz sands, for example, require long-term source area stability as well as the existence of broad, shallow-water epeiric seas that mantle continental blocks. Marine transgressions and regressions across broad stable continental cratons occurred only in Proterozoic and Phanerozoic time; Archean continental blocks were smaller and tectonically unstable, and most likely less granitic than those of today. Consequently, the early Precambrian sedimentary rock record consists largely of volcanogenic sediments, wackes, and arkoses physically disintegrated from small, high-relief island arcs (the Archean greenstone belts of the various Precambrian shields) and microcontinental fragments. The fact that iron formations are restricted to rocks of Archean and Proterozoic time supports the conclusion that atmospheric oxygen levels in earlier stages of Earth history were lower, promoting the dissolution, transport, and precipitation of iron by chemical or biochemical means. The total lack of evaporites from the Archean record and their subsequent steady buildup probably reflects a number of factors. Such deposits can be easily destroyed by metamorphism, and presumably, given enough time, they will have been completely erased. Also, evaporite formation requires seawater with elevated salinity, a condition that is established with time. Finally, significant volumes of bedded evaporites can occur only once broad, stable continents have evolved, because the requisite restricted evaporite basins develop exclusively adjacent to cratons.

CHAPTER 4
METAMORPHIC ROCK

M etamorphic rocks are a class of rocks that result from the alteration of preexisting rocks in response to changing environmental conditions, such as variations in temperature, pressure, and mechanical stress, and the addition or subtraction of chemical components. The preexisting rocks may be igneous, sedimentary, or other metamorphic rocks.

The word metamorphism is taken from the Greek for "change of form"; metamorphic rocks are derived from igneous or sedimentary rocks that have altered their form (recrystallized) as a result of changes in their physical environment. Metamorphism comprises changes both in mineralogy and in the fabric of the original rock. In general, these alterations are brought about either by the intrusion of hot magma into cooler surrounding rocks (contact metamorphism) or by large-scale tectonic movements of Earth's lithospheric plates that alter the pressure-temperature conditions of the rocks (regional metamorphism). Minerals within the original rock, or protolith, respond to the changing conditions by reacting with one another to produce a new mineral assemblage that is thermodynamically stable under the new pressure-temperature conditions. These reactions occur in the solid state but may be facilitated by the presence of a fluid phase lining the grain boundaries of the minerals. In contrast to the formation of igneous rocks, metamorphic rocks do not crystallize from a silicate melt, although high-temperature metamorphism can lead to partial melting of the host rock.

Because metamorphism represents a response to changing physical conditions, those regions of Earth's surface where dynamic processes are most active will also be regions where metamorphic processes are most intense and easily observed. The vast region of the Pacific margin, for example, with its seismic and volcanic activity, is also an area in which materials are being buried and metamorphosed intensely. In general, the margins of continents and regions of mountain building are the regions where metamorphic processes proceed with intensity. But in relatively quiet places, where sediments accumulate at slow rates, less spectacular changes also occur in response to changes in pressure and temperature conditions. Metamorphic rocks are therefore distributed throughout the geologic column.

Because most of Earth's mantle is solid, metamorphic processes may also occur there. Mantle rocks are seldom observed at the surface because they are too dense to rise, but occasionally a glimpse is presented by their inclusion in volcanic materials. Such rocks may represent samples from a depth of a few hundred kilometres, where pressures of about 100 kilobars (10 gigapascal or 3 million inches of mercury) may be operative. Experiments at high pressure have shown that few of the common minerals that occur at the surface will survive at depth within the mantle without changing to new high-density phases in which atoms are packed more closely together. Thus, the common form of SiO_2, quartz, with a density of 2.65 grams per cubic cm (1.53 ounces per cubic inch), transforms to a new phase, stishovite, with a density of 4.29 grams per cubic cm (2.48 ounces per cubic inch). Such changes are of critical significance in the geophysical interpretation of the Earth's interior.

In general, temperatures increase with depth within Earth along curves referred to as geotherms. The specific shape of the geotherm beneath any location on Earth is a function of its corresponding local tectonic regime. Metamorphism can occur either when a rock moves from one position to another along a single geotherm or when the geotherm itself changes form. The former can take place when a rock is buried or uplifted at a rate that permits it to maintain thermal equilibrium with its surroundings; this type of metamorphism occurs beneath slowly subsiding sedimentary basins and also in the descending oceanic plate in some subduction zones. The latter process occurs either when hot magma intrudes and alters the thermal state of a stationary rock or when the rock is rapidly transported by tectonic processes (e.g., thrust faulting or large-scale folding) into a new depth-temperature regime in, for example, areas of collision between two continents. Regardless of which process occurs, the result is that a collection of minerals that are thermodynamically stable at the initial conditions are placed under a new set of conditions at which they may or may not be stable. If they are no longer in equilibrium with one another under the new conditions, the minerals will react in such a way as to approach a new equilibrium state. This may involve a complete change in mineral assemblage or simply a shift in the compositions of the preexisting mineral phases. The resultant mineral assemblage will reflect the chemical composition of the original rock and the new pressure-temperature conditions to which the rock was subjected.

Because protolith compositions and the pressure-temperature conditions under which they may be placed vary widely, the diversity of metamorphic rock types is large. Many of these varieties are repeatedly associated with one another in space and time, however, reflecting a uniformity of geologic processes over hundreds of millions of years. For example, the metamorphic rock associations that developed in the Appalachian Mountains of eastern North America in response to the collision between the North American and African lithospheric plates during the Paleozoic are very similar to those developed in the Alps of south-central Europe during the Mesozoic-Cenozoic collision between the European and African plates. Likewise, the metamorphic rocks exposed in the Alps are grossly similar to metamorphic rocks of the same age in the Himalayas of Asia, which formed during the continental collision between the Indian and Eurasian plates. Metamorphic rocks produced during collisions between oceanic and continental plates from different localities around the world also show striking similarities to each other yet are markedly different from metamorphic rocks produced during continent-continent collisions. Thus, it is often possible to reconstruct tectonic events of the past on the basis of metamorphic rock associations currently exposed at Earth's surface.

METAMORPHIC VARIABLES

Metamorphism results from a complex interplay between physical and chemical processes that operate on a scale ranging from micrometres (e.g., fine mineral grain sizes, thickness of intergranular fluid, diffusion distances for chemical species) to tens or hundreds of kilometres (e.g., crustal thickness, width of collision zone between lithospheric plates, depth to subducting plate). Despite this wide range and the many processes involved in the recrystallization of sedimentary and igneous protoliths into metamorphic rocks, there are relatively few variables that effect metamorphic changes. Those of greatest importance are temperature, pressure, and the original chemical composition of the protolith; each is briefly discussed here.

TEMPERATURE

Temperatures at which metamorphism occurs range from the conditions of diagenesis (approximately 150°–200 °C [about 300–400 °F]) up to the onset of melting. Rocks of different compositions begin to melt at different temperatures, with initial melting occurring at roughly 650–750 °C (about 1,200–1,382 °F) in rocks of granitic or shaley composition and approximately 900–1,200 °C (about 1,650–2,200 °F) in rocks of basaltic composition. Above these temperatures, metamorphic processes gradually give way to igneous processes. Hence, the temperature realm of metamorphism spans an interval of about 150°–1,100 °C (300–2,000 °F) and is strongly dependent on the composition of the protolith.

The temperature at any point within Earth's crust is controlled by the local heat-flow regime, which is a composite function of heat flow upward from the mantle into the crust, heat generated by radioactive decay in nearby regions of the crust, heat transported into the crust by silicate melts, and tectonic transport of hot or cold rocks at rates faster than those needed to maintain thermal equilibrium with the surrounding rocks. The temperature gradient at any location inside Earth, known as the geothermal gradient, is the increase in temperature per unit distance of depth; it is given by the tangent to the local geotherm. The magnitude of the geothermal gradient thus varies with the shape of the geotherm. In regions with high surface heat flow, such as areas of active volcanism or mantle upwelling beneath thinned continental crust, geothermal gradients of 40–100 °C (104–212 °F) per km (0.6 mile) prevail, giving rise to high temperatures at relatively shallow levels of the crust. Within the stable interiors of old continents, geothermal gradients of 25–35 °C (77–95 °F) per km are more typical, and in zones of active subduction, where the relatively cold oceanic crust is rapidly transported to great depths, geothermal gradients range from 10–20 °C (50–68 °F) per km. These large variations in geotherms and geothermal gradients give rise to different metamorphic regimes, or combinations of pressure-temperature conditions, associated with the different tectonic provinces.

In addition to the variation of geotherms as a function of position within Earth, individual geotherms at a single location can vary with time. Geotherms are at steady state (i.e., do not change with time) in tectonically quiescent areas of Earth, such as the middle regions of large continents, and also in areas where tectonic processes such as subduction have operated at similar rates over long periods. Transient geotherms, on the other hand, are generated in tectonically active regions, such as zones of continent-continent collision or rapid uplift and erosion, in which the tectonic processes are relatively short-lived; in these areas, the temperature at a given depth in Earth is time-dependent, and individual geotherms can have very complex shapes that with time approach smooth curves. These complex geotherms can produce wide temperature fluctuations at a given depth within Earth; rocks metamorphosed in response to these variations may show considerable textural and chemical evidence of disequilibrium, reflecting the fact that temperatures changed at rates that were more rapid than reaction rates among the constituent minerals.

Pressure

The pressure experienced by a rock during metamorphism is due primarily to the weight of the overlying rocks (i.e., lithostatic pressure) and is generally reported in units of bars or kilobars. The standard scientific notation for pressure is expressed in pascals or megapascals (1 pascal is equivalent to 10 bars). For typical densities of crustal rocks of 2 to 3 grams per cubic cm (1.15 to 1.72 ounces per cubic inch), 1 kilobar (0.1 gigapascal) of lithostatic pressure is generated by a column of overlying rocks approximately 3.5 km (about 2 miles) high. Typical continental crustal thicknesses are on the order of 30–40 km (about 19–25 miles) but can be as great as 60–80 km (37–50 miles) in mountain belts such as the Alps and Himalayas. Hence, metamorphism of continental crust occurs at pressures from a few hundred bars (adjacent to shallow-level intrusions) to 10–20 kilobars (1–2 gigapascal) at the base of the crust. Oceanic crust is generally 6–10 km (3.7–6 miles) in thickness, and metamorphic pressures within the oceanic crust are therefore considerably less than in continental regions. In subduction zones, however, oceanic and, more rarely, continental crust may be carried down to depths exceeding 100 km (about 60 miles), and metamorphism at very high pressures may occur. Metamorphic recrystallization also occurs in the mantle at pressures up to hundreds of kilobars.

Changes in lithostatic pressure experienced by a rock during metamorphism are brought about by burial or uplift of the sample. Burial can occur in response either to ongoing deposition of sediments above the sample or tectonic loading brought about, for example, by thrust-faulting or large-scale folding of the region. Uplift, or more properly unroofing, takes place when overlying rocks are stripped off by erosional processes or when the overburden is tectonically thinned.

Fluids trapped in the pores of rocks during metamorphism exert pressure on the surrounding grains. At depths greater than a few kilometres within Earth, the magnitude of the fluid pressure is equal to the lithostatic pressure, reflecting the fact that mineral grain boundaries recrystallize in such a way as to minimize pore space and to seal off the fluid channelways by which solutions rise from depth. At shallow depths, however, interconnected pore spaces can exist, and hence the pressure within a pore is related to the weight of an overlying column of fluid rather than rock. Because metamorphic fluids (dominantly composed of water and carbon dioxide) are less dense than rocks, the fluid pressure at these conditions is lower than the lithostatic pressure.

Deformation of rocks during metamorphism occurs when the rock experiences an anisotropic stress—i.e., unequal pressures operating in different directions. Anisotropic stresses rarely exceed more than a few tens or hundreds of bars but have a profound influence on the textural development of metamorphic rocks.

ROCK COMPOSITION

The chemistry of the original igneous or sedimentary rock determines the type of metamorphic rock produced. Although numerous types of igneous and sedimentary rocks can be reformed into metamorphic rocks, most metamorphic rocks develop within the realms of four chemical systems, and the mineral composition of a given metamorphic rock is limited by the laws of thermodynamics. In addition, the original igneous and sedimentary rocks tend not to be radically transformed by the process of metamorphism.

CLASSIFICATION INTO FOUR CHEMICAL SYSTEMS

Common metamorphic rock types have essentially the same chemical composition as what must be their equally common igneous or sedimentary precursors. Common greenschists have roughly the same compositions as basalts; marbles are like limestones; slates are similar to mudstones or shales; and many gneisses are like granodiorites. In general, then, the chemical composition of a metamorphic rock will closely reflect the primary nature of the material that has been metamorphosed. If there are

A marble quarry in Carrara, northern Italy. Heat, pressure, and the action of liquids cause limestone to change into marble. Shutterstock.com

significant differences, they tend to affect only the most mobile (soluble) or volatile elements; water and carbon dioxide contents can change significantly, for example.

Despite the wide variety of igneous and sedimentary rock types that can recrystallize into metamorphic rocks, most metamorphic rocks can be described with reference to only four chemical systems: pelitic, calcareous, felsic, and mafic. Pelitic rocks are derived from mudstone (shale) protoliths and are rich in potassium (K), aluminum (Al), silicon (Si), iron (Fe), magnesium (Mg), and water (H_2O), with lesser amounts of manganese (Mn), titanium (Ti), calcium (Ca), and other constituents. Calcareous rocks are formed from a variety of chemical and detrital sediments such as limestone, dolostone, or marl and are largely composed of calcium oxide (CaO), magnesium oxide (MgO), and carbon dioxide (CO_2), with varying amounts of aluminum, silicon, iron, and water. Felsic rocks can be produced by metamorphism of both igneous and sedimentary protoliths (e.g., granite and arkose, respectively) and are rich in silicon, sodium (Na), potassium, calcium, aluminum, and lesser amounts of iron and magnesium. Mafic rocks derive from basalt protoliths and some volcanogenic sediments and contain an abundance of iron, magnesium, calcium, silicon, and aluminum. Ultramafic metamorphic rocks result from the metamorphism of mantle rocks and some oceanic crust and contain dominantly magnesium, silicon, and carbon dioxide, with smaller amounts of iron, calcium, and aluminum. For the purposes of this discussion, ultramafic rocks are considered to be a subset of the mafic category.

The particular metamorphic minerals that develop in each of these four rock categories are controlled above all by the protolith chemistry. The mineral calcite ($CaCO_3$), for example, can occur only in rocks that contain sufficient quantities of calcium. The specific pressure-temperature conditions to which the rock is subjected will further

COMMON MINERALS OF METAMORPHIC ROCKS	
MINERAL	**MINERAL**
actinolite	kaolinite
adularia**	kyanite**
*albite	lawsonite
andalusite**	magnesite
anorthite	microcline**
anthophyllite	*muscovite
aragonite**	*omphacite
*biotite	orthoclase**
*calcite**	*plagioclase
*chlorite	prehnite
chloritoid	pumpellyite
cordierite	*quartz**
diopside	sanidine**
*dolomite	scapolite
enstatite	serpentine**
*epidote	sillimanite**
forsterite	staurolite
*garnet	stilpnomelane
glaucophane	talc
*hornblende	tremolite
hypersthene	wollastonite
jadeite	

*Indicates wide range of stability.
**Indicates more than one form (polymorph) exists.

influence the minerals that are produced during recrystallization; for example, at high pressures calcite will be replaced by a denser polymorph of $CaCO_3$ called aragonite. In general, increasing pressure favours denser mineral structures, whereas increasing temperature favours anhydrous and less dense mineral phases. Although some minerals, such as quartz, calcite, plagioclase, and biotite, develop under a variety of conditions, other minerals are more restricted in occurrence; examples are lawsonite, which is produced primarily during high-pressure, low-temperature metamorphism of basaltic protoliths, and sillimanite, which develops during relatively high-temperature metamorphism of pelitic rocks.

COMMON METAMORPHIC MINERALS AS A FUNCTION OF PRESSURE, TEMPERATURE, AND PROTOLITH COMPOSITION*			
PROTOLITH	HIGH P/ LOW T	MEDIUM P AND T	LOW P/ HIGH T
shale, mudstone (pelitic)	paragonite, muscovite	muscovite, paragonite	muscovite
	kyanite	chlorite	biotite
	Mg-chloritoid	biotite	andalusite, sillimanite
	Mg-carpholite	chloritoid	cordierite
	jadeite	garnet	plagioclase
	chlorite	staurolite	orthopyroxene
	pyrope garnet	andalusite, kyanite, sillimanite	microcline, sanidine
	talc	plagioclase	mullite
	coesite	alkali feldspar	spinel
		cordierite	tridymite
		orthopyroxene	
limestone, dolostone, marl (calcareous)	aragonite	calcite	wollastonite

PROTOLITH	HIGH P/ LOW T	MEDIUM P AND T	LOW P/ HIGH T
	magnesite	dolomite	grossular garnet
	lawsonite	tremolite	diopside
	zoisite	diopside	plagioclase
	jadeite	epidote, clinozoisite	vesuvianite
	talc	grossular garnet	clinozoisite
			forsterite
			brucite
			talc
granite, grano-diorite, arkose (felsic)	jadeite	plagioclase	plagioclase
	paragonite	alkali feldspar	alkali feldspar
		muscovite	sillimanite
		biotite	cordierite
		garnet	
		sillimanite	
basalt, andes-ite (mafic)	glaucophane	plagioclase	plagioclase
	lawsonite	chlorite	biotite
	garnet	biotite	garnet
	omphacite	garnet	hornblende
	epidote	epidote	diopside
	albite	actinolite	
	chlorite	hornblende	
		diopside	
		orthopyroxene	

*Quartz may be present in all categories. Minor phases such as oxides and sulfides have been omitted.

Thermodynamics of Metamorphic Assemblages

Despite the large number of minerals that can be included in each of the four bulk compositions listed in the previous table, the actual number of minerals present in an individual metamorphic rock is limited by the laws of thermodynamics. The number of mineral phases that can coexist stably in a metamorphic rock at a particular set of pressure-temperature conditions is given by the Gibbs phase rule (named for American physicist J. Willard Gibbs): number of mineral phases = number of chemical components - number of degrees of freedom + 2, where the 2 stands for the two variables of pressure and temperature. The degrees of freedom of the system are the parameters that can be independently varied without changing the mineral assemblage of the rock. For example, a rock with no degrees of freedom can only exist at a single set of pressure-temperature conditions; if either the pressure or the temperature is varied, the minerals will react with one another to change the assemblage. A rock with two degrees of freedom can undergo small changes in pressure or temperature or both without altering the assemblage. Most metamorphic rocks have mineral assemblages that reflect two or more degrees of freedom at the time the rock recrystallized. Thus, a typical pelitic rock made up of the six chemical components silica (SiO_2), aluminum oxide (Al_2O_3), ferrous oxide (FeO), magnesium oxide (MgO), potash (K_2O), and water would contain no more than six minerals; the identity of those minerals would be controlled by the pressure and temperature at which recrystallization occurred. In such a rock taken from Earth's surface, the identity of the six minerals could be used to infer the approximate depth and temperature conditions that prevailed at the time of its recrystallization. Rocks that contain more mineral phases than would be predicted by the phase rule often preserve evidence of chemical disequilibrium in the form of reactions that did not go to completion. Careful examination of such samples under the microscope can often reveal the nature of these reactions and provide useful information on how pressure and temperature conditions changed during the burial and uplift history of the rock.

Metamorphic rocks only rarely exhibit a chemical composition that is characteristically "metamorphic." That is, the diffusion of materials in metamorphism is a slow process, and various chemical units do not mix on any large scale. But occasionally, particularly during contact metamorphism, diffusion may occur across a boundary of chemical dissimilarity, leading to rocks of unique composition. This process is referred to as metasomatism. If a granite is emplaced into a limestone, the contact region may be flooded with silica and other components, leading to the formation of a metasomatic rock. Often such contacts are chemically zoned. A simple example is provided by the metamorphism of magnesium-rich igneous rocks in contact with quartz-rich sediments. A zonation of the type serpentine-talc-quartz may be found such as:

$$Mg_6(Si_4O_{10})(OH)_8 - Mg_3(Si_4O_{10})(OH)_2 - SiO_2.$$

In this case the talc zone has grown by silica diffusion into the more silica-poor environment of the serpentine. Economic deposits are not uncommon in such situations—e.g., the formation of the $CaWO_4$ (calcium tungstate) scheelite when tungstate in the form of WO_3 moves from a granite into a limestone contact. The reaction can be expressed as:

$$CaCO_3 + WO_3 \text{ (solution)} \rightarrow CaWO_4 + CO_2 \text{ (gas)}.$$

calcite   scheelite

METAMORPHIC REACTIONS

The metamorphic reaction process involves burial and heating. As pressure and temperature build, water is released from the rock and the rock's chemistry begins to change. This section provides additional details on this process following the path of kaolinite-quartz. Other aspects of metamorphic reactions—such as the reactions of other mineral systems, the principal types of metamorphic reactions, and the roles that isograds and retrograde metamorphism play—are discussed in the following sections.

REACTIONS IN A KAOLINITE-QUARTZ SYSTEM

A very simple mineralogical system and its response to changing pressure and temperature provide a good illustration of what occurs in metamorphism. An uncomplicated sediment at Earth's surface, a mixture of the clay mineral kaolinite [$Al_4Si_4O_{10}(OH)_8$] and the mineral quartz (SiO_2), provides a good example. Most sediments have small crystals or grain sizes but great porosity and permeability, and the pores are filled with water. As time passes, more sediments are piled on top of the surface layer, and it becomes slowly buried. Accordingly, the pressure to which the layer is subjected increases because of the load on top, known as overburden. At the same time, the temperature will increase because of radioactive heating within the sediment and heat flow from deeper levels within Earth.

In the first stages of incremental burial and heating, few chemical reactions will occur in the sediment layer, but the porosity decreases, and the low-density pore water is squeezed out. This process will be nearly complete by

the time the layer is buried by 5 km (about 3 miles) of overburden. There will be some increase in the size of crystals;
small crystals with a large surface area are more soluble and
less stable than large crystals, and throughout metamorphic processes there is a tendency for crystals to grow in
size with time, particularly if the temperature is rising.

Eventually, when the rock is buried to a depth at which
temperatures of about 300 °C (about 570 °F) obtain, a
chemical reaction sets in, and the kaolinite and quartz are
transformed to pyrophyllite and water:

$$Al_4Si_4O_{10}(OH)_8 + 4SiO_2 \longrightarrow 2Al_2Si_4O_{10}(OH)_2 + 2H_2O.$$

kaolinite   quartz   pyrophyllite   water

The exact temperature at which this occurs depends
on the fluid pressure in the system, but in general the fluid
and rock-load pressures tend to be rather similar during
such reactions. The water virtually fights its way out by
lifting the rocks. Thus, the first chemical reaction is a
dehydration reaction leading to the formation of a new
hydrate. The water released is itself a solvent for silicates
and promotes the crystallization of the product phases.

If heating and burial continue, another dehydration
sets in at about 400 °C (about 750 °F), in which the pyrophyllite is transformed to andalusite, quartz, and water:

$$Al_2Si_4O_{10}(OH)_2 \longrightarrow Al_2SiO_5 + 3SiO_2 + H_2O.$$

pyrophyllite   andalusite quartz water

After the water has escaped, the rock becomes virtually anhydrous, containing only traces of fluid in small
inclusions in the product crystals and along grain boundaries. Both of these dehydration reactions tend to be fast,
because water, a good silicate solvent, is present.

Although the mineral andalusite is indicated as the first product of dehydration of pyrophyllite, there are three minerals with the chemical composition Al_2SiO_5. Each has unique crystal structures, and each is stable under definite pressure-temperature conditions. Such differing forms with identical composition are called polymorphs. If pyrophyllite is dehydrated under high-pressure conditions, the polymorph of Al_2SiO_5 formed would be the mineral kyanite (the most dense polymorph). With continued heating, the original andalusite or kyanite will invert to sillimanite, the highest-temperature Al_2SiO_5 polymorph:

$$Al_2SiO_5 \longrightarrow Al_2SiO_5$$
andalusite   sillimanite
or kyanite

The kinetics of these polymorphic transformations are sufficiently sluggish, however, that kyanite or andalusite may persist well into the stability field of sillimanite.

REACTIONS OF OTHER MINERAL SYSTEMS

Owing to the very simple bulk composition of the protolith in this example (a subset of the pelitic system containing only SiO_2-Al_2O_3-H_2O), no other mineralogical changes will occur with continued heating or burial. The original sediment composed of kaolinite, quartz, and water will thus have been metamorphosed into a rock composed of sillimanite and quartz, and perhaps some metastable andalusite or kyanite, depending on the details of the burial and heating history. In the case of a more typical pelite containing the additional chemical components potash, ferrous oxide, and magnesium oxide, the reaction history would be correspondingly more complex. A typical shale that undergoes burial and heating in response to continent-continent collision would develop the minerals muscovite, chlorite, biotite, garnet, staurolite, kyanite, sillimanite, and alkali feldspar, in approximately that order, before beginning to melt at about 700 °C (about 1,300 °F). Each of these minerals appears in response to a chemical reaction similar to those presented above. Most of these reactions are dehydration reactions, and the shale thus loses water progressively throughout the entire metamorphic event. As discussed above, the total number of minerals present in the rock is controlled by the Gibbs phase rule, and the addition of new minerals generally results from the breakdown of old minerals. For example, the following reaction,

garnet + muscovite + chlorite ⟶

staurolite + biotite + quartz + water,

occurs at temperatures of about 500–550 °C (about 930–1,022 °F) and typically consumes all the preexisting chlorite in the rock, introduces the new mineral staurolite, and adds more biotite and quartz to the biotite and quartz generated by earlier reactions. Some garnet and muscovite usually remain after the reaction, although examination of the sample under the microscope would probably reveal partial corrosion (wearing away due to chemical reactions) of the garnets resulting from their consumption.

ISOGRADS

Reactions that introduce new minerals in rocks of a specific bulk composition are referred to as mineral appearance isograds. Isograds can be mapped in the field as lines across which the metamorphic mineral assemblage changes. Caution must be exercised to note the approximate bulk composition of the rocks throughout the map area, however, because the same mineral can develop at quite different sets of pressure-temperature conditions in rocks of dissimilar chemical composition. For example, garnet generally appears at a lower temperature in pelitic rocks than it does in mafic rocks; hence, the garnet isograd in pelitic rocks will not be the same map line as that in metabasaltic (i.e., metamorphosed basalt) compositions. Isograd patterns are discussed further in the section on structural features.

PRINCIPAL TYPES

Metamorphic reactions can be classified into two types that show different degrees of sensitivity to temperature and pressure changes: net-transfer reactions and exchange reactions. Net-transfer reactions involve the breakdown of preexisting mineral phases and corresponding nucleation and growth of new phases. (Nucleation is the process in which a crystal begins to grow from one or more points, or nuclei.) They can be either solid-solid reactions (mineral A + mineral B = mineral C + mineral D) or devolatilization reactions (hydrous mineral A = anhydrous mineral B + water), but in either case they require significant breaking of bonds and reorganization of material in the rock. They may depend most strongly on either temperature or pressure changes. In general, devolatilization reactions are temperature-sensitive, reflecting the large increase in entropy (disorder) that accompanies release of structurally bound hydroxyl groups (OH) from minerals to produce molecular water. Net-transfer reactions that involve a significant change in density of the participating mineral phases are typically more sensitive to changes in pressure than in temperature. An example is the transformation of albite ($NaAlSi_3O_8$) to the sodic pyroxene jadeite ($NaAlSi_2O_6$) plus quartz (SiO_2); albite and quartz have similar densities of about 2.58 grams per cubic cm (1.49 ounces per cubic inch), whereas jadeite has a density of 3.27 grams per cubic cm (1.89 ounces per cubic inch). The increased density reflects the closer packing of atoms in the jadeite structure. Not surprisingly, the denser phase jadeite is produced during subduction zone (high-pressure) metamorphism. Net-transfer reactions always involve a change in mineral assemblage, and textural evidence of the reaction often remains in the sample; isograd reactions are invariably net-transfer reactions.

In contrast to net-transfer reactions, exchange reactions involve redistribution of atoms between preexisting phases rather than nucleation and growth of new phases. The reactions result simply in compositional changes of minerals already present in the rock and do not modify the mineral assemblage. For example, the reaction

$$Fe_3Al_2Si_3O_{12} + KMg_3AlSi_3O_{10}(OH)_2 \longrightarrow$$
almandine garnet   magnesium-biotite

$$Mg_3Al_2Si_3O_{12} + KFe_3AlSi_3O_{10}(OH)_2$$
pyrope garnet   iron-biotite

results in redistribution of iron and magnesium between garnet and biotite but creates no new phases. This reaction is limited by the rates at which iron and magnesium can diffuse through the garnet and biotite structures. Because diffusion processes are strongly controlled by temperature but are nearly unaffected by pressure, exchange reactions are typically sensitive to changes only in metamorphic temperature. Exchange reactions leave no textual record in the sample and can be determined only by detailed microanalysis of the constituent mineral phases. The compositions of minerals as controlled by exchange reactions can provide a useful record of the temperature history of a metamorphic sample.

The types of reactions cited here are typical of all metamorphic changes. Gases are lost (hydrous minerals lose water, carbonates lose carbon dioxide), and mineral phases undergo polymorphic or other structural changes; low-volume, dense mineral species are formed by high pressures, and less dense phases are favoured by high temperatures. Considering the immense chemical and mineralogical complexity of Earth's crust, it is clear that the number of possible reactions is vast. In any given complex column of crustal materials some chemical reaction is likely for almost any incremental change in pressure and temperature. This is a fact of immense importance in unraveling Earth's history and mechanics, for such changes constitute a vital record and are the primary reason for the study of metamorphic rocks.

RETROGRADE METAMORPHISM

In general, the changes in mineral assemblage and mineral composition that occur during burial and heating are referred to as prograde metamorphism, whereas those that occur during uplift and cooling of a rock represent retrograde metamorphism. If thermodynamic equilibrium were always maintained, one might expect all the reactions that occur during prograde metamorphism to be reversed during subsequent uplift of the rocks and reexposure at Earth's surface; in this case, metamorphic rocks would never be seen in outcrop. Two factors mitigate against complete retrogression of metamorphic rocks, however, during their return to Earth's surface. First is the efficient removal of the water and carbon dioxide released during prograde devolatilization reactions by upward migration of the fluid along grain boundaries and through fractures. Because almost all the water released during heating by reactions such as

$$Fe_9Al_6Si_5O_{20}(OH)_{16} + 4SiO_2 \longrightarrow 3Fe_3Al_2Si_3O_{12} + 8H_2O$$
$$\text{chlorite} \qquad \text{quartz} \qquad \text{garnet} \qquad \text{water}$$

is removed from the site of reaction, the reaction cannot be reversed during cooling unless water is subsequently added to the rock. Thus, garnet can be preserved at Earth's surface even though it is thermodynamically unstable at such low temperatures and pressures. The second reason that metamorphic reactions do not typically operate in reverse during cooling is that reaction rates are increased by rising temperatures. During cooling, reaction kinetics become sluggish, and metastable mineral assemblages and compositions can be preserved well outside their normal stability fields. Thus, prograde reactions are generally more efficient than retrograde reactions, and metamorphic assemblages indicative of even extremely high temperatures or pressures or both are found exposed throughout the world. It is common, however, to find at least some signs of retrogression in most metamorphic rocks. For example, garnets are often rimmed by small amounts of chlorite and quartz, indicating that limited quantities of water were available for the reverse of the reaction given above to proceed during cooling. Retrograde features such as these reaction rims can be mapped to yield information on pathways of fluid migration through the rocks during uplift and cooling. In other rocks, such as high-temperature gneisses, mineral compositions often reflect temperatures too low to be in equilibrium with the preserved mineral assemblage; in these samples, it is clear that certain exchange reactions operated in a retrograde sense even when the net-transfer reactions were frozen in during prograde metamorphism.

TEXTURAL FEATURES

The fabric of a metamorphic rock results from the combined effects of mineral reactions and deformation throughout the metamorphic event and the subsequent return of the rock to the terrestrial surface. The study of metamorphic fabrics in outcrop and under the microscope has become a highly specialized subject aimed at revealing the nature and direction of the forces acting during dynamic processes within Earth. Much of this work is an outgrowth of a classic investigation conducted in 1930 by the Austrian geologist Bruno Sander, coupled with more recent experimental work on the pressure-temperature stabilities of metamorphic minerals and their responses to deformation.

Observations show that pressure is only rarely hydrostatic (equal in all directions) at any point within Earth's crust. In real cases, consequently, anisotropic stresses operate that may lead to flow or fracture of materials. Such occurrences produce certain characteristic fabrics or structures in metamorphic rocks that may be observed at the scale of the orientation of small crystals in a rock or as a pattern of folds in a mountain range. One of the principal characteristics of most metamorphic rocks is that the arrangement of crystals is not isotropic, or random, but that there is a strong preferred orientation related to the direction of stress components of pressure. Such preferred orientation of crystals and mineral grains is perhaps the most striking difference between metamorphic rocks and other rock types.

MAJOR FEATURES

The most obvious features of metamorphic rocks are certain planar features that are often termed s-surfaces. The simplest planar features may be primary bedding (akin to the layering in sedimentary rocks). As the rock crystallizes or recrystallizes under directed pressure, new crystals may grow in some preferred direction, sometimes subparallel to the primary bedding but often at new angles defining new planar structures. At the same time, folding of layers may occur, leading to folds with amplitudes on scales of kilometres or millimetres. Fabric symmetry may be represented by the nature of deformed fossils, pebbles in a conglomerate, or any objects with a known shape prior to deformation.

A few terms that commonly are used to describe several types of preferred orientation in metamorphic rocks include foliation, a general term describing any type of s-surface, bedding, or crystal orientation; slaty cleavage, a planar structure leading to facile cleavage that is normally caused by the preferred orientation of mica crystals; schistosity, a term used to describe repetitive and pronounced foliation of the type that is present in schists; and lineation, which is any linear structure, such as the axis of the fold, grooves on a fault plane, or the direction of stretching of pebbles.

The various mineral phases of a metamorphic rock have different physical properties and symmetries. When a rock is subjected to recrystallization in a stress field, different substances will behave differently according to such physical properties and symmetries. Some minerals always tend to grow in better-formed crystals than others; rates of nucleation may differ, and this can lead to different patterns of growth of crystals—there may be a few large crystals or a mass of small crystals. Minerals can be arranged in order of their tendency to form crystals showing planar surfaces—namely, magnetite, garnet, epidote, mica, calcite, quartz, and feldspar. Minerals that have a tendency to form large single crystals (e.g., garnet) are termed porphyroblasts.

Porphyroblastic crystals may grow before, during, or after an episode of deformation (pre-, syn-, and post-kinematic growth, respectively); the relative timing of mineral growth and deformation can often be determined by examining the sample under a microscope. Prekinematic porphyroblasts may be fractured by subsequent deformation; the orientation of the fractures and any offset of the grains along them provide information on the directed stresses responsible for the deformation. Prekinematic grains may also be surrounded by pressure shadows produced by minerals such as quartz that dissolve in zones of maximum compressive stress and reprecipitate in zones of lesser compressive stress adjacent to the rigid porphyroblasts. The texture of the shadows is different from that of the host rock. Samples exhibiting asymmetric pressure shadows around porphyroblasts can yield information on the orientation of shear stresses during deformation. A spectacular example of synkinematic prophyroblast growth is provided by the so-called snowball garnets, which have spiral trails of inclusions that indicate rotation of either the garnet or the matrix foliation during garnet growth. Postkinematic porphyroblasts typically overgrow all previous fabrics in the rock and may contain trails of mineral inclusions that define microfolds or an earlier schistosity.

In some samples, it is possible to use the compositions of the porphyroblasts to calculate the depth and temperature conditions at which they grew and thereby constrain the conditions at which deformation occurred. Studies of this sort add immeasurably to the understanding of crustal rheologies and the response of rocks to large-scale orogenic events. Because a particular metamorphic event may be accompanied by either several isolated episodes of deformation or a single continuum of deformation, there may be many fabric generations recorded in one sample; individual minerals may be postkinematic with respect to the earliest deformation but prekinematic relative to younger deformation in the same rock. Thus, the study of

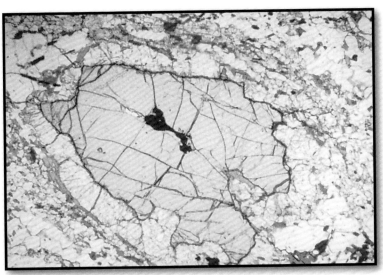

Photomicrograph showing corroded garnet (darker gray) surrounded by a corona of cordierite produced during uplift of the sample. Other minerals present are biotite, plagioclase, sillimanite, alkali feldspar, and ilmenite. The garnet is two millimetres across. Jane Selverstone

porphyroblast fabrics in metamorphic rocks can be complex but has the potential to yield important information on the structural history of metamorphic regions.

Because changes in pressure and temperature often occur at faster rates than those of mineral reaction and recrystallization, metamorphic rocks may display fabrics that result from incomplete reactions. Such disequilibrium features provide a wealth of information on the reaction history of the sample and, by comparison with experimental studies of mineral stabilities, can also constrain the quantitative pressure-temperature history of the rock during metamorphism.

An example of a reaction texture can be described. For example, a corroded garnet is surrounded by a corona (reaction rim) of the mineral cordierite; other minerals present in the matrix include sillimanite, quartz, biotite, and alkali feldspar. The sample does not contain garnet in contact with sillimanite or quartz. These textural features suggest the following reaction relationship between garnet, sillimanite, quartz, and cordierite:

$$2Mg_3Al_2Si_3O_{12} + 4Al_2SiO_5 + 5SiO_2 \rightleftharpoons 3Mg_2Al_4Si_5O_{18}.$$

garnet \quad\quad\quad sillimanite \quad quartz \quad\quad\quad cordierite

This reaction has been shown experimentally to occur at temperatures of approximately $725° \pm 50$ °C ($1{,}337° \pm 122$ °F) and to be very sensitive to pressure, with cordierite occurring under low-pressure conditions. The textural evidence that preexisting garnet was partially replaced by cordierite thus implies that the rock underwent decompression while still at high temperatures and that the decompression occurred too rapidly for the rock to recrystallize completely (i.e., for garnet to be totally replaced by cordierite).

LAMINATION

There is also a tendency for many types of metamorphic rocks to become laminated, and the separate laminae may have distinct chemical compositions. A macroscopically rather homogeneous sediment may prove to be inhomogeneous on a minute scale. When graywackes are metamorphosed within the greenschist facies, for example, laminae rich in quartz and feldspar alternate with others rich in epidote, chlorite, and muscovite. The precise causes of this process are not well known, but it may result from a combination of extensive deformation accompanied by recrystallization. In a sense, it is a type of flow unmixing. It is important to recognize that this type of structure need have no relation to original bedding in the unmetamorphosed sediments.

STRUCTURAL FEATURES

Metamorphic rocks are often intimately related to large-scale (kilometres of tens of kilometres) structural features of Earth. Such features include folds, nappes, and faults with a wide variety of geometries. In many cases, the correlation of metamorphic isograds and their position in the structure implies a genetic relationship between the two. For example, one of the major structural features in the Himalayan mountain belt is the Main Central Thrust, a thrust fault that runs for hundreds of kilometres from east to west and was responsible for the transportation of rocks belonging to the Eurasian Plate southward over those of the Indian Plate. Along much of the length of this fault, the metamorphic rocks in the hanging wall (located above the fault) display a pattern of inverted isograds; i.e., the rocks that reached the highest temperatures of metamorphism overlie rocks that record lower temperatures, implying that metamorphic temperatures decreased with depth to the fault. Several explanations have been proposed to account for this anomalous distribution of temperature with depth. One model suggests the fault transported hot Asian rocks over cooler Indian rocks, which caused cooling of the Asian rocks in the vicinity of the fault. Another model proposes that fluids circulating along the fault zone caused retrograde metamorphism and thus reset the rocks located nearest to the fault to lower temperatures. Although neither of these models provides an adequate explanation for the entire length of the Main Central Thrust, they both emphasize the significant control that structural features can exert on the development of metamorphic rocks.

Metamorphism associated with nappes (large recumbent folds) in the Alps and the Appalachians provides strong evidence that the tectonic transport of rocks typically occurs at rates faster than those of thermal equilibration—in other words, that the nappes can transport hot rocks for large distances without significant cooling. Nappe formation is a major process of crustal thickening during continent-continent collision; emplacement of the nappes results in burial and heating of the underlying rocks. Isograd distributions associated with nappe structures can be either normal or inverted, depending on the relative rates of nappe emplacement and heat transfer.

Isograd maps can provide information on the relative timing of structural and metamorphic events in much the same way that fabric studies constrain the relative timing of deformation episodes and prophyroblast growth. For example, isograd patterns that are cut by faults clearly indicate that metamorphism predated fault displacement, whereas isograd sequences that overprint structural discontinuities imply the reverse. Isograds that parallel major structures suggest some cause-and-effect relationship between the structural and metamorphic development of the region. Since the 1980s, metamorphic petrologists and structural geologists have increasingly worked together to correlate metamorphic and tectonic events and thereby increase understanding of crustal dynamics in tectonically active regions of Earth.

METAMORPHIC FACIES

Metamorphic petrologists studying contact metamorphism early in the 20th century introduced the idea of metamorphic facies to correlate metamorphic events. The concept was first defined in 1914 by a Finnish petrologist, Pentti Eelis Eskola, as any rock of a metamorphic formation that has attained chemical equilibrium through metamorphism at constant temperature and pressure conditions, with its mineral composition controlled only by the chemical composition. In current usage, a metamorphic facies is a set of metamorphic mineral assemblages, repeatedly associated in space and time, such that there is a constant and therefore predictable relation between mineral composition and chemical composition.

The facies concept is more or less observation-based. In a single outcrop, for instance, layers of different chemical composition will display different mineral assemblages despite having all experienced the same pressure and temperature history. A pelitic layer might contain the assemblage garnet + chlorite + biotite + muscovite + quartz, whereas a basaltic horizon a few centimetres away would contain the assemblage chlorite + actinolite + albite. Both of these rocks belong to the same facies, meaning that, in another region, a geologist who observed the assemblage chlorite + actinolite + albite in a metabasalt could predict that associated pelitic rocks would contain the garnet + chlorite + biotite + muscovite + quartz assemblage.

Experimental work on the relative stabilities of metamorphic minerals and assemblages has permitted correlation of the empirically derived facies with quantitative pressure and temperature conditions. The names of metamorphic facies in common usage are derived from the behaviour of a rock of basaltic bulk composition during metamorphism at various sets of pressure-temperature conditions. For example, a basalt metamorphosed during subduction to high pressures at low temperatures recrystallizes into a rock containing glaucophane, lawsonite, and albite; glaucophane is a sodic amphibole that is blue to black in hand sample and lavender to blue under the microscope. Because of their distinctive bluish coloration, such samples are called blueschists. The same rock type metamorphosed at more moderate pressures and temperatures in the range of 400–500 °C (about 750–930 °F) would contain abundant chlorite and actinolite, minerals that are green both in hand sample and under the microscope, and would be referred to as a greenschist. At somewhat higher temperatures, the rock would become an amphibolite, reflecting a mineralogy composed predominantly of the amphibole hornblende along with plagioclase and perhaps some garnet. At still higher temperatures, a metabasalt recrystallizes into a rock containing hypersthene, diopside, and plagioclase; in general, these minerals form relatively equant crystals and hence do not develop a preferred orientation. The granular texture of these rocks has resulted in the name granulite for a high-temperature metabasalt. A pelitic or calcareous rock will develop very different mineral assemblages from a metabasalt, yet the same facies names apply. Thus, one can refer to a greenschist facies pelitic schist, an amphibolite facies calcsilicate rock, or a granulite facies garnet gneiss.

The boundaries between the different facies are regions of pressure and temperature in which chemical reactions occur that would significantly alter the mineralogy of a rock of basaltic bulk composition. For example, the boundary between the greenschist and amphibolite facies marks a transition from amphibole of actinolitic composition to hornblende and of a sodic plagioclase into a more calcic plagioclase. The reactions that bring about these transformations depend on the specific composition of the rock.

FACIES SERIES

Different types of tectonic processes produce different associations of metamorphic facies in the field. For example, regions associated with subduction of oceanic material beneath either oceanic or continental crust are characterized by blueschist, greenschist, and eclogite facies rocks, whereas areas thought to reflect continent-continent collision are more typically distinguished by greenschist and amphibolite facies rocks. Still other regions, usually containing an abundance of intrusive igneous material, show associations of low-pressure greenschist, amphibolite, and granulite facies rocks. These observations led a Japanese petrologist, Akiho Miyashiro, working in the 1960s and '70s, to develop the concept of baric types, or metamorphic facies series. Miyashiro described the three facies associations given above as high-pressure, medium-pressure, and low-pressure facies series, respectively, and correlated the development of these characteristic series with the shape of the geotherm in different tectonic settings. Subsequent thermal modeling studies have shown that metamorphism generally occurs in response to tectonically induced perturbation of geotherms rather than along steady-state geotherms and, hence, that the facies series do not record metamorphic geotherms. Nonetheless, the concept of metamorphic facies series is a useful one in that it emphasizes the strong genetic relationship between metamorphic style and tectonic setting.

Pressure-Temperature-Time Paths

Interaction between metamorphic petrologists and geophysicists in the 1980s led to the realization that each metamorphic rock follows its own unique path through pressure- (depth-) temperature space during metamorphism and that these paths bear little or no resemblance to steady-state geotherms. The specific shape of a pressure-temperature-time (P-T-t) path depends on the tectonic setting in which the rock was metamorphosed, which in turn controls the relative rates at which burial or uplift and heating or cooling occur. For example, a rock that is uplifted rapidly from depth, perhaps in response to extensional faulting (that caused by the stretching of Earth's crust), may transport heat with it to near-surface depths. Its P-T-t path would show a phase of nearly isothermal decompression (uplift at approximately constant temperature), reflecting the fact that uplift rates were more rapid than those of heat transfer. In contrast, if the same rock remained at depth for a long period of time and then experienced very slow uplift, its P-T-t path would show cooling during uplift or even a phase of isobaric (constant-pressure) cooling. Rocks belonging to medium-pressure facies series generally follow P-T-t paths that

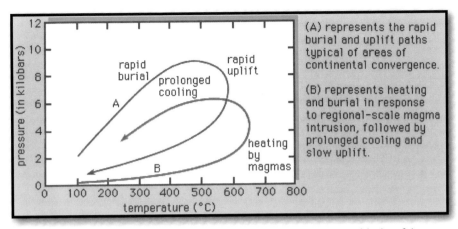

Examples of pressure-temperature-time paths that would be followed by rocks metamorphosed in different environments. Copyright Encyclopædia Britannica, Inc.; rendering for this edition by Rosen Educational Services

are clockwise loops on a pressure-temperature diagram, reflecting rapid burial during a collisional event followed by heating and relatively rapid uplift. In contrast, low-pressure facies series rocks may follow counterclockwise P-T-t paths in response to rapid heating of the crust due to magma intrusion prior to uplift. P-T-t paths followed by rocks of a high-pressure facies series are less predictable and depend strongly on the mechanism by which the rocks are transferred from the subducting slab to the overlying continental crust. In general, the mineral assemblage preserved in a metamorphic rock is frozen at the highest temperature experienced during metamorphism, and thus the facies and facies series to which the rock would be assigned reflect only a single point on its P-T-t path.

One of the principal goals of much of the work that is done on metamorphic rocks is the reconstruction of the P-T-t paths followed by rocks presently exposed at Earth's surface. Because these paths are so strongly linked to dynamic processes, their reconstruction provides a means by which tectonic processes operative in the geologic past may be understood. Owing to the continuous recrystallization of rocks that occurs during progressive metamorphism, much of the early record of metamorphic changes within a sample is eradicated by later events. It is, therefore, not possible to determine the entire P-T-t path followed by an individual sample, but often enough disequilibrium features are preserved to permit reconstruction of a few thousand bars and a couple of hundred degrees of the path; such a portion may represent anywhere from a few million to a hundred million years of Earth history, as revealed by geochronologic determinations involving different minerals or fabric generations in the sample. Techniques for determining the pressure-temperature history of a metamorphic rock include using compositions of coexisting minerals to calculate pressures and temperatures of equilibration (geobarometry and geothermometry, respectively), comparing the mineral assemblage to experimentally determined stability fields for the phases, utilizing mineral inclusions enclosed within porphyroblasts to constrain assemblages present in the early history of the sample, and making use of the densities of small inclusions of fluids trapped within the minerals to determine possible pressures and temperatures experienced at different stages in the burial and uplift history.

ORIGIN OF METAMORPHIC ROCKS: TYPES OF METAMORPHISM

It is convenient to distinguish several general types of metamorphism in order to simplify the description of the various metamorphic phenomena. Recognized here are hydrothermal, dynamic, contact, and regional metamorphism, each of which will be described in turn.

METAMORPHISM

Metamorphism is the process by which mineralogical and structural adjustments occur in solid rocks in response to their current physical and chemical conditions, which differ from those under which the rocks originally formed. Changes produced by surface conditions such as compaction are usually excluded. The most important agents of metamorphism include temperature, pressure, and fluids. Equally as significant are changes in chemical environment that result in two metamorphic processes: (1) mechanical dislocation where a rock is deformed, especially as a consequence of differential stress; and (2) chemical recrystallization where a mineral assemblage becomes out of equilibrium due to temperature and pressure changes and a new mineral assemblage forms.

Three types of metamorphism may occur depending on the relative effect of mechanical and chemical changes. Dynamic metamorphism, or cataclasis, results mainly from mechanical deformation with little long-term temperature change. Textures produced by such adjustments range from breccias composed of angular, shattered rock fragments to very fine-grained, granulated or powdered rocks with obvious foliation and lineation. Large, pre-existing mineral grains may be deformed as a result of stress. Contact metamorphism occurs primarily as a consequence of increases in temperature when differential stress is minor. A common phenomenon is the effect produced adjacent to igneous intrusions where several metamorphic zones represented by changing mineral assemblages reflect the temperature gradient from the high-temperature intrusion to the low-temperature host rocks; these zones are concentric to the intrusion. Because the volume affected is small, the pressure is near constant. Resulting rocks have equidimensional grains because of a lack of stress and are usually fine-grained due to the short duration of metamorphism. Regional metamorphism results from the general increase, usually correlated, of temperature and pressure over a large area. Grades or intensities of metamorphism are represented by different mineral assemblages that either give relative values of temperature or absolute values when calibrated against laboratory experiments. Regional metamorphism can be subdivided into different pressure-temperature conditions based on observed sequences of mineral assemblages. It may include an extreme condition, where partial melting occurs, called anatexis.

Other types of metamorphism can occur. They are retrograde metamorphism, the response of mineral assemblages to decreasing temperature and pressure; metasomatism, the metamorphism that includes the addition or subtraction of components from the original assemblage; poly-metamorphism, the effect of more than one metamorphic event; and hydrothermal metamorphism, the changes that occur in the presence of water at high temperature and pressure which affect the resulting mineralogy and rate of reaction.

HYDROTHERMAL METAMORPHISM

Changes that occur in rocks near the surface, where there is intense activity of hot water, are categorized as hydrothermal metamorphism. Such areas include Yellowstone National Park in the northwestern United States, the Salton Sea in California, and Wairakei in New Zealand. It is now generally recognized that the circulating groundwaters that often become heated by their proximity to igneous materials produce the metamorphism. Migration of chemical elements, vein formation, and other kinds of mineral concentration may be extreme on account of the large volumes of water circulated.

DYNAMIC METAMORPHISM

When directed pressure or stress is the dominant agent of metamorphism, it is termed dynamic; other terms are dislocation, kinematic, and mechanical metamorphism. Mineralogical changes occurring on a fault plane provide an obvious example. In some such cases, the action may simply be a grinding up of existing grains or realignment of minerals that have non-equant crystals. If the action is intense, friction may even lead to melting.

CONTACT METAMORPHISM

Whenever silicate melts (magmas, from which igneous rocks crystallize within Earth) invade the crust at any level, they perturb the normal thermal regime and cause a heat increase in the vicinity. If a mass of basaltic liquid ascending from the upper mantle is trapped in the crust and crystallizes there, it will heat the surrounding area; the amount of heating and its duration will be a direct function of the mass and shape of the igneous material. Contact-metamorphic phenomena thus occur in the vicinity of hot igneous materials and at any depth. Under such circumstances, pressure and temperature are not simply correlated. Thermal gradients are often steep unless the igneous mass is extremely large. Contact aureoles—the surrounding zones of rock that become altered or metamorphosed—vary in thickness from several centimetres (around tabular bodies such as dikes and thin sills) to several kilometres (around large granitic intrusions). The contact metamorphic rocks of the aureole zone often lack any obvious schistosity or foliation.

The facies associated with contact metamorphism include the sanidinite, pyroxenite-hornfels, hornblende-hornfels, and albite-epidote-hornfels facies.

SANIDINITE FACIES

Rocks of the sanidinite facies are represented by small fragments of aureole materials that have often been totally immersed in silicate liquids or by the aureole rocks surrounding volcanic pipes. Very high temperatures are attained, often at very low pressures. The dominant feature of the mineralogy of this facies is an almost complete lack of minerals containing water or carbon dioxide. Many of the minerals show similarity to those of igneous rocks themselves. If the duration of heating is short, adjustment to the imposed temperature is often imperfect.

Pelitic rocks (high in aluminum oxide) contain minerals such as mullite, sillimanite, sanidine, cordierite, spinel, hypersthene, anorthite, tridymite, and even glass. One of the classic localities of such rocks is the island of Mull, off the west coast of Scotland, but these rocks can be found in most regions of volcanism.

Calcareous rocks (originally impure limestones or dolomites) tend to lose nearly all their carbon dioxide, but pure calcite may survive. Typical metamorphic minerals are quartz, wollastonite, anorthite, diopside, periclase, and in some places (the classic is Scawt Hill in Northern Ireland) an array of complex calcium silicates such as spurrite, larnite, rankinite, melilite, merwinite, and monticellite. These minerals result from the addition of varying amounts of silica to impure mixtures of calcite and dolomite. In a general way the minerals of this facies are reminiscent of those of industrial slags.

PYROXENE-HORNFELS FACIES

Rocks of the pyroxene-hornfels facies are characteristically formed near larger granitic or gabbroic bodies at depths of a few kilometres or at pressures of a few hundred bars. The mineral assemblages are again largely anhydrous, but, unlike the sanidinite facies, the minerals reflect distinctly lower temperatures. One of the classic descriptions of such rocks is from the Oslo district of Norway.

In pelitic rocks, minerals such as quartz, orthoclase, andalusite, sillimanite, cordierite, orthopyroxene, and plagioclase occur. Sometimes the hydrate biotite is developed. In calcareous rocks the minerals found include plagioclase, diopside, grossularite, vesuvianite, wollastonite, and sometimes the more complex calcium silicates monticellite, melilite, spurrite, tilleyite, and clinohumite.

HORNBLENDE-HORNFELS FACIES

A generally deeper level of contact metamorphism at pressures of a few kilobars is represented by the hornblende-hornfels facies. Hydrated phases become stable, and the transition to regional metamorphism becomes apparent. Because of the generally greater depth, this type of aureole is often superposed on a metamorphism at more normal pressure-temperature conditions, and the rocks may appear schistose and exhibit new thermally generated minerals on a preexisting assemblage. This type of metamorphism develops the classic "spotted" texture in which new porphyroblasts grow in slates and phyllites of a previous episode of metamorphism. Typically, such rocks are developed near most of the world's large granite batholiths.

Typical minerals of pelitic assemblages include quartz, muscovite, biotite, andalusite, sillimanite, cordierite, plagioclase, microcline, and staurolite. Calcareous assemblages include calcite, quartz, diopside, grossular, plagioclase, wollastonite, brucite, talc, forsterite, tremolite, and clinozoisite. Basaltic compositions include plagioclase, hornblende, diopside, quartz, biotite, and almandine garnet.

When rather pure limestone and dolomite come into direct contact with granitic rocks, elements such as silicon, iron, magnesium, and aluminum diffuse into the limestone, forming spectacular rocks termed skarns. These rocks often consist of large garnet crystals (grossular) with green diopside and vesuvianite or epidote.

SKARN

A skarn is the metamorphic zone developed in the contact area around igneous rock intrusions when carbonate sedimentary rocks are invaded by large amounts of silicon, aluminum, iron, and magnesium. The minerals commonly present in a skarn include iron oxides, calc-silicates (wollastonite, diopside, forsterite), andradite and grossularite garnet, epidote, and calcite. Many skarns also include ore minerals; several productive deposits of copper or other base metals have been found in and adjacent to skarns. Granitic and dioritic magmas are most commonly associated with skarns. Skarns can be zoned, with the inner zones successively replacing the outer ones as the wave of metamorphism moves through the surrounding rocks.

ALBITE-EPIDOTE-HORNFELS FACIES

Rocks of the albite-epidote-hornfels facies are characteristically found as the outer zones of contact aureoles where the thermal episode fades out and the rocks pass into their regional grade of metamorphism. The mineral assemblages are quite similar to those found in regional greenschist-facies metamorphism, except for the presence of low-pressure phases such as andalusite. Characteristic minerals include quartz, muscovite, biotite, chlorite, andalusite, actinolite, calcite, dolomite, albite, and epidote.

REGIONAL METAMORPHISM

Regional metamorphism is associated with the major events of Earth dynamics, and the vast majority of metamorphic rocks are so produced. They are the rocks involved in the cyclic processes of erosion, sedimentation, burial, metamorphism, and mountain building, events that are all related to major convective processes in Earth's mantle.

Most regionally metamorphosed rocks develop primarily in response to continent-continent collision and to collision between oceanic and continental plates. As a result, young metamorphic belts aligned roughly parallel to the present-day continental margins (e.g., the Pacific margin) as well as older metamorphic belts are used to infer the geometries of the continental margins at earlier periods in Earth's history. Most of the world's mountain belts are at least partially composed of regionally metamorphosed rocks, with spectacular examples provided by the Alps, the Himalayas, the northern Appalachians, and the Highlands of Scotland. Although the processes that formed each of these mountain belts are broadly similar, in almost all such crustal events at different times and places, there is uniqueness as well as conformity to a general pattern. Metamorphic events in the Alps, the Urals, and the Himalayas all show specific differences: to unravel such differences and their significance is one of the major tasks of metamorphic petrology.

In areas of collision between oceanic and continental lithospheric plates such as the circum-Pacific region, the denser oceanic plate is subducted (carried into Earth's mantle) beneath the more buoyant continental lithosphere. Rapid subduction of the cool oceanic lithosphere perturbs the thermal regime in such a way that high pressures can be obtained at relatively low temperatures, thereby generating blueschists and eclogites (high-pressure facies series) from ocean-floor basalts transported down the subduction zone. Continued subduction of these rocks to great depth may eventually result in either (1) rising temperatures and partial melting of subducted rocks or (2) the melting of hydrated peridotite created by fluids released from metamorphic reactions in the subduction zone that rise into the overlying mantle wedge. These melts contribute to the formation of the volcanoes that overlie subduction zones in areas such as the Andes of South America, Japan, and the Aleutian Islands. Upward migration of subduction-related magmas also contributes to the development of paired metamorphic belts, in which high-pressure, low-temperature metamorphic rocks are flanked on the continental side by a parallel belt of low-pressure, high-temperature rocks. The latter rocks are thought to reflect perturbation of the crustal thermal regime by the passage of silicate melts generated above the subducting slab. Continued intrusion of magma over a period of time would cause an increase in crustal temperatures at relatively shallow depths and produce the high-temperature rocks adjacent to the high-pressure rocks generated in the subduction zone. Well-developed paired metamorphic belts are exposed in Japan, California, the Alps, and New Zealand.

Data obtained from deep earthquakes in subduction zones indicate that a descending slab of oceanic lithosphere can remain intact to depths of several hundred kilometres before undergoing complete melting or fragmentation or both and being incorporated into the surrounding mantle. Clearly, the blueschists and eclogites exposed in orogenic belts around the world did not undergo such a process and were instead returned to Earth's surface. Most of the high-pressure rocks that have been studied from Japan, California, New Caledonia, the Alps, and Scandinavia record maximum pressures of 10–20 kilobars (1–2 gigapascal), corresponding to subduction to depths of approximately 35–70 km (about 22–44 miles). A few samples have been discovered in Norway, the Alps, and China that contain the mineral coesite, a high-pressure polymorph of quartz. Experimental studies on the stability of coesite imply minimum pressures of 30 kilobars (3 gigapascal) for these rocks, indicating burial or subduction to depths of approximately 100 km (about 60 miles). This is termed ultra-high pressure metamorphism (UHPM). These pressures are particularly noteworthy in that they are recorded in rocks derived from sedimentary rather than basaltic protoliths. Because of the low density, and hence greater buoyancy, of sediments relative to basalts, many geologists have argued that sediment subduction must be a rather limited process; the coesite-bearing metapelites (metamorphosed pelites) provide important evidence that sediment subduction can and does occur under certain circumstances.

The processes by which rocks that have been partially subducted are returned to the surface are not well understood. Models have been proposed to account for uplift and exposure of these high-pressure, high-density rocks; they include scraping material from the subducting plate against the overlying crustal lithosphere, upward flow of material in response to forced convection above the subducted slab, and removal of overlying thickened crust by low-angle extensional faulting. Testing these models requires considerable petrologic and structural work in areas where high-pressure rocks are exposed.

Most of the high-pressure rocks that are currently displayed in metamorphic belts around the world were metamorphosed in Mesozoic or Cenozoic time (e.g., the circum-Pacific belt, the Alps, the Greek Cyclades, and the Cordillera Betica in Spain). Older high-pressure rocks are known from only a few isolated occurrences in, for example, Wales, Bavaria, the Île de Groix off the coast of Brittany, and the Norwegian Caledonides (on the west coast of Norway). The general absence of high-pressure samples in the early rock record raises a number of interesting questions concerning Earth history. Some geologists have argued that the lack of well-developed Precambrian and Paleozoic high-pressure belts indicates that plate tectonic processes have changed significantly throughout geologic time. Specifically, they claim that greater heat production in Archean time (about 4 billion to 2.5 billion years ago) would have produced hotter crustal geotherms, resulting in thin, hot lithospheric plates whose mechanical behaviour may have been quite different from that of the present-day plates and hence may not have permitted formation of subduction zones. The increasing abundance of subduction-related metamorphic rocks with decreasing age in the rock record would thus reflect the gradual onset of plate tectonics as operative today. Others argue that the rock record is biased owing to preferential erosion or thermal over-printing (development of a new mineralogy that may obliterate the original one) of old blueschists and eclogites. Thermal modeling studies suggest that blueschists will generally undergo heating and be converted to greenschist assemblages if exposure at Earth's surface does not occur within 100 million to 200 million years after high-pressure metamorphism. Early exposure at the surface also increases the chances for removal by erosion, however, resulting in a low probability for preserving blueschists greater than 100 million to 200 million years old. Geologists favouring generation of blueschists throughout Earth history but only selective preservation of these rocks also point to crustal rocks more than 2.5 billion years old that record metamorphism at depths of 25–40 km (about 16–25 miles); these medium-pressure facies series rocks imply that crustal thicknesses in the early Earth were similar to those of the present day and thus that modern plate tectonic processes may have operated from the early Precambrian to the present. This debate, though unresolved, emphasizes the substantial knowledge of Earth's thermal structure and plate tectonic processes that can be obtained from the study of metamorphic rocks.

Depending on the original geometry of Earth's lithospheric plates, subduction of oceanic crust beneath continental lithosphere may result in complete consumption of an ocean basin and subsequent collision between two continents. Collisions of this type have a long and complex history that may include initial formation of a paired metamorphic belt followed by extreme crustal thickening in response to the actual collision of the continents. The overthickened crust produced by the collision event will be gravitationally unstable and will undergo subsequent rapid erosion and possibly extensional faulting in order to return to a normal crustal thickness. Rocks metamorphosed in the early stages of collision may belong to a high-pressure facies series, reflecting the final stages of subduction of oceanic lithosphere, whereas the younger facies more typically belong to medium-pressure facies series. Metamorphic rocks exposed in former collision zones may thus have followed a variety of pressure-temperature-time paths, but paths showing rapid burial followed by heating and subsequent unroofing at moderate to high temperatures have been reported from many mountain belts around the world. Owing to the strong directed forces operative during collision, deformation typically accompanies metamorphism; rocks metamorphosed in response to continent-continent collision generally have fabrics showing a strong preferred orientation of mineral grains, folds on a variety of scales, and pre-, syn-, and postkinematic porphyroblasts. Examples of metamorphic belts produced in response to this type of collision include the Paleozoic Appalachian and Caledonides belts and the Mesozoic-Cenozoic Alpine and Himalayan belts.

Regionally metamorphosed rocks are also exposed in areas where the crust has been thinned by extensional faulting, such as the Basin and Range province of the western United States. In this type of occurrence, areas of medium- and low-pressure facies series rocks that measure a few tens of kilometres in diameter are juxtaposed against unmetamorphosed sediments or very low-grade metamorphic rocks along low-angle extensional faults. (Metamorphic grades refer to the degree and intensity of the metamorphism: they are determined by the pressure and temperatures to which the rock has been subjected.) Such areas are generally referred to as metamorphic core complexes. Metamorphism in these complexes may or may not be related to the extensional event. In some instances, metamorphic rocks produced during much earlier events are simply unroofed and exposed by the faulting but show little or no recrystallization related to extension. In other cases, prolonged extension has resulted in an increased crustal geotherm, and relatively high-temperature metamorphism and magmatism is thus directly related to the extensional event. Immediately adjacent to the faults, the rocks may also be affected by dynamic metamorphism.

The facies associated with regional metamorphism include, at low grade, the zeolite and prehnite-pumpellyite facies. In areas belonging to high-pressure facies series, the rocks are predominantly in the blueschist and eclogite facies. Medium- and low-pressure facies series are typified by rocks belonging to the greenschist, amphibolite, and granulite facies.

In the zeolite facies, sediments and volcanic debris show the first major response to burial. Reactions are often not complete, and typical metamorphic fabrics may be poorly developed or not developed at all. This is the facies of burial metamorphism.

The zeolite facies was first described from southern New Zealand, but similar rocks have now been described from many of Earth's younger mountain regions, particularly around the Pacific margin and the European Alps. Typically, the rocks are best developed where reactive volcanic materials (often partly glassy) are common and the characteristic minerals include zeolites, which are low-density, hydrated silicates, stable at temperatures rarely exceeding 300 °C (570 °F). Typical mineral assemblages include heulandite, analcite, quartz with complex clay minerals (montmorillonite), micaceous phases such as chlorite and celadonite, and the potassium feldspar, adularia. At higher grades of metamorphism, the zeolite laumonite and the feldspar albite dominate the mineral assemblage. In New Zealand these are developed in a rock column that is about 15 km (about 9 miles) thick. Calcareous rocks (impure limestones) show very little response to this grade of metamorphism.

PREHNITE-PUMPELLYITE FACIES

Along with the zeolite facies, the prehnite-pumpellyite facies received little attention until about 1950. The first rocks of the facies were described in New Zealand and Celebes. The facies is transitional, bridging the path to the blueschist facies or the greenschist facies. It is particularly well developed in graywacke-type sediments. The two minerals prehnite and pumpellyite replace the zeolite minerals of the zeolite facies and are themselves replaced by epidote minerals in the greenschist facies and by lawsonite and pyroxenes in the blueschist facies. Typical minerals in this facies are quartz, albite, prehnite, pumpellyite, chlorite, stilpnomelane, muscovite, and actinolite. Almost all the minerals are hydrated, and, except for chlorite, they bear little resemblance to the minerals of sediments. This facies has been most described from younger mountain ranges of the Pacific margin.

Blueschist Facies

Rocks of the blueschist facies represent deep metamorphism under conditions of a low thermal gradient. The characteristic locale for this type of metamorphism appears to be along a continental margin being underthrust by an oceanic plate. Regions in which blueschists are found are also regions of great seismic and volcanic activity, such as the Pacific margin. The best described examples of this class of metamorphism come from California, Japan, New Caledonia, Celebes, the Alps, and the Mediterranean region. At present there are no confirmed examples of glaucophane schists predating the Paleozoic Era. Because of the presence of the blue amphibole glaucophane and minerals such as garnet and jadeite, these schists are among the most attractive of metamorphic rocks.

Characteristic minerals of the facies include quartz, glaucophane, lawsonite, jadeite, omphacite, garnet, albite, chlorite, muscovite, paragonite, epidote, and kyanite. In calcareous rocks, calcite may be replaced by the high-pressure polymorph aragonite. In general, the facies is characterized by many high-density minerals reflecting a high pressure of formation.

Eclogite Facies

The eclogite facies was initially recognized in rocks only of basaltic composition, which are transformed at the pressure-temperature conditions of the eclogite facies into spectacular red and green rocks composed of the anhydrous mineral assemblage garnet plus omphacite. The garnet is rich in the high-pressure species pyrope, and the omphacite is rich in the high-pressure pyroxene jadeite. Small amounts of minerals such as kyanite, zoisite, and hornblende may be present. The rocks are of high density and frequently show little or no schistosity. It is now known that protoliths other than basalt also can be metamorphosed to pressures and temperatures characteristic of the eclogite facies, and a wide variety of mineral assemblages can be stable at these conditions, including several hydrous mineral phases. Minerals that have been observed in metapelites include magnesium-rich chloritoid and staurolite, kyanite, garnet, phengite (a muscovite mica with high magnesium and silicon and low aluminum content), chlorite, and talc. Experimental work shows that pelitic rocks composed primarily of talc and kyanite, which are referred to as whiteschists, can be stable from pressures of approximately 6 kilobars (0.6 gigapascal) up to greater than 30 kilobars (3 gigapascal). Minerals observed in eclogite-facies calcareous rocks include magnesite, dolomite, zoisite or epidote, and omphacite.

Because of the high density and composition, it was proposed long ago that part of the upper mantle might be made of eclogite. Such a view is supported by eclogitic intrusions in volcanic rocks and by eclogitic inclusions in diamond-bearing kimberlite, which must come from the upper mantle. Some workers also think that eclogites found in metamorphic terrains in Norway, California, U.S., and the European Alps could also come from the mantle by tectonic processes.

Early experimental work on eclogites of basaltic bulk composition suggested that eclogites could generally only be stable if water pressure was much lower than the lithostatic pressure, and the facies was thus thought to represent dry, high-pressure metamorphism of basaltic protoliths. Subsequent work on the more diverse pro-tolith compositions reveals, however, that a wide range of water pressures are possible in the eclogite facies and that fluid compositions in equilibrium with the eclogite minerals also probably vary greatly. Indeed, fluid inclu-sions (tiny bubbles of fluid trapped within mineral grains) in eclogite samples provide evidence of fluids containing nitrogen, salts, and carbon dioxide in addition to water. Eclogite metamorphism is therefore not confined to dry environments but results instead from metamorphism of a variety of rock types at pressures above about 10 kilobars (1 gigapascal), corresponding to burial to approximately 35 km (about 22 miles), and at temperatures ranging from about 400 to 1,000 °C (about 750 to 1,830 °F). The tempera-tures of the eclogite facies overlap those of the greenschist, amphibolite, and granulite facies, but the higher pressures result in distinctly different mineral assemblages charac-terized by high-density mineral phases.

Greenschist Facies

The greenschist facies was once considered the first major facies of metamorphism proper. The name comes from the abundance of the green mineral chlorite in such rocks. Because chlorite and muscovite are ubiqui-tous and because both exhibit a platy crystal habit, these rocks normally show a highly developed foliation and often exhibit strong metamorphic differentiation. They have been described from practically every metamorphic terrain on Earth, from earliest Precambrian to the young mountain regions. In fact, many of Earth's oldest rocks (about three billion years old) of the continental shield areas are in this facies, classic examples of which are in the Appalachians, the Highlands of Scotland, New Zealand, the European Alps, Japan, and Norway.

The dominant minerals of greenschists formed from silicate-rich sediments include quartz, albite, muscovite, chlorite, epidote, calcite, actinolite, magnetite, biotite, and paragonite. Minerals less common include the manganese-rich garnet spessartine, stilpnomelane, kyanite, rutile, sphene, pyrophyllite, and chloritoid. Calcareous rocks are dominated by calcite, dolomite, and quartz; the major carbonate minerals are thermally stable. It is only when large quantities of water flush away carbon dioxide or keep its partial pressure low that carbonate-silicate reactions take place and liberate carbon dioxide. The typical minerals of this facies have low water contents as compared with the zeolite facies minerals.

AMPHIBOLITE FACIES

The amphibolite facies is the common high-grade facies of regional metamorphism, and, like the greenschist facies, such rocks are present in all ages from all over the world. Their characteristic feature is the development of the most common amphibole, hornblende, in the presence of a plagioclase feldspar and garnet. The rocks are normally highly foliated or schistose. Many zones or isograds subdividing the facies have been recognized, and classic studies have been made in the Highlands of Scotland, New Hampshire and Vermont in the United States, Switzerland, and the Himalayas.

Characteristic minerals derived from pelitic rocks are quartz, muscovite, biotite, garnet, plagioclase, kyanite, sillimanite, staurolite, and orthoclase. Minerals derived from basaltic rocks include hornblende, plagioclase, garnet, epidote, and biotite. Those derived from calcareous rocks are calcite, diopside, grossular (garnet), zoisite, actinolite (hornblende), scapolite, and phlogopite. Minerals from magnesium-rich ultramafic rocks are chlorite, anthophyllite, and talc. In most common types, water is present in minerals only of the mica and amphibole families, and, with their water contents of only about 1 to 3 percent, dehydration is nearing its metamorphic climax.

GRANULITE FACIES

In rocks of basaltic composition, the granulite facies is an anhydrous facies that results from progressive dehydration of amphibolites at high temperature. Rocks of other bulk compositions may retain some hydrous minerals, such as biotite and hornblende, but it is likely that water pressure is lower than lithostatic pressure during most granulite facies metamorphism. Evidence for relatively low water pressures comes from fluid inclusion data indicating carbon dioxide-rich fluid compositions and from preservation of some bulk compositions that should have undergone nearly total melting at granulite temperatures if water pressure had been equal to lithostatic pressure.

Rocks of this facies frequently have a granular texture quite similar to plutonic igneous rocks. Schistosity is only weakly developed. Typical minerals of the facies are quartz, alkali feldspar, garnet, plagioclase, cordierite, sillimanite, and orthopyroxene. In calcareous members, dolomite, calcite, diopside, and forsterite occur; and it is in this facies that minerals of the scapolite family are best developed. Small amounts of hornblende are often present. A rare mineral occurring in this facies is sapphirine. The rock type charnockite (from Tamil Nadu, India), essentially an orthopyroxene granite, is normally included in this facies.

It appears from experimental studies that during ultrametamorphism, when melting starts, the basic reactions which take place are of the type

biotite + other minerals $\to$ melt + residue
hornblende + other minerals $\to$ melt + residue.

The first melts to form are partly wet granitic or granodioritic melts, and phases such as biotite and hornblende break down by producing a partly wet melt from the least refractory phases in the rocks. They would persist to much higher temperatures in other systems of their own composition. The residue in the above equations is a granulite-facies metamorphic rock containing phases such as pyroxene and sillimanite. Thus it is probable, but certainly not universally accepted, that many granulites are formed only in the presence of a silicate liquid. This liquid may, of course, move to higher crustal levels.

Large areas of granulite facies rocks are confined almost entirely to Precambrian areas of the continents (those areas that were formed more than 542 million years ago), with well-developed areas exposed in Canada, India, Africa, Antarctica, Greenland, and the Adirondack Mountains of New York in the northeastern United States. Smaller areas of granulite facies rocks occur in younger mountain belts, with Paleozoic examples in New England (U.S.) and Brittany and Paleogene and Neogene examples (those formed between about 65.5 million and 2.6 million years ago) in British Columbia (Can.) and Timor. The apparent decrease in the volume of granulite facies rocks with decreasing age of metamorphism has led some geologists to postulate, as mentioned above, that plate-tectonic processes might have changed significantly with time—specifically that steady-state continental geotherms were hotter in the Precambrian than at the present time. Some work on pressure-temperature-time paths in granulites also suggests that Precambrian granulites were metamorphosed along distinctly different paths than younger granulites, lending credence to models invoking changes in tectonic processes. An alternative hypothesis is that large volumes of granulites have been formed throughout Earth's history but that they have not yet been exposed by erosion. Pressures calculated from fragments of granulite-facies metamorphic rocks carried to the surface in young volcanic eruptions suggest that the fragments were derived from the lower crust. It is likely that the lower crust is currently composed largely of granulite-facies rocks that may be exposed by future episodes of mountain building, but it is also possible that these granulites will prove to be different from their Precambrian counterparts. In order to resolve some of the controversies surrounding the origin and composition of granulites, it is necessary that considerable studies of these rocks be conducted in the future.

DISTRIBUTION OF METAMORPHIC ROCKS

A high-grade metamorphic rock is one that formed at a depth of tens of kilometres and later returned to the surface. Hence, metamorphic regions are also regions of former or recent intense orogeny. More stable regions of Earth's crust tend to be covered with sediments, and only deep drilling will reveal the metamorphic rocks below.

Earth's crust is made up of two basic units, the continents and ocean basins. Exploration of ocean floors has revealed that old, thick sedimentary piles are missing. Doubtless this is related to the processes of continental drift or seafloor spreading; sediments are continuously swept up by continental motion and are added to the continents or returned to the upper mantle. Nearly all studies of metamorphic rocks have concentrated on the continents for this reason.

There are few large areas of Earth's crust that are not affected by some type of igneous event from time to time. Although the intensity of volcanism may be focused in certain geographic regions (e.g., the Pacific margin), volcanism appears to be a rather random phenomenon, at times even occurring in the stable shield areas of the continents. In this sense, contact-metamorphic events

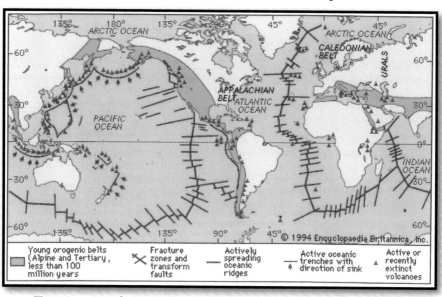

Tectonic units of the continents: shields and the present-day configuration of the continents and Earth's major lithospheric plates. Copyright Encyclopædia Britannica, Inc.; rendering for this edition by Rosen Educational Services

may be found almost everywhere at almost any time on Earth. But these metamorphic events are of trivial volumetric significance compared with those of regional metamorphism.

During the past 500 million years or so of Earth's history, major tectonic, seismic, igneous, and metamorphic events have been concentrated on continental margins. This has been a period of depression and uplift of Earth's crust associated with the formation of the present continental distribution. The processes are still going on at dramatic rates in ocean trench environments. These modern regions of activity form immense linear belts. One such belt runs around virtually the entire Pacific margin and another through the Mediterranean and southern Asia to fuse with the circum-Pacific belt. It is in these belts that the spectacular development of zeolite facies, prehnite-pumpellyite facies, blueschist facies, and, occasionally, eclogite facies, as well as the more universal facies of regional metamorphism, have occurred. The granulite facies is almost missing.

The central and often dominant feature of most continents is their vast Precambrian shield area; examples include the Canadian Shield, Brazilian Shield, African Shield, and Australian Shield. In these rocks, dating reveals ages of 1 billion to 3.5 billion years, and they have been little affected by tectonic events postdating the Cambrian. But these shield areas are themselves complex. They consist of vast areas of granitic or granodioritic gneisses. Inside them, between them, and overlapping onto them are belts of sedimentary rocks quite like those in modern sedimentary belts of the Pacific margin or European Alps. These rocks are frequently metamorphosed in the greenschist, amphibolite, and granulite facies. Low-temperature facies and, in particular, low-temperature–high-pressure facies are missing—or have not yet been found. From marginal areas of these stable shield areas, a complex array of processes has been documented covering the past few hundred million years. The Caledonian orogeny (at the close of the Silurian Period) produced tectonic-metamorphic events along the east coast of North America, Greenland, the British Isles, Fennoscandia, Central Asia, and Australia. The Hercynian, or Variscan, orogeny followed about 300 million years ago, affecting subparallel regions and the Urals and European Alps. In fact, the shield margins appear to have been subjected to a more or less constant battering by forces both destroying and rebuilding the margins of these protocontinents. As geologists study Precambrian areas in greater detail, the number of metamorphic and orogenic events recognized on a global scale increases.

It is the great task and problem of those who study metamorphic rocks to deduce the record of Earth dynamics and thermal history from metamorphic rocks. Among the questions to be answered are (1) whether the pattern of facies development through time—e.g., the granulite facies in the Archean to blueschist facies in the early Cenozoic—is a reflection of a cooling Earth and the decline of radioactivity in the crust, and (2) whether the increase in size of global tectonic-metamorphic belts through time reflects changes in convective patterns in the mantle.

As understanding of the pressure-temperature regimes of metamorphism increases, and as knowledge of rock mechanics and fluid motion during metamorphism also increases through field and laboratory studies, it may become possible to understand the details of the motion of the chemical elements during such processes and hence much of the subject of economic geology, or the search for our essential raw materials.

CLASSIFICATION OF METAMORPHIC ROCKS

Because of the diverse chemistry, mineralogy, and primary origin of metamorphic rocks and because of the diverse fabrics or textures that may develop depending on the stresses that may operate during their formation, there is no simple, universally used classification of these rocks. Any classification of metamorphic rocks tends to stress either their fabric, mineralogy, or primary origin. Some common metamorphic rock types are described here.

SCHIST

Rocks in which metamorphic minerals are easily seen by eye or hand lens and in which the mineral grains have a highly orientated fabric are called schists. Grains of acicular (needlelike) or platy minerals (e.g., amphiboles and micas) tend to lie with their long directions parallel or their planar directions parallel. Often the rocks show a pronounced mineralogical layering; quartz layers a few millimetres or centimetres in thickness may lie between mica layers, for example. Other words often qualify schist: as described earlier, greenschist is a schist rich in the green mineral chlorite; blueschist is rich in the blue amphibole, glaucophane; mica-schist is rich in mica; and a graphite-schist is rich in graphite. Schists that are rich in the amphibole hornblende and are often derived by metamorphism of common igneous rocks of the basalt-gabbro type are called amphibolites.

SLATE

Slate is a fine-grained, clayey metamorphic rock that cleaves, or splits, readily into thin slabs. Each slab has great tensile strength and durability. Some other rocks that occur in thin beds are improperly called slate because they can be used for roofing and similar purposes. True slates do not, as a rule, split along the bedding plane but along planes of cleavage, which may intersect the bedding plane at high angles. Slate was formed under low-grade metamorphic conditions— i.e., under relatively low temperature and pressure. The original material was a fine clay, sometimes with sand or volcanic dust, usually in the form of a sedimentary rock (e.g., a mudstone or shale). The parent rock may be only partially altered so that some of the original mineralogy and sedimentary bedding are preserved; the bedding of the sediment as originally laid down may be indicated by alternating bands, sometimes seen on the cleavage faces. Cleavage is a super-induced structure, the result of pressure acting on the rock at some time when it was deeply buried beneath Earth's surface. On this account, slates occur chiefly among older rocks, although some occur in

Slate, a metamorphic rock, showing typical splintery fracture and thin layering (slightly larger than life size). John H. Gerard

regions in which comparatively recent rocks have been folded and compressed as a result of mountain-building movements. The direction of cleavage depends upon the direction of the stresses applied during metamorphism.

Slates may be black, blue, purple, red, green, or gray. Dark slates usually owe their colour to carbonaceous material or to finely divided iron sulfide. Reddish and purple varieties owe their colour to the presence of hematite (iron oxide), and green varieties owe theirs to the presence of much chlorite, a green micaceous clay mineral. The principal minerals in slate are mica (in small, irregular scales), chlorite (in flakes), and quartz (in lens-shaped grains).

Slates are split from quarried blocks about 7.5 cm (3 inches) thick. A chisel, placed in position against the edge of the block, is lightly tapped with a mallet; a crack appears in the direction of cleavage, and slight leverage with the chisel serves to split the block into two pieces with smooth and even surfaces. This is repeated until the original block is converted into 16 or 18 pieces, which are afterward trimmed to size either by hand or by means of machine-driven rotating knives.

Slate is sometimes marketed as dimension slate and crushed slate (granules and flour). Dimension slate is used mainly for electrical panels, laboratory tabletops, roofing and flooring, and blackboards. Crushed slate is used on composition roofing, in aggregates, and as a filler. Principal production in the United States is from Pennsylvania and Vermont; northern Wales provides most of the slate used in the British Isles.

GNEISSES

Gneisses are metamorphic rocks that possess a distinct banding, which is apparent in hand specimen or on a microscopic scale. Gneiss usually is distinguished from schist by its foliation and schistosity; gneiss displays a well-developed foliation and a poorly developed schistosity and cleavage. For the casual student, it is convenient to think of a gneiss as a rock with parallel, somewhat irregular banding which has little tendency to split along planes. In contrast, schist typically is composed of platy minerals with a parallel to subparallel geometric orientation that gives the rock a tendency to split along planes; banding is usually not present.

Gneiss is medium- to coarse-grained and may contain abundant quartz and feldspar, which some petrographers regard as essential components. The banding is usually due to the presence of differing proportions of minerals in the various bands; dark and light bands may alternate because of the separation of mafic (dark) and felsic (light) minerals. Banding can also be caused by differing grain sizes of the same minerals. The mineralogy of a particular gneiss is a result of the complex interaction of original rock composition, pressure and temperature of metamorphism, and the addition or loss of components.

Gneiss is the principal rock over extensive metamorphic terrains. The banding may be oriented nearly parallel to Earth's surface (horizontal dip) or may have a steep dip. Such orientations can be interpreted in terms of the stresses that prevailed during the formation of the rock.

Gneiss can be classified on the basis of minerals that are present, presumed formational processes, chemical composition, or probable parent material. Orthogneiss is formed by the metamorphism of igneous rocks; paragneiss results from the metamorphism of sedimentary rocks. Pencil gneiss contains rod-shaped individual minerals or segregations of minerals, and augen gneiss contains stubby lenses of feldspar and quartz having the appearance of eyes scattered through the rock. The identification of gneiss as a product of metamorphism is usually clear, but some primary gneiss can be formed by the flow of a viscous, partially crystallized magma.

Hornfels

The hornfels are formed by contact metamorphism and typically show little sign of the action of directed pressure. They are fine-grained rocks in which crystals display little orientation.

Marble

Rocks derived from the metamorphism of carbonate sediments containing calcite or dolomite are marbles. The main result of metamorphism is an increase in grain size. Because of the rather equidimensional habit of calcite and dolomite crystals, they rarely appear schistose unless they contain other minerals such as mica.

Mylonites and Cataclastites

These are rocks in which the texture is the result of ductile shearing or mechanical shattering of grains. They often show only slight, if any, development of new minerals. They form on fault planes or in zones of intense shearing. If the crustal rocks have an appropriate composition, phyllonites may develop where new mica crystals grow parallel to the shearing direction. If shearing is extreme, melting may occur, locally producing a pseudo-tachylite. Tachylite is a term applied to certain types of glass formed by rapid cooling of molten rocks.

OTHER CLASSES

Most of the terms used throughout this chapter indicate structural or fabric classification of metamorphic rocks. Sometimes terms are used to indicate chemical features. Several types of schists, for example, include the following: pelitic schists contain much aluminum oxide and often are derivatives of clay-rich sediments; quartz-ofeldspathic schists are high in quartz and feldspars and often are derivatives of sandstones or quartz-rich igneous rocks; calcareous schists have a high content of lime (CaO) and often are derivatives of impure limestones, dolomites, or calcareous muds; and mafic schists contain the elements of mafic igneous rocks—namely, calcium, magnesium, and iron.

$$2Mg_3Al_2Si_3O_{12} + 4Al_2SiO_5 + 5SiO_2 \rightleftharpoons 3Mg_2Al_4Si_5O_{18}.$$

gamet   sillimanite   quartz   cordierite

$$Al_2Si_4O_{10}(OH)_2 \longrightarrow Al_2SiO_5 + 3SiO_2 + H_2O.$$

pyrophyllite   andalusite   quartz   water

$$Fe_9Al_6Si_5O_{20}(OH)_{16} + 4SiO_2 \longrightarrow 3Fe_3Al_2Si_3O_{12} + 8H_2O.$$

chlorite   quartz   gamet   water

$$Al_4Si_4O_{10}(OH)_8 + 4SiO_2 \longrightarrow 2Al_2Si_4O_{10}(OH)_2 + 2H_2O.$$

kaolinite   quartz   pyrophyllite   water

$$Fe_3Al_2Si_3O_{12} + KMg_3AlSi_3O_{10}(OH)_2 \longrightarrow$$

almandine gamet   magnesium-biotite

$$Mg_3Al_2Si_3O_{12} + KFe_3AlSi_3O_{10}(OH)_2.$$

pyrope gamet   iron-biotite

$$CaCO_3 + WO_3 \text{ (solution)} \rightarrow CaWO_4 + CO_2 \text{ (gas)}.$$

calcite ·   scheelite

garnet + muscovite + chlorite $\longrightarrow$

staurolite + biotite + quartz + water.

$$Al_2SiO_5 \longrightarrow Al_2SiO_5$$
andalusite   sillimanite
or kyanite

$$Mg_6(Si_4O_{10})(OH)_8 - Mg_3(Si_4O_{10})(OH)_2 - SiO_2.$$

QUARTZITE

Quartzite is a sandstone that has been converted into a solid quartz rock. Unlike sandstones, quartzites are free from pores and have a smooth fracture; when struck, they break through, not around, the sand grains, producing a smooth surface instead of a rough and granular one. Conversion of sandstone to quartzite may be accomplished by precipitation of silica from interstitial waters below Earth's surface; these rocks are called quartz arenites, whereas those produced by recrystallization under high temperatures and pressures are metaquartzites.

Quartzites are snowy white, less often pink or gray; they commonly have a fine angular jointing and break up into rubble under frost action. They yield a thin and very barren soil and, because they weather slowly, tend to project as hills or mountain masses. Many prominent ridges in the Appalachian Mountains are composed of highly resistant tilted beds of quartzite.

The term quartzite implies not only a high degree of hardening (induration), or "welding," but also a high content of quartz; similar rocks that contain appreciable quantities of other minerals and rock particles are impure quartzites, more appropriately called graywacke, lithic arenite, sandstone, or the like. Most quartzites contain

90 percent or more quartz, but some contain 99 percent and are the largest and purest concentrations of silica in Earth's crust. Pure quartzites are a source of silica for metallurgical purposes and for the manufacture of silica brick. Quartzite is also quarried for paving blocks, riprap, road metal (crushed stone), railroad ballast, and roofing granules.

In microscopic section the clastic structure of some quartzites is well preserved; the rounded sand grains are seen with quartz overgrowths deposited in crystalline continuity, so that optical properties of the grains are similar to those of the material surrounding them. In some cases a line of iron oxides may indicate the boundary of the original sand grain. Many quartzites, however, have been crushed, and the quartz largely is a mosaic of small, irregularly shaped crystalline fragments with interlocking margins; if these sheared quartzites contain white mica in parallel crystalline flakes, they become more fissile (easily broken apart) and pass into quartz schists.

CONCLUSION

Rocks are the tangible foundation upon which Earth's ecosystems rest. They are storehouses for minerals and nutrients for living things, and they also serve as substrates from which plants grow and as abodes in which many kinds of animals den. In the human realm, rocks are used to construct roads, buildings, seawalls, and other structures. Limestone, in particular, is useful in the development of fertilizers, glass manufacturing, and in the construction of building interiors and exteriors. The first tools created by early human beings were probably made of rock.

Rocks are also quite useful in the field of paleontology. Much of the knowledge related to extinct life began with investigations of fossils encased in layers of sedimentary rock. Using radioactive dating techniques, the age of the rock layer and thus the age of the fossil organism contained within the rock layer could be calculated. This process allows scientists to fix both the rock and the fossil in geologic time, a process that assists in the understanding of the evolution of life on Earth. Rocks also provide the clues to Earth's age and the origin and development of its landmasses and its ocean basins. Rocks therefore are the foundation upon and means by which we can come to understand our world, our history, and ourselves.

Encyclopædia Britannica, Inc. Source: International Commission on Stratigraphy (ICS)

APPENDIX

GEOLOGIC TIME SCALE

Precambrian time — Paleozoic Era · Cenozoic Era · Mesozoic Era · present

| 4,600[1] | 4,000[1] | 3,000[1] | 2,000[1] | 1,000[1] | present |

[1] Millions of years ago.
[2] Both the Mississippian and Pennsylvanian time units are formally designated as sub-periods within the Carboniferous Period.
[3] Several Cambrian unit age boundaries are informal and are awaiting ratified definitions.

Published with permission from the International Commission on Stratigraphy (ICS). International chronostratigraphic units, ranks, names, and formal status are approved by the ICS and ratified by the International Union of Geological Sciences (IUGS).
Source: 2009 International Stratigraphic Chart produced by the ICS.

Phanerozoic (Mesozoic / Cenozoic)

Eonothem/Eon	Erathem/Era	System/Period	Series/Epoch	Stage/Age	mya[1]
Phanerozoic	Mesozoic	Cretaceous	Lower	Berriasian	145.5 ± 4.0
				Valanginian	140.2 ± 3.0
				Hauterivian	~133.9
				Barremian	130.0 ± 1.5
				Aptian	125.0 ± 1.0
				Albian	112.0 ± 1.0
			Upper	Cenomanian	99.6 ± 0.9
				Turonian	93.6 ± 0.8
				Coniacian	~88.6
				Santonian	85.8 ± 0.7
				Campanian	83.5 ± 0.7
				Maastrichtian	70.6 ± 0.6
	Cenozoic	Paleogene	Paleocene	Danian	65.5 ± 0.3
				Selandian	61.1
				Thanetian	58.7 ± 0.2
			Eocene	Ypresian	55.8 ± 0.2
				Lutetian	48.6 ± 0.2
				Bartonian	40.4 ± 0.2
				Priabonian	37.2 ± 0.1
			Oligocene	Rupelian	33.9 ± 0.1
				Chattian	28.4 ± 0.1
		Neogene	Miocene	Aquitanian	23.03
				Burdigalian	20.43
				Langhian	15.97
				Serravallian	13.82
				Tortonian	11.608
				Messinian	7.246
			Pliocene	Zanclean	5.332
				Piacenzian	3.600
		Quaternary	Pleistocene	Gelasian	2.588
				Calabrian	1.806
				"Ionian"	0.781
				Tarantian	0.126
			Holocene		0.0117

Phanerozoic (Paleozoic / Mesozoic)

Eonothem/Eon	Erathem/Era	System/Period	Series/Epoch	Stage/Age	mya[1]
Phanerozoic	Paleozoic	Carboniferous — Mississippian[2]	Lower	Tournaisian	359.2 ± 2.5
			Middle	Visean	345.3 ± 2.1
			Upper	Serpukhovian	328.3 ± 1.6
		Carboniferous — Pennsylvanian[2]	Lower	Bashkirian	318.1 ± 1.3
			Middle	Moscovian	311.7 ± 1.1
			Upper	Kasimovian	307.2 ± 1.0
				Gzhelian	303.4 ± 0.9
		Permian	Cisuralian	Asselian	299.0 ± 0.8
				Sakmarian	294.6 ± 0.8
				Artinskian	284.4 ± 0.7
				Kungurian	275.6 ± 0.7
			Guadalupian	Roadian	270.6 ± 0.7
				Wordian	268.0 ± 0.7
				Capitanian	265.8 ± 0.7
			Lopingian	Wuchiapingian	260.4 ± 0.7
				Changhsingian	253.8 ± 0.7
	Mesozoic	Triassic	Lower	Induan	251.0 ± 0.4
				Olenekian	~249.5
			Middle	Anisian	~245.9
				Ladinian	237.0 ± 2.0
			Upper	Carnian	~228.7
				Norian	216.5 ± 2.0
				Rhaetian	203.6 ± 1.5
		Jurassic	Lower	Hettangian	199.6 ± 0.6
				Sinemurian	196.5 ± 1.0
				Pliensbachian	189.6 ± 1.5
				Toarcian	183.0 ± 1.5
			Middle	Aalenian	175.6 ± 2.0
				Bajocian	171.6 ± 3.0
				Bathonian	167.7 ± 3.5
				Callovian	164.7 ± 4.0
			Upper	Oxfordian	161.2 ± 4.0
				Kimmeridgian	~155.6
				Tithonian	150.8 ± 4.0
					145.5 ± 4.0

Phanerozoic (Paleozoic: Cambrian–Devonian)

Eonothem/Eon	Erathem/Era	System/Period	Series/Epoch	Stage/Age	mya[1]
Phanerozoic	Paleozoic	Cambrian[3]	Terreneuvian	Fortunian	~542.0 ± 1.0
				Stage 2	~528.0
			Series 2	Stage 3	~521.0
				Stage 4	~515.0
			Series 3	Stage 5	~510.0
				Drumian	~506.5
				Guzhangian	~503.0
			Furongian	Paibian	~499.0
				Stage 9	~496.0
				Stage 10	~492.0
		Ordovician	Lower	Tremadocian	488.3 ± 1.7
				Floian	478.6 ± 1.7
			Middle	Dapingian	471.8 ± 1.6
				Darriwilian	468.1 ± 1.6
			Upper	Sandbian	460.9 ± 1.6
				Katian	455.8 ± 1.6
				Hirnantian	445.6 ± 1.5
		Silurian	Llandovery	Rhuddanian	443.7 ± 1.5
				Aeronian	439.0 ± 1.8
				Telychian	436.0 ± 1.9
			Wenlock	Sheinwoodian	428.2 ± 2.3
				Homerian	426.2 ± 2.4
			Ludlow	Gorstian	422.9 ± 2.5
				Ludfordian	418.7 ± 2.7
			Pridoli		416.0 ± 2.8
		Devonian	Lower	Lochkovian	411.2 ± 2.8
				Pragian	407.0 ± 2.8
				Emsian	397.5 ± 2.7
			Middle	Eifelian	391.8 ± 2.7
				Givetian	385.3 ± 2.6
			Upper	Frasnian	374.5 ± 2.6
				Famennian	359.2 ± 2.5

Precambrian

Eonothem/Eon	Erathem/Era	System/Period	mya[1]
Hadean (informal)			4,600
Archean	Eoarchean		4,000
	Paleoarchean		3,600
	Mesoarchean		3,200
	Neoarchean		2,800
Proterozoic	Paleoproterozoic	Siderian	2,500
		Rhyacian	2,300
		Orosirian	2,050
		Statherian	1,800
	Mesoproterozoic	Calymmian	1,600
		Ectasian	1,400
		Stenian	1,200
	Neoproterozoic	Tonian	1,000
		Cryogenian	850
		Ediacaran	~635
			542

alluvial Relating to or composed of alluvium, which is clay, silt, sand, gravel, or similar loose material deposited by running water.

anhedral Also known as allotriomorphic, mineral grains of igneous rocks whose mutual growths have prevented the assumption of outward crystal form.

antiferromagnetism Magnetic behaviour characteristic of certain feebly magnetic substances (as manganese monoxide and chromium sesquioxide) thought to have two oppositely directed electron spins not quite neutralizing each other with the result that the magnetic susceptibility at first increases and then decreases as the substance is heated.

batholith A great mass of intruded igneous rock that for the most part stopped in its rise a considerable distance below the surface and that extends downward to unknown depth.

biogenic Produced by the action of living organisms.

calcareous Like calcite or calcium carbonate especially in hardness.

crystallographer A specialist in crystallography, the science of crystallization dealing with the system of forms among crystals, their structure, and their forms of aggregation.

cuneiform Composed of strokes having the form of a wedge or arrowhead.

curie temperature Also known as curie point, the temperature at which there is a transition in a substance from one phase to another of markedly different magnetic properties.

devitrification The conversion of glassy matter into crystalline (as by slow cooling or by pressure, action of water, or chemical changes).

devolatilize To remove volatile (unstable) material from (as coal).

diagenesis The recombination or rearrangement of constituents (as of a chemical or mineral) resulting in a new product.

dielectric constant A measure of the ability of a dielectric material (a nonconductor of direct electric current) to store electrical potential energy under the influence of an electric field, measured by the ratio of the capacitance of a condenser with the material as dielectric to its capacitance with vacuum as dielectric.

distal Remote from the point of attachment or origin.

ductile Capable of being permanently drawn out without breaking; malleable.

eolian Borne, deposited, produced, or eroded by the wind.

equant Of, being, or relating to a crystal having equal or nearly equal diameters in all directions.

escarpment A long cliff or steep slope separating two comparatively level or more gently sloping surfaces and resulting from erosion or faulting.

euhedral Minerals the growth of whose crystals in a rock has not been interfered with.

exsolve To separate or precipitate from a solid crystalline phase; unmix.

flocculate To cause to aggregate into a flocculent (loosely aggregated) mass.

fluvial Produced by river action.

Fourier analysis Named for nineteenth-century French geometrician and physicist Joseph Fourier, the process of using the terms of a Fourier series to find a function that approximates periodic data.

hydrostatic Of or relating to liquids at rest or to the pressures they exert or transmit.

hypabyssal Of or relating to a fine-grained igneous rock intermediate in texture between the plutonites and extrusive rocks and usually formed at a moderate distance below Earth's surface.

in situ In the natural or original position.

lacustrine Of, relating to, or formed in lakes.

lathlike Consisting of thin, narrow, flat strips, much like thin strips of wood known as lath.

lithify To change to stone.

maria Plural form of mare, meaning one of several dark areas of considerable extent on the surface of either the moon or Mars.

mole In chemistry, a standard scientific unit for measuring large quantities of very small entities such as atoms, molecules, or other specified particles.

monolith A mountain or large hill apparently composed of one kind of rock, usually a coarse-grained igneous rock.

Néel temperature The antiferromagnetic Curie point is called the Néel temperature in honour of the French physicist Louis Néel, who in 1936 successfully explained antiferromagnetism.

ovoid Egg-shaped.

petrologist A geologist who specializes in petrology, the science that deals with the origin, history, occurrence, structure, chemical composition, and classification of rocks.

planar Having a flat two-dimensional quality.

platy Consisting of plates or flaky layers. Used chiefly to describe soil or mineral formations.

plumose Having feathers or plumes.

Poisson's ratio Named for nineteenth century French mathematician Siméon-Denis Poisson, the ratio of transverse to longitudinal strain in a material under tension.

potash Potassium carbonate especially from wood ashes.

premonitory Giving previous warning or notice.

pyrometamorphism Change produced in rocks by the action of heat but without the action of pressure or mineralizers.

subduction The action or process of the edge of one crustal plate descending below the edge of another.

subhedral Incompletely bounded by crystal planes, partly faced.

substrate The base on which an organism lives. The soil is the substrate of most seed plants while rocks, soil, water, tissues, or other media are substrates for various other organisms.

Udden-Wentworth scale The scale devised (1898) by the American sedimentary petrologist J.A. Udden was adapted (1922) by C.K. Wentworth, who expanded the definitions of the various grades to conform with actual usage by researchers; most sedimentologists have adopted the Udden scale with the Wentworth modifications.

ROCKS

Standard mineralogical reference works include Frederick H. Pough, *Field Guide to Rocks and Minerals*, 5th ed. (1998); Dexter Perkins, *Mineralogy*, 2nd ed. (2001); James R. Craig, David J. Vaughan, and Brian J. Skinner, *Earth Resources and the Environment*, 4th ed. (2010); Chris Pellant, *Smithsonian Handbooks: Rocks & Minerals* (2002); and W.A. Deer, R.A. Howie, and J. Zussman, *Rock-forming Minerals*, 2nd ed. (1997). Useful texts and monographs include Harvey Blatt, *Sedimentary Petrology* (1992); Anthony Hall, *Igneous Petrology*, 2nd ed. (1996); Cornelis Klein, *Minerals and Rocks: Exercises in Crystallography, Mineralogy, and Hand Specimen Petrology* (1989); *Manual of Mineralogy (after James D. Dana)*, 23rd ed. by Cornelis Klein and Barbara Dutrow (2007); and Harvey Blatt and Robert J. Tracy, *Petrology: Igneous, Sedimentary and Metamorphic*, 2nd ed. (1996).

Cornelis Klein, *Minerals and Rocks: Exercises in Crystal and Mineral Chemistry, Crystallography, X-ray Powder Diffraction, Mineral and Rock Identification, and Ore Mineralogy*, 3rd ed. (2007); Robert S. Carmichael (ed.), *Handbook of Physical Properties of Rocks*, 3 vol. (1982–84), also available in a 1-vol. abridged ed., *Practical Handbook of Physical Properties of Rocks and Minerals* (1989); Edgar W. Spencer, *Introduction to the Structure of the Earth*, 3rd ed. (1988); and D.R. Bowes (ed.), *The Encyclopedia of Igneous and Metamorphic Petrology* (1989), may also be consulted.

IGNEOUS ROCKS

Treatments of igneous rocks are included in Robin Gill, *Igneous Rocks and Processes* (2010); B.M. Wilson, *Igneous Petrogenesis: A Global Tectonic Approach* (2010); Alexander R. McBirney, *Igneous Petrology*, 3rd ed. (2006); Paul C. Hess, *Origins of Igneous Rocks* (1989); Anthony R. Philpotts, *Principles of Igneous and Metamorphic Petrology* (1990); Marjorie Wilson, *Igneous Petrogenesis* (1989); Robert Decker and Barbara Decker, *Volcanoes*, 3rd ed. (1998); Alexander R. McBirney, *Igneous Petrology*, 2nd ed. (1993); Jacques-Marie Bardintzeff and Alexander R. McBirney, *Volcanology,* 2nd ed. (2000).

SEDIMENTARY ROCKS

Sedimentary rocks are described in Donald R. Prothero and Fred Schwab, *Sedimentary Geology* (2003); Sam Boggs, Jr., *Petrology of Sedimentary Rocks*, 2nd ed. (2009); Sam Boggs, Jr., *Principles of Sedimentology and Stratigraphy*, 4th ed. (2005); C.J.R. Braithwaite, *Carbonate Sediments and Rocks: A Manual for Geologists and Engineers* (2005); Maurice E. Tucker and V. Paul Wright, *Carbonate Sedimentology* (1991); Andrew D. Miall, *Principles of Sedimentary Basin Analysis*, 2nd ed. (1990); Donald R. Prothero, *Interpreting the Stratigraphic Record* (1989); Maurice E. Tucker and V.P. Wright, *Carbonate Sedimentology* (1990); and Maurice E. Tucker, *Sedimentary Petrology: An Introduction to the Origin of Sedimentary Rocks*, 3rd ed. (2001).

METAMORPHIC ROCKS

Standard references and basic textbooks include Anthony Philpotts and Jay Ague, *Principles of Igneous and Metamorphic Petrology*, 2nd ed. (2009); John D. Winter, *Introduction to Igneous and Metamorphic Petrology* (2001); Ron H. Vernon and Geoffrey Clarke, *Principles of Metamorphic Petrology* (2008); Jacques Kornprobst, *Metamorphic Rocks and Their Geodynamic Significance: A Petrological Handbook* (2002); Roger Mason, *Petrology of the Metamorphic Rocks*, 2nd ed. (1990); Bruce W.D. Yardley, *An Introduction to Metamorphic Petrology* (1989); K. Bucher and M. Frey, *Petrogenesis of Metamorphic Rocks*, 6th ed. (1994); Martin Frey and Doug Robinson (eds.), *Low-grade Metamorphism: An Overview* (1999); and Frank S. Spear, *Metamorphic Phase Equilibria and Pressure-Temperature-Time Paths* (1995). Metamorphic fabric development is discussed in Ralph Kretz, *Metamorphic Crystallization* (1994); and C.W. Passchier and R.A.J. Truow, *Micro-tectonics* (1996). Major techniques for studying metamorphic rocks and the metamorphic histories of many of the world's mountain belts are reviewed in J.S. Daly, R.A. Cliff, and Bruce W.D. Yardley (eds.), *Evolution of Metamorphic Belts* (1988); and Peter J. Treloar and Patrick J. O'Brien (eds.), *What Drives Metamorphism and Metamorphic Reactions* (1998).

INDEX

G

H